CHALLENGING Communication Research

international
communication
association

Annual Conference Theme Book Series

Vol. 1

The ICA Annual Conference Theme Book Series
is part of the Peter Lang Media and Communication list.
Every volume is peer reviewed and meets
the highest quality standards for content and production.

PETER LANG
New York • Washington, D.C./Baltimore • Bern
Frankfurt • Berlin • Brussels • Vienna • Oxford

CHALLENGING Communication Research

EDITED BY

Leah A. Lievrouw

PETER LANG
New York • Washington, D.C./Baltimore • Bern
Frankfurt • Berlin • Brussels • Vienna • Oxford

Library of Congress Cataloging-in-Publication Data

International Communication Association.
Annual Conference (63rd: 2013: London, England)
Challenging communication research / edited by Leah A. Lievrouw.
pages cm. — (ICA annual conference theme book series; vol. 1)
Selected papers presented at the 63rd annual conference of the
International Communication Association (ICA) held June 2013 in London.
Includes bibliographical references and index.
1. Communication—Research—Congresses.
2. Communication—Research—Methodology—Congresses.
I. Lievrouw, Leah A., editor of compilation.
II. International Communication Association. III. Title.
P91.3.I53 302.2'0721—dc23 2013042395
ISBN 978-1-4331-2536-2 (hardcover)
ISBN 978-1-4331-2535-5 (paperback)
ISBN 978-1-4539-1273-7 (e-book)
ISSN 2330-4529

Bibliographic information published by **Die Deutsche Nationalbibliothek.**
Die Deutsche Nationalbibliothek lists this publication in the "Deutsche
Nationalbibliografie"; detailed bibliographic data is available
on the Internet at http://dnb.d-nb.de/.

Cover design by the International Communication Association

Peter Lang Publishing, Inc., New York
29 Broadway, 18th floor, New York, NY 10006
www.peterlang.com

Table of Contents

Acknowledgements

The planning and editorial work on this volume went remarkably quickly and smoothly. I want to acknowledge my wonderful collaboration with François Heinderyckx, who conceived the theme for ICA 2013, and worked with me on the details of the call for papers. I appreciate the great support of all the ICA division and interest group chairs who responded to my own call for their very best papers, and their eagerness to have the work of their section members represented in the book. ICA Executive Director Michael Haley has provided outstanding and immediate administrative support for the project, including funding that allowed me to enlist the help of my colleague, student, and editorial assistant wunderkind, Diana Ascher. Michael also led the negotiations with Peter Lang Publishing, which takes over as publisher for the ICA Theme Books with this edition. And finally, many thanks to Mary Savigar, our commissioning editor at Peter Lang, for her enthusiasm for the Theme Book series and for this volume in particular—we all look forward to a productive and creative collaboration on the series in the future.

Foreword

Challenging Communication Research

FRANÇOIS HEINDERYCKX, PRESIDENT OF
INTERNATIONAL COMMUNICATION ASSOCIATION (ICA),
(2013–2014)

Communication research traditions are recent, by scholarly standards, and in a perennial state of flux that can call the whole idea of "traditions" into question. It is fundamentally multifaceted and consistently receptive to a range of disciplines, methods, scholarly traditions, and epistemologies. This dynamic state is no transitional phase on the way to some definitive, ultimate form of the field. Rather, the morphing nature of media and communication research reflects the changing nature of communication itself and its participants, stakeholders, and contexts. Communication and media are multidimensional phenomena, open to the wider society beyond the research community; and communication research is a fundamentally dynamic space where disciplines meet, share, conflict, and engage. Communication scholars are destined continually to reinvent the field and its questions, interests, and methods.

These developments are generating a variety of challenges that both hinder and stimulate us as researchers, teachers, citizens, creative professionals, and cultural participants. These challenges can be identified at different levels: how research is conducted (approaches, perspectives, assumptions, and methods); how research identifies, classifies, and understands its objects of study; how research challenges society and public discourses that are increasingly dominated by powerful economic, political, and technical interests; how research challenges authority, privilege, and power in times of uncertainty and change; how research challenges common, taken-for-granted conceptions about the communication process itself; how research itself is challenged by financial pressures, by political and power shifts, by technological change and the reconfiguration and control of communication infrastructures and systems, and by cultural debates and conflicts.

The complexity of these challenges, their implications, and their evolution cannot be catalogued, let alone modeled in any integrated form. Instead, we offer to illustrate the diversity underlying the notion of challenge is this particular context. This volume draws from the work presented during the 63rd annual conference of the International Communication Association (ICA) that took place in London in June 2013. The chapters explore a broad range of topics from a diversity of perspectives to provide a rich set of thought-provoking considerations about not just the challenges that we face as communication scholars but also the challenges that we prompt and carry along. Challenging is in the DNA of scholarship, and this volume is intended to spur that particular characteristic.

Editor's Introduction

Challenge and Change in Communication Research

LEAH L. LIEVROUW

From the start, communication scholarship has not enjoyed the same kind of theoretical cohesion or ontological security as some other disciplines. Its origin stories feature disciplinary crossovers, reinventions, and hybrid projects, ranging from Chicago School pragmatism and ethnomethods, to the experiments and surveys of Columbia's Bureau of Applied Social Research, to the disciplinary heteroglossia of cybernetics and the Macy Conferences. Its early adherents left the certainties of a dozen established fields, ranging from rhetoric, theater, literary criticism, and philosophy, to social psychology, engineering, speech therapy, political science, sociology, and anthropology. They ventured into a barely defined but apparently irresistible arena of research, scholarship, practice, and critique dedicated to understanding just how, under what circumstances, and with what tools people make, share, and unmake meaning.

Moreover, the longstanding disconnect between the field's dramatic institutional success after the Second World War (the global proliferation of schools, degree programs, academic departments, journals, academic and professional societies and conferences), and its intellectual "roving eye" and resistance to establishing a single core body of knowledge, has inspired serial rounds of soul-searching and existential doubt among communication scholars, on one hand, and celebration and intellectual adventurism, on the other. As new modes of mediation and interaction have emerged, the field has adapted its agendas and methods accordingly. Younger scholars often lead the way.

So the theme of the 2013 annual conference of the International Communication Association, "Challenging Communication Research," begs an interesting question. For a field that is perpetually in flux and "decentered," what exactly is, or should be, challenged? How and by whom?

The chapters in this collection, chosen from among the top papers presented in London in June 2013, suggest that in communication research and scholarship, the challenges themselves are multifaceted. Indeed, challenge may be part of something more like the continuous process of reinvention, breakdown, and reorganization posited by the early systems theorists. The communication discipline can be seen as *emergent*, in an ongoing state of change, rather than as an orderly, stepwise path toward the neat, complete accumulation of knowledge.

Of course, not everything changes at once. Some benchmarks in communication scholarship have endured because they remain persuasive and useful, fostering a sort of Kuhnian "normal" scholarship. Here, we might include nuanced media effects theories like uses and gratifications; the insights into human language and culture offered by linguistics and semiotics; the lattices of microstructures and practices that comprise conversation; the networks of relations that form the social and cultural architecture of communities; the skills that endow people with communicative competence and effectiveness; and, of course, a deep skepticism toward the power of the state or private sector to shape public discourse and politics.

Still, communication researchers are just as likely to treat these ideas as useful constraints to spur creativity, something to test and push against, as they are to be considered unimpeachable "classics" enshrined in master texts or handed down through generations of comprehensive exams. Communication—as a phenomenon, an object of study, a field, an intellectual tradition, or principles for practice and intervention—is a moving target. Scholars seeking intellectual stability, respectability, or, indeed, ontological security should probably look elsewhere.

In that spirit, the chapters here all challenge familiar approaches, notions, or assumptions in communication research and scholarship. In the 2013 conference call for papers, ICA President Elect-Select François Heinderyckx and I asked contributors to "reflect on the field's multifaceted and increasingly open character in an era of shifting social relations, formations and technologies." In particular, we asked colleagues to consider:

- How communication research is conducted: its approaches, perspectives, assumptions, and methods
- How communication research identifies, classifies, and understands its objects of study
- How communication research challenges society and public discourses that are increasingly dominated by powerful economic, political, and technical interests

- How communication research challenges authority, privilege, and power in times of uncertainty and change
- How communication research challenges common, taken-for-granted conceptions about the communication process itself
- How communication research itself is challenged: by financial pressures, by political and power shifts, by technological change and the reconfiguration and control of communication infrastructures and systems, and by cultural debates and conflicts.

The following chapters do not—cannot—answer all of these questions, but they do provide an intriguing indication of the field's current sense of challenge, and some directions the discipline may take in its second century.

EDITORIAL PROCESS

The London conference was the largest ever held by the International Communication Association, with more than 2,800 registered delegates and thousands of papers, posters, panels, and presentations. Fully 60% of the ICA membership attended the meeting. Clearly, the present volume contains only a tiny selection of the vast array of work presented at the conference. However, like earlier editions of the ICA theme books, this book is specifically not a comprehensive collection of conference proceedings. Rather, the purpose is to present work that explores and reflects in some depth on the year's chosen theme, as a way to chart the discipline's evolving concerns, problem areas, and research fronts.

Thus, the principal challenge for assembling this collection was to identify a set of outstanding chapters that would address the theme, hold together as a collection, and give readers a sense of the enormous variety of work presented by ICA's 25 divisions, interest groups, and specially designated conference theme sessions. As theme chair for the London conference and theme book editor, I also wanted to highlight the high quality of student papers that ICA customarily accepts for the conference, and to emphasize the "I" in ICA (International)—the latter a perennial challenge for an organization historically based in North America. Last but not least, the whole book needed to fit the length requirements set by our enthusiastic new publisher, Peter Lang. Our commissioning editor, Mary Savigar, set a deadline for delivering the manuscript barely three months after the close of the London meeting so the book would appear in print in time for the 2014 ICA Conference in Seattle.

Work began in earnest in early 2013, after conference paper submissions had been reviewed and the best selected by the various divisions and interest groups, and section chairs had organized their sessions. In the months leading up to the conference, I scanned the full program to identify potentially relevant papers. I asked all section chairs to nominate top-quality papers that they considered most relevant and appropriate for the theme book. Chairs of 14 divisions and interest groups responded; they nominated anywhere from two to a dozen papers each, many of which were top papers or top student papers. Armed with this long list, I read and reviewed the nominees and attended conference sessions in London to hear the presentations, as well as others that just seemed like interesting possibilities.

After the conference, the real work began on narrowing the choices and extending invitations to authors. Several in the first round of about 20 short-listed papers were unavailable because they were already accepted by journals or promised to other book projects. One or two did not respond to the invitation. I searched the program again for strong papers I may have overlooked that would round out the collection.

Ultimately, the authors of 14 papers accepted the invitation to publish. They worked with me throughout the summer of 2013 to revise their papers for length and style. (Regrettably, one author had to withdraw his paper very late in the process due to a personal matter.) The final group of 13 chapters includes seven top papers, four of which are by students, from various ICA sections and the theme sessions. Many of the authors are affiliated with American institutions; however, the authors or coauthors of seven chapters have appointments outside the United States, in Australia, Austria, Canada, Denmark, Germany, New Zealand, and the United Kingdom. Beyond their institutional affiliations, several authors are nationals of other countries as well.

Although I made the final selections for the 2013 theme book, all of the papers included here have been fully refereed and recommended: first by reviewers for the various ICA divisions and interest groups, who recommended the papers for the conference; and then by the section chairs who nominated the best of them for inclusion in the theme book (or by my choice from the conference program). I provided further editorial comments and guidance to the authors as they revised their conference papers for the book. Deadline constraints did not permit a further round of outside reviews; nonetheless, readers will certainly recognize the consistently high quality of the resulting chapters.

Overview and Themes

As noted above, each of the papers included in *Challenging Communication Research* considers some aspect of communication research, scholarship, or practice from a critical or novel perspective. They present nonobvious, counterintuitive viewpoints that help us to rethink taken-for-granted methods, theories, and critical and practical interventions. Ideally, they are not "more like this" papers that extend existing frameworks and projects but, instead, offer genuinely new—and sometimes contrary—insights on established topics. And in many cases, they do so by deliberately crossing boundaries or situating their arguments at the intersections among specializations within the communication field, or between communication and other disciplines.

The chapters were not chosen with any particular thematic framework in mind. However, as I worked with them and looked for parallels or intersections, I found that they could be organized around four broad themes: challenging *core concepts*, challenging *discourses*, challenging *action and agency*, and challenging the *record*.

In Part I, on core concepts, Anita Varma asks readers to consider how one of the cornerstones of cultural and media studies, Stuart Hall's *encoding/decoding* model, has become something of a shibboleth among critical scholars. In her chapter—which was the top-ranked paper in the London theme sessions and a student paper as well—she points out the ironies implicit in scholarship that treats Hall's model as a law-like principle of culture rather than the heuristic tool-to-think-with that Hall himself always insisted it should be, subject to critique and adaptation. In a similar spirit, Sean Phelan traces a tendency among critical communication scholars to use "neoliberalism" as an all-purpose, and increasingly hollow, category and label for conservative, Western, or market-driven economics, politics, and culture—indeed any stance that departs from a progressive, emancipatory, neo-Marxist or critical viewpoint. He reviews several trenchant critiques of "neoliberal" discourse, and suggests ways to renew and reclaim the critical power of the term. Methodology is the focus of the chapter by David Karpf, Daniel Kreiss, and Rasmus Kleis Nielsen. They describe the near-total reliance on quantitative methods in political communication research over the last few decades, which has prompted concerns among prominent scholars that dependence on quantification has stymied the development of new theory in the area. Karpf, Kreiss, and Nielsen trace the roots of political communication research to qualitative fieldwork like that conducted by Gladys and Kurt Lang and Paul Lazarsfeld in the 1940s and 1950s, and suggest that a revival of a more balanced methodological approach to the study of political communication, incorporating both qualitative and quantitative methods, is long overdue.

In Part II, the focus shifts to challenges to larger media-driven political and cultural discourses. Two chapters address the formation and representation of political norms. In their chapter, which was a top paper in the Ethnicity and Race in Communication interest group, Alex Balch, Ekaterina Balabanova, and Ruxandra Trandafoiu examine media coverage of the Roma people in Europe, particularly the expulsion policies advanced in France by the government of Nicolas Sarkozy. They compare press reporting and opinion about the Roma population in Romania and Bulgaria and discover some unexpected normative frames that may be shaping news about the Roma in Europe. The chapter by Udo Göttlich and Martin Rolf Herbers, a top paper in the Mass Communication division, reviews the normative underpinnings of the idea of the democratic public sphere, particularly Jürgen Habermas's contention that political discourse shaped by market-driven media becomes just one more form of consumption that trivializes "serious" politics and disempowers citizens. Göttlich and Herbers suggest that certain forms of political "infotainment," such as *The Daily Show* in the United States, may actually inform viewers about issues they might not otherwise have known about, and indeed encourage political engagement. Humor is also the focus of Chapter 6, which was a top student paper in the Public Relations division. Katharina Wolf argues that humor is an important feature of effective public communication. Based on a case study of the West Australian anti-nuclear movement, she finds that humor plays a major role in the movement's ability to communicate with and persuade wider audiences. She notes that corporate communications practitioners have largely avoided humor in efforts to foster a "serious" image for corporate firms. However, Wolf believes that they should take a page from activist movements as a model for designing more effective public communication campaigns.

Communicative action and agency are the central issues in Part III, particularly the shifting nature of communicative practices online. Aram Sinnreich and Mark Latonero present survey data that document Americans' knowledge about and engagement in what the authors call "configurable culture," that is, practices of making and sharing appropriated, recombined, or customized content online. They find that configurable culture is more nuanced and contested than might be suggested by popular celebrations of "remix culture." Individuals participate in a range of content-related activities from simple consumption to original production; traditional media and content industries not only use expanded intellectual property regimes to constrain such practices but also seek to re-appropriate and commodify such "home built" content to create new products.

Katharine Sarikakis and Joan Ramon Rodriguez-Amat also consider intellectual property regimes. In their chapter, they survey the history of the idea of authorship, particularly as it has been enshrined in U.S. and European copyright regimes. They argue that the familiar notion of "the author" is becoming less meaningful, and less useful, as modes of creative work become more collaborative, distributed, and diffuse, and creative works themselves become less fixed and more dynamic. In the following chapter, a top student paper in the Communication Law and Policy division, Nora Draper considers how the growth of markets in personal information online has required people to become more aware of and cautious about the reputational risks of having such information in open circulation. She charts the rise and rationale of commercial online reputation management (ORM) services that claim to help their customers assess and manage those risks.

The final section of the book deals with an area that is often overlooked by communication scholars: how communication and knowledge are transformed into cultural records and data; the practical and ethical implications of creating, selecting, sharing, and retaining records; and what difference communication technologies make in all these processes. David Phillips, Brian Harding, and Danielle Leighton provide a look into the burgeoning quantified self movement, where individuals monitor, capture, and publicly post the minutest details of their daily lives, from physiological changes to feelings, attitudes, and interactions. The authors consider the prospects for such self-surveillance as a way to resist or "queer" the use of centralized information infrastructure by powerful state authorities and corporate interests as a tool of pervasive, and invasive, surveillance. In her history of Britain's mass observation movement, Annie Rudd recalls what might seem like a "kinder, gentler" regime of surveillance and photographic data gathering between the world wars, intended to capture a comprehensive, detailed, and unobtrusive picture of everyday life in 1930s Britain. Rudd's chapter was the top student paper in the Communication History division, the second consecutive year that her work has been so recognized. In the closing chapter, again a top paper in the 2013 theme sessions, Gina Neff, Brittany Fiore-Silfvast, and Carrie Sturts Dossick draw on a rich ethnography of a large construction site to demonstrate the crucial operational role of documentary records—particularly informal records like sketches, doodles, lists, or mobile phone photos—as indispensable tools of organizational communication. They show how these everyday records and uses contrast with the formal, "official" records that are often generated for external stakeholders and internal reporting. The authors argue that by focusing on "immaterial" digital records, or privileging the meaning and interpretation of records over their material functions and uses, communication scholars may overlook or neglect the fundamental materiality of workplace communication practices.

Obviously these papers cover a great deal of intellectual and empirical territory. But in addition to the section themes, various chapters also share some other cross-cutting concerns, including news production and journalism; challenges to the foundations of communication law and policy; the role of creativity in communication and the generation of knowledge; the changing nature of self-presentation via digital communication technologies, particularly questions of visibility and transparency; and what we might call the "critique of critique."

Taken together, the chapters suggest that while contemporary communication research and scholarship is grounded in enduring questions—the nature of identity, interaction, and community; how meaning is represented and conveyed; how time, space, and embodiment shape human expression; how value is assigned to particular practices and forms of communication—other classic concepts and objects of study are being redefined. The traditional levels of analysis in communication research (individuals, dyads, small groups, organizations, communities, audiences, masses) are no longer easily distinguished. Analysts must be ready to move across levels or conceptualize new hybrid approaches as required. The historical divides in the discipline that drew bright lines between the study of interpersonal communication and the process and effects of media technologies and institutions are increasingly difficult to sustain in an era of personal mobile communication devices, Twitter feeds and followers, and the computational power to capture, aggregate, circulate, and characterize patterns within minutely detailed "big data" repositories of personal information.

Indeed, the notion of mediation itself is in play. No longer the simple imposition of a channel between a sender and a receiver, the concept has expanded to include intercession in interpersonal relations and group processes, modes of governance and governmentality that define and shape the relations between members of a society and its powerful institutional interests, and the complex interplay among people's communicative action, the design and deployment of devices and systems, and patterns of social organization and institutionalization in which those practices and devices are implicated.

Clearly, the field's brief has expanded far beyond Harold Lasswell's classical formulation of "who says what to whom in what channel with what effect." And challenges to communication research like those presented in this book will ensure that the field's intellectual cosmopolitanism and vitality will continue and grow into a second century.

PART ONE

Challenging Core Concepts

CHAPTER ONE

The Ironic Incongruity of Canonical Common Sense in Critical Communication

The Case of Stuart Hall's "Encoding/Decoding" Model

ANITA VARMA[1]

There is an ironic incongruity between critical models of communication seeking to challenge "crudely conservative" common sense (Gramsci & Forgacs, 1988, p. 346) and uncritical applications of these models. A case study of this incongruity lies in contemporary usage of Stuart Hall's "Encoding/Decoding" model (1993/1973, 1980). The troubling irony beneath the surface of applications of Hall's model only becomes visible when the studies are juxtaposed with the historical moment in which Hall wrote "Encoding/Decoding." Beyond Hall's particular model, this chapter proposes that "being critical" means reflexively looking for such incongruities. Without a critical approach to the foundations of critical studies that attends carefully to the irony of incongruity, these foundations may be rendered stale, weighty anchors that stagnate the field instead of serving as compelling starting points for substantive elaboration and revision.

Foundational texts like Hall's originally sought to destabilize—not neatly replace—existing dominant theories because, as Hall (1992) argued, "the only theory worth having is that which you have to fight off, not that which you speak with profound fluency" (pp. 265–266). Hall's encoding/decoding model has become fraught with fluency over the past three decades, making continued critical scrutiny imperative. As communication scholars study new media settings using critical models, these scholars should incorporate critical reflexivity about the origins and intentions of existing frameworks in order to avoid applying them uncritically and reifying what Briankle Chang (2011) called "blueprints" for scholarship that these frameworks originally sought to challenge (p. 86).

Regarded as a seminal work in cultural studies, "Encoding/Decoding" provided a new way to conceptualize media producers, audiences, and embedded ideologies by transgressing the unspoken presumptions of the dominant positivist media effects tradition (Gurevitch & Scannell, 2002). As Gurevitch and Scannell argue, "Encoding/Decoding" has attained canonic status because of its "capacity to open new doors and trigger new questions" (p. 245). This capacity was partly energized by Hall's use of the familiar communication terminology of encoding/decoding, which is present in work as early as C. E. Osgood and Wilbur Schramm's 1954 circular model (McQuail & Windahl, 1993, p. 19). Hall's model "suggested continuity, even as it subverted the older conceptual frameworks" (Gurevitch & Scannell, p. 245). Hall himself acknowledged that "Encoding/Decoding" warranted further refinement, yet many subsequent researchers have treated his model as if it were an indisputable law rather than a theoretical work in progress. As a result, encoding/decoding appears to "have a growth of its own" even though such growth divorced from historical context is incompatible with critical theory (Horkheimer, 1972/1937, p. 240). Hall's work has been mistaken for a universal formula, which is precisely the kind of domineering ideology he argued against.

I will begin by exploring what it means to be "critical" by using Antonio Gramsci's discussion of common sense and extending D. C. Muecke's definition of the irony of incongruity. Then, I will summarize Hall's encoding/decoding model and place "Encoding/Decoding" in its historical context. This context will support my argument that critical scholars should approach Hall's model as a work in progress rather than cast in stone, and that not doing so presents a troubling irony of incongruity. Finally, I will critique two studies that use Hall's model. The first study, "Interpreting Slavery Tourism" (Buzinde & Santos, 2009), treats Hall's framework as complete and final, which ultimately stifles the critical contribution of the authors' interpretation as it makes an (unintentionally) ironic contribution instead. The second study, "Social Movements, Political Goals, and the May 1 Marches: Communicating Protest in Polysemous Media Environments" (Edgerly, Toft, & Veden, 2011), on the other hand, interrogates and recasts Hall's categories, thus avoiding an incongruously uncritical execution of Hall's critical model. I will conclude with remarks about the continued significance of "being critical," and the role that critical canonic texts might play in future critical scholarship.

The main contribution of this chapter is to encourage critical mindfulness of how the field's foundational texts are used and applied. Canonical texts should be used as starting points rather than as universal frameworks, lest today's critical communication scholars inadvertently re-create a status quo that its forerunners vehemently transgressed against.

WHAT DOES IT MEAN TO BE *CRITICAL*?

Advocating that critical studies remain critical of its canonical models raises the question of how to define the slippery term "critical." An established definition of critical theory is elusive since, as Joe L. Kincheloe and Peter McLaren (2005) note, "to lay out a set of fixed characteristics of the position is contrary to the desire of such theorists to avoid the production of blueprints of sociopolitical and epistemological beliefs" (p. 287). The crux of critical studies is resistance to—and even refusal of—fixed blueprints. That said, as Chang (2011) and Hanno Hardt (1986) have explained, the badge of "critical" can be easily co-opted and lose its meaning if it remains ambiguously defined. Even research that purports to be critical can actually proceed uncritically, which underscores the importance of developing a working definition of critical studies.

Critical, common sense, and irony are all "conceptually foggy" terms with lofty aspirations to explain complex dynamics (Chang, 2011, p. 85; Muecke, 1969, p. 3). By coupling existing definitions of "critical" with the concepts of common sense and irony, I will develop a new conception of what it means to *be critical.*

Critical theory has meant envisioning a transformed future by transgressing against the status quo. Critical scholars of communication often trace their roots to the Frankfurt School of the 1930s, in which scholars "developed a critical and transdisciplinary approach to cultural and communications studies, combining critique of political economy of the media, analysis of texts, and audience reception studies of the social and ideological effects of mass culture and communications" (Kellner, 2002, p. 32). According to Frankfurt School historian Martin Jay (1973), the Frankfurt School's visions for a transformed future were "less blueprints for action than sources of critical distance from the gravitational pull of the prevailing reality" (p. 279).

The motivating drive behind "being critical" stems from a desire to challenge structural limitations that constrain how people imagine the future. These limitations ensure that certain perspectives are marginalized or excluded while others are privileged—frequently for no expressed reason other than the common sense justification of "the way it has always been." Toppling these limitations requires rejecting the logic of presuming that the status quo is natural and necessary. Without maintaining an impassioned commitment to seeking the good, critical theory would crumble and would closely resemble traditional theory with a different façade (Horkheimer, 1972/1937). Premised upon the need to question and disrupt the commonsensical status quo, being critical means seeking to "expose the meanings of the 'what-goes-without-saying'" (Kincheloe & McLaren, 2005, p. 297). Put another way, being critical means opposing the presumptions that undergird taken-for-granted common sense.

Rather than dismissing common sense altogether, being critical also involves "rehabilitating common sense" (Glasser & Ettema, 2008, pp. 522–523). As Gramsci (1988) wrote in *Prison Notebooks*, the result of competing common senses has been for one form of common sense "to transcend … and to create another which was closer to the conception of the world of the leading group" (p. 345). If critical thinkers using Hall have become a leading group, this might appear to herald a positive shift in common sense. But common sense alone is still a hidden force of a domineering establishment—particularly when divorced from historical context. Ignoring or omitting the history that led to the emergence of a new form of common sense may lead to a path of reification rather than critically rehabilitated common sense. Critical reflexivity pushes against the "crudely conservative" (p. 346) specter that lurks behind the establishment of common sense. In the field of critical studies, the presence of unquestioned common sense is particularly ironic.

Irony, like critical scrutiny of common sense, is what D. C. Muecke (1969) calls "an art that gets its effects from below the surface" (p. 5). As Muecke explains in his catalog of ironies, "It is ironic when we meet what we set out to avoid, especially when the means we take to avoid something turns out to be the very means of bringing about what we sought to avoid" (p. 102). For instance, the "means" of Hall's model (which set out to avoid totalizing notions of audiences) leading to totalizing notions of audiences is an example of irony as Muecke defines it.

The irony of incongruity emerges through juxtaposition: for instance, an audience study that treats a model's three categories as natural and fixed placed next to a sign that says "the model's three categories are neither natural nor fixed" would be an ironic incongruity. Muecke (1969) characterizes the "Irony of Simple Incongruity" as "irony in its barest and simplest terms" (p. 100). A subtle—yet crucial—disconnect between what a critical model sets out to do and resulting applications of it only becomes visible through a lens of ironic incongruity. Certainly, any study can be placed against the backdrop of its historical context. But being sensitive to ironic incongruity goes a step further by carefully identifying "incompatible phenomena" (Muecke, 1970, p. 61). The contribution of this lens is its magnification of otherwise imperceptible incongruity.

The ironist and criticalist have a shared pursuit of bringing latent and contradictory discourses to light. By using historical context, the ironist can illuminate a subtly problematic situation beneath the surface of a present state—which the criticalist seeks to transform. "Being critical" means looking for ironic incongruities beneath the common-sense surface of a situation. Contextualizing Hall's encoding/decoding model and evaluating applications of it will demonstrate the usefulness of a lens of ironic incongruity in critique.

HALL'S ENCODING/DECODING MODEL

Hall's model emerged as a critical departure from the effects tradition and was met with both celebration and consternation in the field of communication research. "Encoding/Decoding" (1993/1973) was originally published as a work in progress for a colloquium (Deacon, Fenton, & Bryman, 1999, p. 5; Gurevitch & Scannell, 2002, p. 235). Amidst a sea of effects research using the sender-message-receiver linear model, Hall's encoding/decoding model has received ample attention in the field over the past forty years; according to Google Scholar, "Encoding/Decoding" has been cited more than 5,000 times. The model is used so frequently that it is sometimes referenced without an explicit citation, which clouds the perceptibility of the encoding/decoding frame.

Hall's schematic consists of a set of *encoding* meaning structures and a separate *decoding* set of meaning structures, which contain no necessary symmetry (1993/1973, p. 94). The crux of the encoding/decoding model is its three decoding positions: (1) dominant-hegemonic, (2) negotiated, and (3) oppositional.[2]

The dominant-hegemonic position is "when the viewer takes the connoted meaning … and decodes the message in terms of the reference code in which it has been encoded. We might say that the viewer *is operating inside the dominant code*" (Hall, 1993/1973, p. 101). Here, Hall was making a daring statement: dominant-hegemonic positions are what most would regard as "normal" or "legitimate" readings. Hall argued instead that these "normal" readings contain hidden (and oppressive) ideologies:

> The definition of a hegemonic viewpoint is (a) that it defines within its terms the mental horizon, the universe, of possible meanings … and (b) that it carries with it the stamp of legitimacy—it appears coterminous with what is "natural," "inevitable," "taken for granted" about the social order. (p. 102)

Hall drew a landscape in which meaning is always being created—rather than existing naturally—and thus always operating through dynamics of power.

Conversely, the oppositional position is when an individual decodes a message "in a *globally* contrary way" (Hall, 1993/1973, p. 103). Rather than decoding in dutiful accordance with preferred codes, an oppositional reader "detotalizes the message in the preferred code in order to retotalize the message within some alternative framework of reference" (p. 103). For example, an oppositional news reader might replace all mentions of "protect nations around the world from terror through intervention" with "advance American capitalist interests abroad."

The negotiated position, on the other hand, mixes dominant and oppositional elements. Hall (1993/1973) explained, "It acknowledges the legitimacy of the hegemonic definitions to make the grand significations (abstract), while, at a more restricted, situational (situated) level, it makes its own ground rules—it operates with exceptions to the rule" (p. 102). Rife with contradictions, negotiated decoding may lead to people behaving counterintuitively. For instance, a worker who broadly accepts that cheaper labor is better for the economy may still protest a wage cut (p. 102). Here, the worker has accepted the dominant capitalist code, but has mixed in elements of an oppositional decoding (since capitalist gain leads to the worker's personal loss).

The thrust of Hall's model was threefold: (1) all meaning is created through discourse (and power operates thickly throughout discourse); (2) there is no necessary symmetry between encoded meaning structures and decoded meaning structures; and (3) decoding may ensue from a variety of positions categorized as dominant, negotiated, or oppositional.

HISTORICAL CONTEXT AND RECEPTION OF ENCODING/DECODING

Hall's model grew out of a particular set of circumstances in a specific historical moment in cultural studies—which is often overlooked in applications of his model. That said, narrating a definitive history of "Encoding/Decoding" (and of Hall's work) is challenging for reasons that Hall (2007) identifies in a volume of collected working papers of the Centre for Contemporary Cultural Studies (CCCS):

> What claims are being made—about origin ("this is where it all started"), or authenticity ("this is what really happened") or authority ("we are in a better position to know what cultural studies is than you")? These remain contested issues in the Centre's history. … This is hardly surprising, given the anti-foundational, anti-essentialist theoretical ethos in which Cultural Studies has matured, its instinctive inclination to critique and deconstruct "grand narratives." (p. x)

Hall's rejection of "grand narratives" is reflected in the absence of a published comprehensive anthology of his works. Procter (2004) suggests that this absence is consistent with Hall's desire to avoid "impos[ing] upon his thinking a false unity and coherence. … Hall's dispersed essays do not add up to a complete or finished position but are full of contradictions, discrepancies and U-turns" (p. 8). What follows is a brief historical sketch of Hall's work in the period when he wrote and published "Encoding/Decoding."

Hall was the director of the Centre for Contemporary Cultural Studies (CCCS) at the University of Birmingham in the late 1960s and 1970s (Gurevitch & Scannell, 2002, p. 234). As a beacon of British cultural studies, CCCS transformed as Hall "challenged the national boundaries of cultural studies and paved the way for both the consolidation and globalization of cultural studies as a field" (Alexander, 2009, p. 463).

Upon its founding, the Centre received a chilly reception from established departments at the university. Hall (1990) recalled, "We received [a] rather sharp … letter from the sociologists saying, in effect, 'We have read *The Uses of Literacy* and we hope you don't think you're doing sociology, because that's not what you're doing at all'" (p. 13). Though startling, this terse reaction to critical studies is not unique to CCCS. According to Horkheimer (1972/1937), friction often begins with critical theorists when they diverge from "verification and classification by means of categories which are as neutral as possible, that is, categories which are indispensable to inherited ways of life" (p. 232). A critical model's categories becoming "the most familiar" (in the case of Hall's trio of decoding positions) underlines the incongruous irony of Hall becoming part of the sediment of an entrenched status quo.

Hall himself has said that his model is a starting point that provides a basic map rather than a comprehensive, fixed framework. In 1994, Hall reflected on "Encoding/Decoding" and its unanticipated persistence in the field of communication:

> The encoding/decoding model wasn't a grand model. I had in my sights the Centre of Mass Communications Research—that was who I was trying to blow out of the water. I didn't think of it as generating a model which would last for the next twenty-five years for research. I don't think it has the theoretical rigor, the internal logic and conceptual consistency for that. If it's of any purchase, now and later, it's a model because of what it suggests. It suggests an approach; it opens up new questions. It maps the terrain. But it's a model, which has to be worked with and developed and changed. (Hall, quoted in Davis, 2004, p. 65)

Despite Hall's own acknowledgement of the insufficiency of his model as a standalone tool, his work is frequently used as a "toolbox" of readily accessible (and acceptable) theoretical frames (Alexander, 2009, pp. 459–460). Using Hall's work as a toolbox has, as Claire Alexander argues, "stripped the depth and complexity of the originals, reducing them to … convenient, oft-rehearsed and repeated epigrams that substitute for rigorous analysis, more a store cupboard than a toolbox" (pp. 459–460). Because of the revered status that Hall and his work have achieved, "Encoding/Decoding" is poised for consumption as a convenient "conceptual shorthand" (Alexander, p. 460; Gurevitch & Scannell, 2002, p. 244). The potential consequence of such conceptual shorthand is that Hall's model may become a hidden ideology lurking in the background. As Hall (1982) argues, "Extensive empirical work is required to demonstrate the adequacy of [the critical paradigm's] explanatory terms, and to *refine*, *elaborate* and *develop* its infant insights" (p. 88). Stopping at the first clause of "demonstrating the adequacy of … explanatory tools" without "refining, elaborating, and developing its infant insights" is how Hall's model may ironically become a roadblock rather than a catalyst for further critical development.

The climate in which Hall wrote—where few voices were questioning prevailing presumptions in the field—can easily return if critical communication scholars do not insist on being critical of canonical models rather than reifying them. Studies that simply reaffirm Hall's model (even in new settings) remain at the starting point that the now-canonical model provided, which amounts to repeating the model with a new illustration. This is perhaps pedagogically useful, but it stops short of contributing to the critical pursuit of a transformed future.

The irony of using Hall's model in an uncritical way lies in the implicit "forgetting" of encoding/decoding's fairly recent history. Obeying the "laws" of encoding/decoding by unquestioningly conforming to the categories set forth in Hall's model effectively amounts to forgetting a crucial element of encoding/decoding: the model was a work in progress that sought to challenge prevailing common sense assumptions.

EVALUATING APPLICATIONS OF ENCODING/DECODING

Encoding/decoding has been applied across subfields ranging from journalism studies to tourism studies. Most applications of the canonical model contain a brief paragraph about its structure and Hall's iconic status in cultural studies. Few reflect upon or contextualize Hall's three decoding categories. This leads to an ironic incongruity between the critical drive behind Hall's model and the (unintended) function of such studies of reifying his categories as unquestioned common sense. Such verifications are ultimately less enriching than interpretations that reimagine and develop Hall's categories. Being critical begins with using critical models, but cannot end there: being critical also entails being mindful of ironic incongruity between the conceptual contribution of a model and how the model is applied.

For instance, in "Interpreting Slavery Tourism" (2009), Christine Buzinde and Carla Almeida Santos look at how tourists visiting former plantations participate in meaning-making. Buzinde and Santos are critical of the status quo of interpreting slavery tourism sites as tools for a homogenous "conspiratorial heritage system" (p. 440). Attending heavily to polysemous interpretations, they conclude that dominant readers affirm American nationalism and nostalgia, whereas oppositional readers understand the slavery site as a place where racist atrocities occurred (p. 454). Despite their critical frame, the authors ultimately fall prey to the same totalizing inclination they seek to contest. They plainly "categorize decodings as dominant, negotiated, or oppositional based on the degree of divergence from the original encoding (Hall 1980)" (p. 455), which creates an ironic incongruity of deploying a critical model uncritically.

Although "Interpreting Slavery Tourism" is a clear application of Hall's model and a worthwhile step toward deeper engagement with polysemous readings among tourist audiences, the structure of plainly deploying Hall's three categories severely limits the *critical* depth of the analysis. For instance, the authors might have considered ways that dominant decodings include multiple ideologies (such as pro-slavery, which might be distinct from nationalism), or moments when tourists occupy multiple decoding positions at once. With no discussion of ways to conceptually develop Hall's categories, the study instead provides a straightforward verification of Hall's work.

The analysis in "Interpreting Slavery Tourism" reifies Hall's decoding categories as if the categories were facts of how audiences decode rather than propositions. Here, the authors seem to fall into the trap in which "ideology … moves constantly within a closed circle, producing, not knowledge, but a *recognition* of the things we already knew. It did so because it took as already established fact exactly the premises which ought to have been put in question" (Hall, 1982, p. 75; emphasis added). Ironically, in this case the ideology moving in a circle is Hall's model rather than moving in a circle around the dominant established meaning of slavery tourism sites.

Arguably, researchers who use encoding/decoding without destabilizing its categories could respond that they are reporting what the audiences said, and are not interested in creating new categories simply for the sake of complexity. Furthermore, authors of studies like "Interpreting Slavery Tourism" could respond that they are not forcing their observations to fit a predefined "Encoding/Decoding" frame. "Interpreting Slavery Tourism," for instance, does not include any examples of the negotiated position since the authors find that none of the audience responses map onto a negotiated position. Yet the refutation that a direct application of Hall's model merely "reflects reality" remains doubly ironic given critical studies' history of disputing objectivism that purports to reflect reality. As James Ettema and Theodore Glasser (1998) point out in the context of journalism, "Because irony works through objectivity, journalists may assert that irony is merely, as one investigative reporter said, 'in the facts that you find' … the reporter might better have said that irony is 'the finding that you factualize'" (p. 92).

The starting point and end point for critical work are not verification and falsification (Pollock & Cox, 1991, p. 172). Instead, a nucleus of interrogating, contextualizing, and juxtaposing is what makes an empirical study critical. Approaching audience studies as if it were possible to simply recognize or verify the dominant, negotiated, or oppositional categories implies veiled consent to a hidden ideology, which Hall expressly discouraged. Critical theory appears to be safely insulated and even buttressed with verification studies that reaffirm canonic critical models—but these studies may instead erode critical pillars beneath the surface.

That said, Hall's model does have a place in a study like "Interpreting Slavery Tourism," since it provides a starting point for conceptual elaboration. More broadly, it is not the case that Hall's model should be relegated to the dusty archives of once-apt models of communication. The contribution that Hall's model has made through nearly a half-century of research supports retaining it, while also challenging it. Challenging a seminal model of communication is not the same as jettisoning it from the field altogether, which would be a brash move, even in the service of mindfully avoiding ironic incongruities. Hall's model can be used in the service of advancing critical scholarship by pairing it with the researcher's reflexivity, as the following study illustrates.

"Social Movements, Political Goals, and the May 1 Marches: Communicating Protest in Polysemous Media Environments" (Edgerly, Toft, & Veden, 2011) uses Hall's model but avoids falling into the ironic trap of using the decoding categories as fixed or already existing in discourse. This study is of news coverage of the boycott on May 1, 2006 ("The Day without Immigrants"), in which Edgerly, Toft, and Veden explore "the implications of *polysemy* in political actions both for journalistic coverage and audience reception" (p. 315). Ultimately, they argue that the "strategic ambiguity of organizers' preferred messages resulted in three discrete reading positions" (p. 328)—but these positions are not dominant, negotiated, and oppositional. Instead, they effectively reimagine and develop the categories in Hall's model.

Replacing Hall's categories of *dominant*, *negotiated*, and *oppositional* with *aligned*, *negotiated*, and *resistive*, the authors reconsider the encoding/decoding model in the context of the May 1 protests. This example is particularly nuanced because while the protest organizers played an active (arguably dominant) role in encoding media meanings, they were simultaneously members of a marginalized, subjugated group of Latino undocumented workers. Edgerly and colleagues (2011) explain the revised "reading positions":

> [Since] the primary text of the protests was encoded by a group that is not socially or politically dominant, we modified Hall's (1973/1980) classification of reading positions. *Aligned*—rather than *dominant*—refers to a reading position that endorses the meanings of the message producers; *negotiated* refers to a reading position that acknowledges but does not completely endorse the meanings of the message producers; and *resistive* refers to a reading position that activates the polysemous potential in the text and presents a meaning counter to that of the message producers. (p. 320)[3]

Relabeling the categories may seem like a nominal change, but this move has substantial impact on the analysis that follows. For example, under the modified categories, conservative media producers like then-CNN news anchor Lou Dobbs became *resistive* readers. Using Hall's original categories unchanged, Dobbs simply would have been cast in the dominant-hegemonic position since he decoded the media event of May 1, 2006 using a hegemonic ideology of the legitimizing function of legal immigration. When framed instead as activists in favor of immigrant rights versus conservative interests, Dobbs was resistive. Dobbs' shifting decoding positions illustrates and extends Hall's argument about the fluidity of these categories.

The critical crux of "Social Movements" is when Edgerly and colleagues (2011) reflect on the limitations of their (and Hall's) conceptual structure of discrete reading positions:

> Our analysis highlights the difficulty in using the terms dominant or oppositional/resistive, to denote reading positions when the primary text has been encoded by a marginalized group, and received by both mainstream and partisan journalistic audiences. ... This case demonstrates the need for more careful examination and labeling of reading positions that fully consider both the perspective of the message creators, the wider hegemonic structure within which their message is created, and the possibility that reading positions presenting themselves as "subversive" reinforce the status quo. (p. 328)

Although this passage does not contain an explicit discussion of the origins of critical studies or the particular context in which Hall wrote "Encoding/Decoding," the authors capture the spirit of inquiry that Hall's model set in motion. Through allusion rather than direct reference to how they define "being critical," the authors reflexively examine the reading positions and consider limitations of these positions by juxtaposing their case study against wider hegemonic structures. Their eye toward dynamics beneath the surface illustrates how a reflexive lens enables critical engagement with canonical models. Unlike "Interpreting Slavery Tourism," there is not an ironic incongruity when "Social Movements" is placed against the backdrop of the context of Hall's work.

REMAINING CRITICAL OF CRITICAL MODELS

A lens of ironic incongruity is a sharpened conceptual resource for the pursuit of being critical. The case study of Hall's "Encoding/Decoding" model (and applications of it) illustrates how this lens can be used to remain critical of critical models, which is particularly important given the historical context of Hall's work. Applying a canonic critical model leads to an understandable tension between faithfully using the model and being critical of it. A lens of ironic incongruity is key for perceiving underlying presumptions that might otherwise remain uninterrogated.

The lessons about the potential for multiple meanings and decoding positions that Hall's model teaches have a rightly established place in the communication canon, but it is nevertheless problematic (and troublingly ironic) to use Hall's model as a set of uncontestable fixed categories. Certainly, simplification through fixed categories is often unavoidable in empirical research. Using categories, however, does not preclude critical reflexivity about them. Empirical studies that use critical models of communication should be leading the fore in insisting on reflexivity rather than reconstructing uncritical common sense.

Canonic models of communication can either stagnate or advance a field, depends entirely on how they are used. Starting every empirical study by creating completely new models would be needlessly arduous and stagnating, and would dissolve burgeoning cohesion in an already-fractured field. Building upon canonical models of communication is key for having a clear starting point while bearing in mind that, as Hall (1982) argued,

> The world has to be *made to mean*. … Because meaning was not given but produced, it followed that different kinds of meaning could be ascribed to the same events. Thus, in order for one meaning to be regularly produced, it had to win a kind of credibility, legitimacy or taken-for-grantedness for itself. (p. 67)

Similarly, Hall's model has to be "*made to mean*" (p. 67). Critical communication scholars should continue to use Hall's model, but in a critical way. Otherwise, empirical studies that employ Hall's model may end up wielding it as a tool for reification of a status quo instead of a springboard for developing new explanations. The irony of incongruity demonstrates how, without vigilant reflexivity, critical research might thwart its own hopes for transformation. Continuing the conversation that Hall set in motion with "Encoding/Decoding" requires rebuttals, revisions, and recasting—with an eye toward ironic incongruities that may stymie a critical endeavor.

That said, one could argue that not every study must be a critical interrogation. Developing illustrations of a seminal model like Hall's can certainly be useful for demonstrating the model's continued relevance. However, confirmatory studies cannot sustain the field of critical studies on their own. Verification of a model is an important step, but is only an initial step: verification as an end point has a grave potential downside of reifying a new form of entrenched common sense. Critical studies rejects the claim that there is only one way to interpret or understand, and studies that affirm canonic (critical) common sense may recreate the exclusionary mindset that led to critical studies in the first place, effectively regressing the field instead of advancing it. This is not to suggest that canonic models must be abandoned altogether. Instead, reflexivity that is attentive and aware of ironic incongruities is the toehold to advance critical studies while retaining canonical models. Critical models should be treated as frameworks for interpretation and elaboration rather than sacrosanct schematics.

"Critical" is an amorphous, tenuous, contradictory—yet potentially powerful—label for research (Chang, 2011; Ono, 2009; Hardt, 1986). Some research may appear to be critical, particularly when it cites a work in the critical canon, but is not substantively critical. Looking for ironic incongruity serves as a litmus test for discerning the subtle difference between the *appearance* of a critical study and a *substantively* critical study. Often a critical study's contribution appears, on the surface, to be a clear affirmation of a critical theory. Beneath the surface, however, a study that uses the critical canon in an uncritical way is whittling away at a support beam of critical studies. Being critical means seeking out ironic incongruity between the meaning of a canonical text and its usage. Only by reflexively considering ironic incongruities when using canonic models can critical studies build upon these models to move toward transformation instead of stagnation.

Critical studies are fueled by both idealism and dissatisfaction. Rather than being purely idyllic or purely cynical, critical studies has historically sought to reconcile these contradictions without blunting the force of either hopefulness for the future or suspicion of the present state. Rejecting the notion that academic research must simplify the world by smoothing out ridges of contradiction and complication, critical studies should continue to embrace contradictions while challenging common-sense frameworks. Idealism coupled with resistance to the status quo (and a lens that attends to ironic incongruity) is what constitutes a critical approach. An intellectual approach that does not constantly interrogate underlying presumptions—irrespective of what the particular presumptions happen to be—is not critical.

The field of critical studies will continue to mature, and we should bear in mind the struggles that took place in order for critical cultural studies to coalesce as a field just a few decades ago. As Gurevitch and Scannell (2002) have noted: "The impact of a given work is revealed in the works that follow it, are inspired by it, or carry its ideas further" (p. 232). The impact of critical canonical works should be scholarship that moves beyond simply deploying these foundational texts in the service of illustrating their continued applicability and, instead, should advance the field toward crafting critically transformative interpretations.

NOTES

1. The author gratefully acknowledges Theodore L. Glasser and Christine Larson for their feedback throughout the writing process.
2. Hall drew on Frank Parkin's model to develop these three positions. See Parkin, F. (1973), *Class inequality and political order: Social stratification in capitalist and communist societies.* London: Paladin.
3. These positions are expansions of Leah Ceccarelli's (1998) work on polysemy types. See Ceccarelli, L. (1998), "Polysemy: Multiple Meanings in Rhetorical Criticism," *Quarterly Journal of Speech, 84*, 395–415.

BIBLIOGRAPHY

Alexander, C. (2009, July). Introduction: Stuart Hall and "race." *Cultural Studies, 23*(4), 457–482.

Bernstein, R. (1976). Empirical theory. In *The restructuring of social and political theory* (pp. 1–54). New York, NY: Harcourt.

Brown, M. E. (1997). Feminism and cultural politics: Television audiences and Hillary Rodham Clinton. *Political Communication, 14*(2), 255–270.

Buzinde, C., & Santos, C. A. (2009). Interpreting slavery tourism. *Annals of Tourism Research, 36*(3), 439–458.

Carey, J. W. (2009). *Communication as culture*. New York, NY: Routledge.

Chang, B. G. (2011, March). Introduction: Sixteen and a half questions on "Being Critical." *Communication and Critical/Cultural Studies, 8*(1), 85–87.

Davis, H. (2004). *Understanding Stuart Hall.* London, England: Sage.

Deacon, D., Fenton, N., & Bryman, A. (1999). From inception to reception: The natural history of a news item. *Media, Culture & Society, 21*(1), 5–31.

Delia, J. (1987). Communication research: A history. In C. R. Berger & S. H. Chaffee (Eds.), *Handbook of communication science* (pp. 20–97). Newbury Park, CA: Sage.

Denzin, N. (1994). The art and politics of interpretation. In N. K. Denzin & Y. S. Lincoln (Eds.), *Handbook of qualitative research* (pp. 500–515). Thousand Oaks, CA: Sage.

Edgerly L., Toft, A., & Veden, M. L. (2011). Social movements, political goals and the May 1 marches: Communicating protest in polysemous media environments. *International Journal of Press and Politics, 20*(10), 1–21.

Ettema, J. S., & Glasser, T. L. (1998). *Custodians of conscience: Investigative journalism and public virtue.* New York, NY: Columbia University Press.

Geertz, C. (1973). *The interpretation of cultures.* New York, NY: Basic Books.

Glasser, T. L., & Ettema, J. S. (2008). Ethics and eloquence in journalism. *Journalism Studies, 9*(4), 512–534.

Gramsci, A., & Forgacs, D. (1988). *An Antonio Gramsci reader: Selected writings, 1916–1935.* New York, NY: Schocken.

Gurevitch, M., & Scannell, P. (2002). Canonization achieved? Stuart Hall's "Encoding/Decoding." In E. Katz, J. Durham, T. Liebes, & A. Orloff (Eds.), *Canonic texts in media research: Are there any? Should there be? How about these?* (pp. 231–247). Cambridge, England: Polity.

Hall, S. (1980). Encoding/decoding. In S. Hall, D. Hobson, A. Lowe, & P. Willis (Eds.), *Culture, media, language* (pp. 117–127). London, England: Hutchinson.

Hall, S. (1982). The rediscovery of ideology: The return of the "repressed" in media studies. In T. Bennett, J. Curran, M. Gurevitch, & J. Wollacott (Eds.), *Culture, society and the media* (pp. 56–90). London, England: Methuen.

Hall, S. (1987, June). Gramsci and us. *Marxism Today,* 16–21.

Hall, S. (1990). The emergence of cultural studies and the crisis of the humanities. *October, 53*, 11–23.

Hall, S. (1992). Cultural studies and its theoretical legacies. In D. Morley & K. Chen (Eds.), *Stuart Hall: Critical dialogues in cultural studies* (pp. 262–275). New York, NY: Routledge.

Hall, S. (1993/1973). Encoding, decoding. In S. During (Ed.), *The cultural studies reader* (pp. 90–103). New York, NY: Routledge.

Hall, S. (2007). Preface. In A. Gray, J. Campbell, M. Erickson, S. Hanson, & H. Wood (Eds.), *CCCS selected working papers.* Vol. 1 (pp. ix–xiv). New York, NY: Routledge.

Hardt, H. (1986). British cultural studies and the return of the "critical" in American mass communication research: Accommodation or radical change? *Journal of Communication Inquiry, 10*(2), 117–124.

Horkheimer, M. (1972/1937). Traditional and critical theory. In *Critical theory: Selected essays* (M. J. O'Connell et al., Trans.) (pp. 188–243). New York, NY: Continuum.

Jay, M. (1973). *The dialectical imagination: A history of the Frankfurt School and the Institute of Social Research, 1923–1950.* Boston, MA: Little, Brown.

Kellner, D. (2002). The Frankfurt School and British cultural studies: The missed articulation. In J. T. Nealon & C. Irr (Eds.), *Rethinking the Frankfurt School: Alternative legacies of cultural critique* (pp. 31–57). Albany: State University of New York Press.

Kincheloe, J. L., & McLaren, P. (2005). Rethinking critical theory and qualitative research. Reprinted in Kecia Hayes, Shirley R. Steinberg, & Kenneth Tobin (Eds.), *Key work in critical pedagogy* (pp. 285–326). Rotterdam, the Netherlands: Sense.

Kincheloe, J. L., & McLaren, P. (2011). Rethinking critical theory and qualitative research. In J. L. Kincheloe, K. Hayes, S. R. Steinberg, & K. G. Tobin (Eds.), *Key works in critical pedagogy: Joe L. Kincheloe* (15th ed., pp. 285–326). Rotterdam, the Netherlands: Sense.

McQuail, D., & Windahl, S. (1993). *Communication models for the study of mass communication.* New York, NY: Longman.

Morley, D., & Brunsdon, C. (1999). *The nationwide television studies.* London, England: Routledge.

Muecke, D. C. (1969). *The compass of irony.* London, England: Methuen.

Muecke, D. C. (1970). *Irony.* London, England: Methuen.

Ono, K. (2009). Critical/cultural approaches to communication. In W. F. Eadie (Ed.), *21st century communication: A reference handbook* (pp. 74–80). Los Angeles, CA: Sage.

Ono, K. (2011). Critical: A finer edge. *Communication and Critical/Cultural Studies, 8*(1), 93–96.

Pollock, D., & Cox, J. R. (1991). Historicizing "reason": Critical theory, practice, and postmodernity. *Communication Monographs, 58*(2), 170–178.

Procter, J. (2004). *Stuart Hall.* London, England: Routledge.

Turner, G. (1992). *British cultural studies: An introduction.* New York, NY: Routledge.

CHAPTER TWO

Critiquing "Neoliberalism"

Three Interrogations and a Defense

SEAN PHELAN[1]

Looked at broadly, we can identify two distinct discourses about neoliberalism[2] in communication and media studies and elsewhere. The first deploys the term to enact a familiar critical narrative, where neoliberalism signifies a social order dominated by the logic of the market. This narrative has been given different inflections in communication and media research. Neoliberalism has functioned as a descriptive and explanatory category in analyses of topics such as infotainment (Thussu, 2007), media ownership (Herman & McChesney, 1997), multiculturalism (Lentin & Titley, 2011), reality television (Ouellette & Hay, 2008), political marketing (Savigny, 2008), intellectual property rights (Hesmondhalgh, 2008), and the cultural politics of voice (Couldry, 2010). Others have examined the communicative dynamics of "free market" regimes without explicitly deploying the term "neoliberalism" (Aune, 2001). More generally, the role of media and communication practices in the ideological constitution of neoliberalism is taken for granted in the wider literature (see Birch & Mykhnenko, 2010; Harvey, 2005).

Yet, the authority of neoliberalism as a critical signifier has been interrogated by a second discourse. This critique has sometimes been made by those distancing themselves from critical research traditions, in some cases defending their work against the charge of ideological complicity with neoliberalism. However, frustration with the open-ended scope of the term has also been articulated by those who retain a clear commitment to interrogating what might otherwise be named as neoliberal norms. For example, one author analyzed in this essay, Lawrence Grossberg, argues that a fixation on neoliberalism and neoliberalization can impede critical analysis. As he observes in an interview with Cho (2008):

> Too often, the context is just described in terms of the dialectic between the global and the local or in terms of the neoliberalization of just about everything, a particularly unhelpful phrase, whether it is understood economically or governmentally. These are too glib and too easy. We need to find better ways of talking about regional, transnational, or even global contexts. Perhaps we should be looking at all of them but surely we have to figure out how to map the interconnections, the articulations. (p. 107)

This chapter examines three articulations of the second discourse in communication, media, and cultural analysis. I ask: what is justified, and what is problematic, about the claim that appeals to neoliberalism often produce little more than a formulaic mode of critique? I argue that skepticism about how the term is used is in one respect justified. As in other fields, neoliberalism is too often invoked as a "summary label," a "metaphor for the ideological air we all (must) breathe" (Peck, 2010, p. xii). At the same time, I argue that it would be a mistake to discard the concept; rather, we need to interrogate its formulaic iteration, yet try to operationalize it in a more critically illuminating way. I conclude by briefly outlining a theoretical and methodological rationale for recuperating the concept.

THE CRITIQUE OF CRITIQUE

Skepticism about the term "neoliberalism" is contextualized by a more general turn in social and political theory interrogating the condition of critique. Much that is performed in the name of critique has simply "run out steam," Latour (2004) suggests, "like those mechanical toys that endlessly make the same gesture when everything else has changed around them" (p. 225). He blames a popularization of critique and "quick readings" of critical social theory for normalizing a post–9/11 conspiracy theory culture: an "absurd deformation" of the weapons of social critique that—in a reproach of his own earlier work—"are our weapons nonetheless" (p. 230). Ranciere (2009) offers his own "critique of critique," though he retains a much sharper focus on the political constitution of the social order (p. 25). Interrogating the condescending nature of a critical posture that "demystifies" on behalf of the apparently mystified, he argues much critique betrays an authentic critical tradition because it assumes a depoliticized and ironized form "entirely disconnected from [a] horizon of emancipation" (p. 32). Billig (2003) discusses the paradoxes resulting from the institutional success of critical identities in the academy. A default critical hostility toward marketized discourses can obscure how the critical has become something of a brand label in its own right; a marketing strategy blind to its own participation in the cultures it interrogates.

This chapter ultimately affirms the value of critique and, in particular, the value of critiquing something called "neoliberalism." My work remains centered on neoliberalism as an object of critical communication and media studies, from a theoretical perspective indebted to Laclau and Bourdieu (Phelan, 2011). At the same time, I want to recognize how the critique of neoliberalism can be banal and predictable. Clive Barnett (2005) puts the point provocatively when he characterizes neoliberalism as a "consolation term" that facilitates the ritual enactment of a rote critical identity. Barnett's critique is one of three positions evaluated in this chapter resonating with the interdisciplinary field of media, communication, and cultural studies. The others are the critiques of Flew, Cunningham, and the already mentioned Grossberg.[3] Instead of dismissing those who question the value of the term or, worse, simply denouncing them as neoliberal collaborators, I want to explore what future critical theoretical work in communication and media studies can productively learn from these critiques.

The chapter follows a two-pronged analytical approach: I attempt to understand the internal logic of each position, while simultaneously interrogating some presuppositions and blind spots. My approach is loosely informed by Glynos and Howarth (2007). They commend a mode of critical interpretivist analysis that passes through agents' self-interpretations of social practices, but that also asks: What makes a particular interpretation possible? How is neoliberalism constituted and presupposed as a discursive object? What other objects are implicated in rendering neoliberalism a problematic object? My objective is to recognize some problems in the critique of neoliberalism but to also insist on its enduring importance as an object of productive critique.

DEFENDING CREATIVE INDUSTRIES

Terry Flew questions the value of the concept of neoliberalism in a number of articles, including one coauthored with Stuart Cunningham. Both are members of the Creative Industries faculty at the Queensland University of Technology (QUT). The establishment of the faculty in the early 2000s saw the parallel disestablishment of the University's arts faculty, and the subsequent closure of its School of Humanities and Human Services (Bahnisch, 2007). QUT's articulation of a creative industries identity has sometimes been the target of scathing critiques for its perceived capitulation to neoliberalized norms and renunciation of a critical scholarly ethos (see McGuigan, 2006). Not surprisingly, a defense of the concept of the creative industries explicitly features in Flew and Cunningham's discussion of neoliberalism.

Flew voices concerns about the concept of neoliberalism in his review of Des Freedman's (2008) book, *The Politics of Media Policy*. Flew (2008) is not dismissive of the book, describing it as a "valuable contribution to … [the] international literature on comparative media policies" (p. 127). However, he interrogates Freedman's reliance on neoliberalism as an "omnibus term," a "single organizing prism" for mapping the relationship between media policy regimes in the "two quite different countries" of the United Kingdom and United States (p. 128). "All roads … seem to point towards the implementation of some or other form of neoliberal policy," Flew concludes, so that "even when policies would appear to be quite different, they are in fact quite the same, all explicable under the rubric of variants of neoliberalism" (p. 128).

Flew (2009) refines his critique in an essay reflecting on "the rise of *cultural economy* as a key organizing concept over the 2000s" (p. 1). Maintaining that "the development of neoliberalism as a meta-concept in critical theory constitutes a substantive barrier to more sustained engagement between cultural studies and economics" (p. 1), Flew's argument against the critique of neoliberalism rests on three interlinked propositions. First, he criticizes researchers for propagating "one-dimensional caricatures" (p. 5) of economics, which reduce the political and methodological heterogeneity of economics to the tenets of neoclassical economics and rational choice theory. Second, this fosters a view of economics as an "ideology" that serves dominant economic and class interests "through the mystification of social reality" (p. 5). Third, these two assumptions converge in appeals to the "all-pervasive term" neoliberalism that disparages, among other targets, "creative industries discourse" (p. 5). Flew specifically interrogates a neo-Marxist analysis that frames the popularization of Chicago School economics, the rise of Thatcher and Reagan, and the articulation of a Third Way political identity as linear developments in the emergence of neoliberalism as a ruling-class ideology. Against this narrative, Flew suggests Foucault's (2008) analysis of ordoliberalism—the neoliberalism of the post-war West German state—illustrates a vision of a "social market economy" quite different from neo-Marxists' conception of neoliberalism through a strong "opposition between the state and the market" (2009, p. 6). Foucault's governmentality approach "may provide more focus on what neoliberalism actually is, rather than it becoming a category prone to analytical hyperinflation" (p. 6).

Flew and Cunningham develop these arguments further in a more comprehensive defense of creative industries against the charge of neoliberal collusion. Here the critique of the concept of neoliberalism morphs into a sharper indictment of the analytical posture of critical identities. They cite Nonini's sarcastic observations about the utility and malleability of the term for "progressive scholars" who can at least "agree that whatever neoliberalism is, they don't like it" (cited in Flew & Cunningham, 2010, p. 119). Flew and Cunningham suggest "universalizing claims about neoliberalism may in fact rest upon a kind of Marxist functionalism, whereby an all-encompassing dominant ideology is developed to 'serve' capital in its latest phase, which is deemed to be global and flexible" (p. 120). Citing Chinese specifics, they highlight the problems with the concept of neoliberalism when "taken outside of the Anglo-American framework in which it originated" (p. 113). The contingency of the Chinese state's commitment to "private property rights, free markets, and free trade," the lack of "popular support for a neoliberal policy program," and the country's strong "developmental state" are listed as evidence of the limitations of reducing the complexity of the world to a single theoretical concept (pp. 119–120).

The different views of the critique of neoliberalism are evaluated as a whole later in the chapter. But bracketing out the question of how accurately they represent the arguments of Freedman and others, Flew and Cunningham identify a number of problems with neoliberalism's use as a catch-all term, noted by others who affirm the value of the concept. Peck (2010) recognizes how neoliberalism can be articulated in a totalizing way that obscures the messiness and contradictions of different social formations. He also cautions against over-relying on a "big picture ... story of neoliberalism" cast in "broad political-economic strokes" (p. xii), implicitly echoing Flew and Cunningham's apprehensions about the universalizing sweep of neo-Marxist arguments.

Nonetheless, Flew and Cunningham make a number of problematic assumptions that, in some cases, paradoxically reproduce dichotomies they are critiquing. They criticize neo-Marxist analyses of neoliberalism for presupposing a strong opposition between state and market. Yet they reproduce a similar opposition when they cite the developmental character of the Chinese state as an exception to neoliberalism, as if there were not examples of a developmental state logic in the embedding of neoliberalism in Western contexts.[4] Their counterargument also obscures how neoliberalism has been a "political project of state-crafting" (Wacquant, 2012, p. 66) rather than one consistent with "official" free market doctrine. The narrow conception of neoliberalism as an economic ideology is reinforced by Flew's (2009) strong alignment of neoliberalism with economics, deemphasizing its significance as a political, social, and cultural project (Couldry, 2010; Brown, 2003).

Second, Flew is correct to identify differences between the social market vision of ordoliberalism and a stylized 1980s representation of neoliberalism as a market ideology antagonistic to the social and the state (see also Crouch, 2011), even if his reading of Foucault exaggerates and decontextualizes them.[5] However, in suggesting ordoliberalism offers a more accurate account of what "neoliberalism actually is"—as if neoliberalism can be reduced to an essentialist form—Flew misrecognizes the contextually *articulated* nature of neoliberal identities and appeals to a "myth of origin" that is hard to square with his citation of Foucault. The idea that there is a *real* neoliberalism, which renders other attributions of the concept inauthentic, is indicative of a general tendency to define the concept though abstract ideological blueprints and typologies, which are then taken to be the most authentic embodiments of neoliberalism. This approach denies what Brenner and

Theodore (2002) describe as the ideological impurity of "actually existing neoliberalism," occluding how neoliberalized regimes are often—if not always—politically institutionalized in ways that deviate from abstract doctrinal prescriptions (see also Peck, 2010).

NEOLIBERALISM-AS-HEGEMONY *AND* NEOLIBERALISM-AS-GOVERNMENTALITY

Although most clearly situated within the field of human geography, Clive Barnett explores the politics of culture and the role of media infrastructures in the constitution of public space (Barnett, 2003). His widely cited polemic (Barnett, 2005) against the critique of neoliberalism echoes Flew and Cunningham in a number of respects: He laments its use as a convenient catch-all term for a bundle of distinct processes; he questions the tendency to define neoliberalism through simplistic oppositions between state and market, individual and collective; and, most provocatively, he wonders if it functions as a consolation term for leftist academics engaging in revelatory interventions that are not half as revealing as they think. Nonetheless, Barnett's (2003) work affirms a critical sensibility, alert to the political conditions of public life. His skepticism about the reliance on neoliberalism as a "descriptive concept" and neoliberalization as an "explanatory concept" (Barnett, 2005, p. 8) is motivated by a concern that the possibility of radicalizing a liberal democratic inheritance can be obscured by critical discourses that disparage values like individualism and freedom as neoliberal proxies.

"There is no such thing as neoliberalism," Barnett (2005) insists; indeed, he assumes an ironic distance from the term by persistently citing it in scare quotes, performatively illustrating how the reified object called "neoliberalism" is partly made by critics themselves (p. 9). Contra Flew, he interrogates a trend (see Larner, 2003) toward reconciling a Marxist political economy analysis of neoliberalism with "post-structuralist ideas of discourse and governmentality derived from Foucault" (p. 7). Barnett argues Marxist and Foucauldian accounts of neoliberalism have been articulated together in a way that remains lodged in Marxist functionalist assumptions, but in a fashion that now communicates a reassuring sensitivity to difference and the openness of neoliberalism to diverse articulations (p. 7). Maintaining that the different ontological, epistemological, and normative assumptions of both theoretical traditions should not be elided, he claims Foucault's account of governmentality has been mainly "instrumentalized for the purposes of shoring up the holes in the Marxist narrative" (p. 8).

The appeal of Foucault as a theoretical supplement to Marx is twofold, Barnett suggests. First, conceptualizing neoliberalism as a dispersed, contextually articulated discourse is "understood instrumentality" as a synonym for a conception of ideology more alert to the role of language and ideas in the constitution of social reality. Second, the notion of governmentality helps explain how a macro-level shift to a market-driven political economy is articulated with mundane everyday practices. What is missing in this neat conjunction of top-down and quotidian perspectives, Barnett argues, is "a set of questions about various middle ranges of agency"—a conception of social relations irreducible to the instrumentalist effects of elite-driven neoliberal hegemony (p. 9). The result is a disabling narrative that presupposes simplistic binaries between state and market, and individual and collective, which enacts the ritualistic performance of a formulaic critique. Barnett even wonders if "we should try to do without the concept of neoliberalism, because it might actually compound rather than aid in the task of figuring out how the world works and how it changes" (p. 10).

Barnett's critique of neoliberalism, as an object of analysis, is productive in at least two respects. First, he highlights how totalizing articulations of the concept are not simply a feature of Marxist analysis but also evident in research indebted to Foucault. What are obscured in such analyses for Barnett are satisfactory explanations of the institutional, agented, and rhetorical processes linking narratives of neoliberal hegemony and institutional cooption to "everyday routines" (p. 9). Both theoretical discourses are generically dependent on Althusserian notions of "hailing and interpellation" (p. 9) in explaining the social reproduction of neoliberalism, even if Foucauldian analysis comes with its own distinct rhetoric of biopolitics and disciplinary power. Both approaches reproduce a romantic antagonism pitching the forces of neoliberalism against the forces of resistance, foreclosing a more imaginative consideration of how neoliberalized cultures might be productively reconfigured and politicized.

Second, Barnett's criticism of how neoliberalism is represented as a singular and "coherent ideological project" with "clear unambiguous origins" is also useful. His citation of a scare-quoted "neoliberalism" highlights the limitations of mundane rhetorical formulations that construct neoliberalism as a singular "it" or thing-like entity with causal effects in its own right. Neoliberalism is construed as a "static type," the master signifier of a whole epoch, rather than a dynamic material-discursive construction(s), more structurally precarious than a grand narrative of neoliberal hegemony might suggest (Clarke, 2010, p. 340). Critical interventions can ironically reinforce a logic of neoliberal inevitability by obscuring the political contingency and contradictions of neoliberal regimes, failing to explore how the world could be otherwise (Clarke, 2008).

There is much to reflect on in Barnett's strong polemic. However, the coherence of his argument rests on several conceptual shortcuts and stylizations. Barnett aligns the Marxist account of neoliberalism with the concept of hegemony, with "neoliberalism-as-hegemony" as the master code for a singular ideological project determined by a top-down infrastructure of power. Barnett's theoretical understanding of hegemony is unclear. The abstract anticipates a discussion of plural "theories of hegemony" (p. 7). Yet, aside from cursory references to "Gramscian state theory" and "French regulation theory," his critique is directed toward a generic Marxist "political economy conceptualization of 'hegemony'" (p. 8), defined by a conflation of ruling-class power, functionalist and mechanical models of consent, the mystifying power of ideologies, the cooption of politics by the logic of capital, and the global diffusive power of a Western political architecture.

The irony is that Stuart Hall, one of the few analysts of neoliberalism cited favorably by Barnett, is also perhaps the best-known proponent of the concept of hegemony in communication and media studies. Not only did Hall play a key role in popularizing Gramsci's ideas in the 1970s, his work was also influenced by the post-Marxist account of hegemony developed by Laclau and Mouffe (2001) in the 1980s (see Morley & Chen, 1996). Barnett commends Hall's work on Thatcherite neoliberalism for its attentiveness to the social specificity and popular mood of the time, in contrast to "elite-focused analyses of state bureaucracies, policy networks and the like" (p. 10) in the recent neoliberalism literature.

I cite Hall simply to highlight how Barnett's critique is directed against a particular conceptual understanding of hegemony, built on stylized assumptions not easily transposed to other theoretical accounts. The point applies equally to Barnett's generic treatment of the concept of discourse. For instance, Ernesto Laclau (1990) would reject aligning the concept of hegemony to a rigid Marxist economism and a priori privileging of class as the defining locus of political identification.[6] Laclau would also pluralize the political in a way that echoes Barnett's (2005) desire for "a bottom-up governmentality" (p. 10) to counter the top-down view of power attributed to the fusion of neoliberalism-as-hegemony and neoliberalism-as-governmentality.[7] Qualifiers of this kind do not make for good polemic, of course, and some aspects of Barnett's critique (such as his criticism of abstract psychoanalytical accounts of subject formation) could be attributed more plausibly to Laclau. Nonetheless, Barnett's provocation needs to be understood as a critique of how particular concepts are articulated (including perhaps the concept of neoliberalism), rather than an indictment of the concept as such, as illustrated by his own valorization of the idea of a "bottom-up governmentality."

LETTING US OFF THE HOOK?

The final author I discuss, Lawrence Grossberg, articulates more of a broadstroke and impressionistic critique of how neoliberalism is used, a frustration voiced as fragmentary observations in different publications (Cho, 2008; Grossberg, 2010). His overriding concern is how rote appeals to neoliberalism can foster a heavy-handed and prefabricated mode of critique rather than alertness to contextual specificity, emerging social phenomena, and a politics of becoming. Like Barnett, his target is the condition of critique itself, and the adequacy of the critical vocabulary of neoliberalism and neoliberalization in illuminating the challenges of the current historical conjuncture.

Grossberg's (2010) problem with the term is articulated as part of a more general dissatisfaction with the condition of cultural studies and the preprogrammed nature of some of its dominant concepts and terminologies. Appeals to neoliberalism are "lazy" (p. 2), as they work to subsume diverse phenomena under a prefabricated critical analytic rather than opening up the "political-intellectual" (p. 2) work of cultural studies to the "empirical complexity of the real" (p. 4). The reduction of everything to the same and the given is contrasted with Grossberg's vision of a cultural studies "that reshapes itself in and attempts to respond to new conjunctures as problem-spaces" (p. 1), an articulation of "theory [that] is always in the service of the concrete" (p. 2).

Grossberg follows Barnett in criticizing Marxist and governmental articulations of the term (and the work of Clarke [2008, 2010] is an important reference for both authors). Both theoretical traditions invoke neoliberalism and neoliberalization in totalizing ways that reduce the particular and the novel to the terms of the already known (Grossberg, 2010, p. 141). Different discourses and practices are constructed as "equivalent and identical" (p. 132), all merely symptomatic of an a priori neoliberal logic rather than different contextual articulations whose relationships to each other necessitate open-ended analysis and exposition. Echoing Flew's concerns about the dismissive view of economics engendered in cultural critique, Grossberg argues that the unitary discourse of neoliberalism obscures both the contingency of economic practices and the need for more sophisticated conversations between cultural studies and heterogeneous economic identities.

Grossberg reaches a similar conclusion to Barnett, wondering if the project of critically understanding the world needs a term that "can be placed in front of almost anything" (2010, p. 141). Appealing to neoliberalism "lets us off the hook," he suggests, and "we would be better off without it unless its meaning is always specified and contextually located" (p. 141). Curiously, he underlines the incoherence of the term by casually observing in parenthesis: "It is a term—certainly not a concept" (p. 141).

Like Barnett's, Grossberg's intervention is a deliberatively provocative one—intended to unsettle the potentially complacent nature of work done under the sign of critique and imagine a mode of critical intervention that goes beyond stock-in-trade appeals and formulations. Nonetheless, he balks at declaring neoliberalism an entirely redundant term; rather, it can still enable useful conjunctural analysis so long as it is responsive to the particular empirical context. "Whatever it [neoliberalism] is," the focus has to be on the "question [of] how is it dis- and re-articulated to existing practices, projects and discourses, or onto specific—old and new configurations" rather than prefabricated explanations and discourses (2010, p. 141).

Grossberg's insistence that we focus on how particular contexts are neoliberalized, but not reducible to the descriptive category of neoliberalism, is well made. He anchors the claim in an affirmation of a "radically contextualist" cultural studies, which holds "that the identity, significance, and effects of any practice or event (including cultural practices and events) are defined only by the complex set of relations that surround, interpenetrate, and shape it, and make it what it is" (2010, p. 20). Radical contextuality is about more than simply exalting the "local" and "particular," Grossberg suggests, for that would occlude how the particular context is always situated within a multiplicity of contexts that "transcend particular sites and territories" (p. 28). A similar relational logic underpins his proposal for negotiating the inevitability of conceptual abstraction: "abstract or general categories" should be understood as "always contextual" and open to different articulations (p. 28).

Listing "commodification, racism, or colonization" (2010, p. 28) as examples of categories that transcend specific contexts, Grossberg omits the category of neoliberalization lest the rhetorical force of his critique be undermined. This is reinforced by his perfunctory dismissal of neoliberalism's conceptual status, seemingly rendering any talk of a generalized neoliberalism incoherent. In denying neoliberalism conceptual status, Grossberg invokes a strong idea of concept that seems at odds with his commitment to a radical contextual appreciation of how concepts can be articulated differently. He seems, in effect, to be valorizing a notion of concept, somehow more real or accurate than how the idea of concept is articulated by others.

Grossberg's hyperbolic aversion to neoliberalism as a general concept is a product of the strong suspicion of the universal evident in his work. This takes the form of an antipathy to a universal neoliberal story recycled in essentialized ways from context to context, and a more general suspicion of analytical discourses that privilege a particular "founding concept" in "a purely theoretical or even ontological way" that then purports to explain "everything … everywhere" (2010, p. 19). Grossberg's suspicion of universality in this strong form is justified. However, his critique forecloses a different conception of the universal, one more consistent with his own ontological commitment to the universality of articulatory relations and radically contextual practices (see Glynos & Howarth, 2007; Laclau, 1990). Such an approach might enable a more nuanced analysis of the universalizing "equivalences" between different neoliberalized contexts, but without denying the specificity of each contextual articulation or leaving us with nothing but singular cases that bear no relation to each other. We can critique totalizing appeals to a singular neoliberalism without displacing how neoliberal logics do have totalizing effects that reduce, but do not eliminate, the differences between one context and another.

RECUPERATING NEOLIBERALISM AS AN OBJECT OF CRITIQUE

I examined three articulations of a discourse questioning the usefulness of the concept of neoliberalism in communication, media, and cultural studies. All three critiques are, in some respects, perfectly justified. Flew is right to suggest neoliberalism often functions as an "omnibus term." Barnett is right to maintain that appeals to a reified neoliberalism can simplify the analysis of social change. And Grossberg is right to argue that the category can "let us off the hook" and cultivate a formulaic reliance on a generic neoliberal story.

Yet the most obvious comeback is that similar arguments have been made by others who continue to privilege neoliberalism as an object of critique. Peck (2010) recognizes the inadequacy of a sweeping grand narrative in understanding the variegated trajectories of neoliberal reason. Wacquant (2012) notes the reductive tendencies in both Marxist and governmentality accounts. And Crouch (2011) critiques the limits of a commonplace state–free market binary for defining neoliberalism, because it obscures the corporatized and anticompetitive tendencies of neoliberal regimes and the state's internalization of neoliberal logics.

In response to our critics, we might therefore suggest the problem with the concept of neoliberalism is not with the category as such; rather, as with all categories, the problem is with how the category is *articulated*. The category is too often articulated in a way that does too much analytic work on its own, obscures the specificity and paradoxes of different social formations, or remains lodged in a denunciatory mode of critique that, as Clarke (2010) observes, becomes so "fascinated [with] tracing the dominant" it ends up simply "confirm[ing] its dominance" (p. 340).

The critique of the critique of neoliberalism does not offer a convincing case for discarding the category from our critical vocabulary (as if categories are easily discarded). If we purge it on the grounds that it signifies a unitary object that is not really a unitary object, well, then, we might have to discard a whole lot of other categories too: society, economy, culture, media, capitalism, and so on.

At the same time, the critique should not be dismissed because it highlights problems with how the term is articulated as a loose signifier for everything and nothing. Let me end by quickly describing how future work on neoliberalism could respond productively to our critics.

The concept of neoliberalism offers a particular way of critically naming the social, more likely to be used by critics of neoliberalism than any putative neoliberals themselves. The name gives analytical and narrative shape to myriad social changes and processes that cannot be pinned down to a single empirical horizon or referent. Barnett is, therefore, right: "There is no such thing as neoliberalism," *if* by that we mean a unitary object with an unambiguous real-world referent or constitutive status (see also Castree, 2006). We might describe it instead as an "impossible object" that "only exists … as an effort to construct that impossible object" (Laclau & Mouffe, 2001, p. 112).[8] The name takes on the analytically necessary, yet also "impossible," task of describing and explaining social changes that are irreducible to discrete empirical objects or subjects, or abstract doctrinal prescriptions. Questions like *what is* neoliberalism, *where* is it located and *how* is it articulated are inherently contestable. In suggesting problems with the term, my argument is not to suggest there is a "correct" way of using it somehow missed by others.

Constructing neoliberalism *as if it were* a unitary object has an obvious polemical and political value. It helps us identify ideological features of particular social formations and highlight similarities between one formation and another. Moreover, if we want to talk about neoliberalism at all (write articles and books about it), we cannot but sometimes speak of it in simplifying and abstract ways. However attentive we are to particular contextual articulations, analyzing neoliberalism necessarily entails a labor of conceptual abstraction.

Nonetheless, as critical analysts of neoliberalism, we should be wary of over-relying on abstract discourses or, as Grossberg suggests, letting our political commitments override our empirical analysis. Identifying social objects and practices as neoliberal can engender a form of "aspect blindness" (Wittgenstein, 1973, p. 213), where other ways of naming the social disappear from view. Empirical phenomena labeled "neoliberal" are too often cursorily disparaged rather than deemed worthy of additional analysis and scrutiny. One defensive response to our critics would be to suggest that no one has argued neoliberalism exists in a monolithic form, and their critical target is therefore a straw man. Yet, while few would explicitly argue that there *is* a singular neoliberalism, the category is routinely rendered as such in banal rhetorical formulations that represent the "impossible" object as a fully present structure or agent with the totalizing power to cause, make, determine, and act on a variety of social objects and practices. Reified discourses of this kind often leave us with little more than a new telling of a familiar neoliberal story rather than productively illuminating the immanent political logics of neoliberalized formations.

Against an excessive use of the reified category of neoliberalism, it might be more productive to speak of neoliberal and neoliberalized logics that are always contextually articulated with other political, social, and fantasmatic logics. Glynos and Howarth (2007) describe "*the logic of a practice [as] the rules or grammar of the practice*, as well as *the conditions which make the practice both possible and vulnerable*" (p. 136). To conceptualize neoliberalism as a series of constitutive logics, dialectically articulated with other logics, underscores the limits of reducing our analysis of social life to the convenient nominalization "neoliberalism." It might also heighten our alertness to how the logic of "things" could be articulated as other than neoliberal, as a counter to the kind of fatalism that often permeates critical discourses (Clarke, 2008).

Yet we also need to go beyond a still relatively abstract analysis of neoliberal "logics." We need to formulate an analysis of neoliberalism that "keeps agents and agency in sight" (Peck, 2010, p. xi) and, as Barnett suggests, encourages productive forms of midlevel theorizing to bridge the gap between the two dominant accounts of neoliberalism. This point is particularly important in a communication and media studies context given the role of the media in mythically connecting the quotidian experiences of everyday social life to a macro-level infrastructure of power (Couldry, 2003). Bringing the concept of neoliberalism "to earth" (Peck, 2010, p. xi) might enable us to better understand how neoliberalized logics are produced by social institutions and agents that do not see themselves as neoliberal. It might also help us develop a critical theory that does more than condemn a sedimented social infrastructure for being neoliberal, perhaps enabling a mode of critical analysis that can both oppose *and* reckon with the given.

NOTES

1. This research was supported by the Massey University Research Fund. Correspondence concerning this article should be addressed to Sean Phelan, School of Communication, Journalism and Marketing, Massey University, Room 5E07, PO Box 756, Wellington, New Zealand. E-mail: s.phelan@massey.ac.nz
2. For consistency's sake, all hyphenated versions of the term "neoliberalism" have been changed in this chapter.
3. One perspective not considered here is a Marxist critique of the term. For example, Garland and Harper (2012) suggest we should be critiquing "capitalism," not the politically obfuscating term "neoliberalism."
4. One example is the Irish case. See Ging, Cronin, and Kirby (2009).
5. Flew downplays at least two elements noted by Foucault (2008): the need for some affirmative conception of the German state after the collapse of the Third Reich, and the character of the ordoliberal state as a "radically economic state" (p. 86).
6. Laclau and Laclau and Mouffe's critique of a Marxist conception of class and economy was never meant as a disavowal of the politics of economy and class, as their critics sometimes imply. Critiquing how we talk about economy and class should not mean we stop talking about them.
7. Barnett (2006) might contest my claim that Laclau and Mouffe offer a poststructuralist conception of hegemony sufficiently different to the one assumed in his critique. In a debate with Thomassen (2005), Barnett (2006) cites Laclau and Mouffe's work as an example of a general poststructuralist tendency to construct rigid dichotomies between the world of the contingent and the possible and the world of the given and the inherited: "What is given is aligned against what is possible, so that the given is understood as what needs to be negated or transcended by unleashing the suppressed potential of what is possible" (p. 640). Barnett contrasts this binary logic with Jacques Derrida's valorization of a patient mode of analysis that pauses "before deciding that all inherited modes of life should be wholly re-made" (p. 64) and "reck[ons] with the

given." What Barnett misses in this critique of a generic poststructuralism is how this Derridean sensibility *is* evident in Laclau's work. Consider, for instance, the following Laclau (1990) quote: "The construction of an alternative project is *based on* the ground created by [capitalist] transformations, not on *opposition* to them" (pp. 55–56).

8. Here I directly transpose Laclau and Mouffe's conception of society as an impossible object, implying any discursive articulation of society will always fail to capture the totality of the relations and processes potentially attributable to society.

BIBLIOGRAPHY

Aune, J. A. (2001). *Selling the free market: The rhetoric of economic correctness*. New York, NY: Guilford.

Bahnisch, M. (2007). QUT farewells the "old" humanities? *Larvatus Prodeo*. Retrieved from http://larvatusprodeo.net/archives/2007/04/23/qut-farewells-the-old-humanities/

Barnett, C. (2003). *Culture and democracy: Media, space and representation*. Edinburgh, Scotland: Edinburgh University Press.

Barnett, C. (2005). The consolations of neoliberalism. *Geoforum, 36*(1), 7–12.

Barnett, C. (2006). Temporality and the paradoxes of democracy. *Political Geography, 24*(5), 641–647.

Billig, M. (2003). Critical discourse analysis and the rhetoric of critique. In G. Weiss & R. Wodak (Eds.), *Critical discourse analysis: Theory and interdisciplinarity* (pp. 35–46). London, England: Palgrave Macmillan.

Birch, K., & Mykhnenko, V. (Eds.). (2010). *The rise and fall of neoliberalism: The collapse of an economic order?* London, England: Zed.

Brenner, N., & Theodore, N. (2002). Cities and the geographies of "actually existing neoliberalism." *Antipode, 34*, 349–79.

Brown, W. (2003). Neo-liberalism and the end of liberal democracy. *Theory & Event, 7*(1). Retrieved from http://muse.jhu.edu/journals/theory_and_event/v007/7.1brown.html

Castree, N. (2006). From neoliberalism to neoliberalisation: Confusions, consolations and necessary illusions. *Environment and Planning, 38*(1), 1–6.

Cho, Y. (2008). We know where we're going, but we don't know where we are: An interview with Lawrence Grossberg. *Journal of Communication Inquiry, 32*(2), 102–122.

Clarke, J. (2008, Summer). Living with/in and without neo-liberalism. *Focaal, 51*, 135–147.

Clarke, J. (2010). Of crises and conjunctures: The problem of the present. *Journal of Communication Inquiry, 34*(4), 337–354.

Couldry, N. (2003). *Media rituals: A critical approach*. London, England: Routledge.

Couldry, N. (2010). *Why voice matters: Culture and politics after neoliberalism*. London, England: Sage.

Crouch, C. (2011). *The strange non-death of neoliberalism*. Cambridge, England: Polity.

Flew, T. (2008). A game of two halves [Review of the book *The politics of media policy*]. *Australian Journalism Review, 30*(2), 127–129.

Flew, T. (2009). The cultural economy moment? *Cultural Science, 2*(1). Retrieved from http://culturalscience.org/journal/index.php/culturalscience/article/view/23/79

Flew, T., & Cunningham, S. (2010). Creative industries after a decade of debate. *Information Society, 26*(2), 113–123.

Foucault, M. (2008). *The birth of biopolitics*. Basingstoke, England: Palgrave Macmillan.

Freedman, D. (2008). *The politics of media policy*. London, England: Polity.

Garland, C., & Harper, S. (2012). Did somebody say neoliberalism? On the uses and limitations of a critical concept in media and communication studies. *tripleC: Cognition, Communication, Co-operation, 10*(2), 413–424. Retrieved from http://www.triplec.at/index.php/tripleC/article/view/396/369

Ging, D., Cronin, M., & Kirby, P. (Eds.). (2009). *Transforming Ireland: Challenges, critique and resources.* Manchester, England: Manchester University Press.

Glynos, J., & Howarth, D. (2007). *Logics of critical explanation in social and political theory.* London, England: Routledge.

Grossberg, L. (2010). *Cultural studies in the future tense.* Durham, NC: Duke University Press.

Harvey, D. (2005). *A brief history of neoliberalism.* Oxford, England: Oxford University Press.

Herman, E. S., & McChesney, R. W. (1997). *The global media: The new missionaries of corporate capitalism.* London, England: Cassell.

Hesmondhalgh, D. (2008). Neoliberalism, imperialism and the media. In D. Hesmondhalgh & J. Toynbee (Eds.), *The media and social theory* (pp. 95–111). London, England: Routledge.

Laclau, E. (1990). *New reflections on the revolution of our time.* London, England: Verso.

Laclau, E., & Mouffe, C. (2001). *Hegemony and socialist strategy* (2nd ed.). London, England: Verso.

Larner, W. (2003). Neoliberalism? *Environment and Planning: Society and Space, 21*(5), 509–512.

Latour, B. (2004, Winter). Why has critique run out of steam? From matters of fact to matters of concern. *Critical Inquiry, 30*, 225–248.

Lentin, A., & Titley, G. (2011). *The crisis of multiculturalism: Racism in a neoliberal age.* London, England: Zed.

McGuigan, J. (2006). Book Review: Creative Industries. *Global Media and Communication, 2*(3), 372–374. doi:10.1177/1742766506069585

Morley, D., & Chen, K. H. (Eds.). (1996). *Stuart Hall: Critical dialogues in cultural studies.* London, England: Routledge.

Ouellette, L., & Hay, J. (2008). *Better living through reality TV: Television and post-welfare citizenship.* Malden, MA: Blackwell.

Peck, J. (2010). *Constructions of neoliberal reason.* Oxford, England: Oxford University Press.

Phelan, S. (2011). The media as the neoliberalized sediment: Articulating Laclau's discourse theory with Bourdieu's field theory. In L. Dahlberg & S. Phelan (Eds.), *Discourse theory and critical media politics* (pp. 128–153). New York, NY: Palgrave Macmillan.

Ranciere, J. (2009). *The emancipated spectator.* London, England: Verso.

Savigny, H. (2008). *The problem of political marketing.* London, England. Continuum.

Thomassen, L. (2005). Reading radical democracy: A commentary on Clive Barnett. *Political Geography, 24*(5), 631–639.

Thussu, D. (2007). *News as entertainment: The rise of global infotainment.* London, England: Sage.

Wacquant, L. (2012). Three steps to a historical anthropology of actually existing neoliberalism. *Social Anthropology, 19*(4), 66–79.

Wittgenstein, L. (1973). *Philosophical investigations.* Oxford, England. Blackwell.

CHAPTER THREE

A New Era of Field Research in Political Communication?

DAVID KARPF, DANIEL KREISS, AND RASMUS KLEIS NIELSEN

For 40 years, a particular methodological consensus has dominated the study of political communication. Quantitative research methods generally, and content analysis, surveys, and experiments in particular, have defined the core of legitimate research, especially in the United States.[1] While some scholars have produced qualitative work—and some of it has been very influential—most political communication research is quantitative, and quantitative methodologies provide the standards by which most political communication research is judged. This methodological consensus not only provides the main tools scholars have at their disposal for empirical work on political communication, it also shapes the very questions they ask, the answers they provide, and the theories they develop.

Since the 1970s, scholars working within this consensus have generated a remarkable body of findings. Scholars have advanced our understandings of agenda setting, the dynamics of public opinion, the influence of news media and campaign communications upon political behavior, and the limits of both citizens' independent reasoning and elites' ability to manipulate people. Political communication research has uncovered with increasing sophistication the cognitive and affective processes that underlie many kinds of political attitudes and assessed the relative importance of mediated appeals versus other factors in shaping political outcomes. Normatively, scholars have made forceful arguments, backed by data, about journalistic and political practices, detailing the corrosive effects of negative campaigning and many shortcomings of the news media when it comes to serving American democracy.

And yet, despite these advances, over the last decade cracks have appeared in the edifice of political communication research. In a sweeping essay aimed at the very foundations of the field as it exists today, two leading figures, W. Lance Bennett and Shanto Iyengar (2008), point out that theoretical advances have not kept pace with social and technological changes over the past decade. Kevin Barnhurst (2011) argues the field faces a crisis because of its reliance on theories and methods developed to understand the media environment of the mid-twentieth century. Patricia Moy and her coauthors (2012) state that political communication research is facing a "critical moment" as it struggles to make sense of a changing world. Ten years ago, Steven Chafee foreshadowed these concerns when, in one of his final essays, he argued that the transition away from a mass media environment challenged many of our core assumptions (Chafee & Metzger, 2001). The concerns shared by all these critics of the field are that we as political communication researchers (1) are not always well equipped to understand our objects, and (2) have not kept pace with a world that looks radically different politically, socially, and technologically from what it looked like at the founding of the field as we knew it in the 1970s (or even as recently as the early 1990s). News media organizations, political campaigns, and interest groups have all changed, as have the tools and techniques they use to communicate with citizens and the broader social, technological, and economic structures within which elites and ordinary people operate. The rise of the Internet and associated digital technologies and social practices is only one of the more visible manifestations of these changes.

In this chapter, we argue that the problems political communication researchers face today stem in part from the very same methodological consensus that has helped facilitate advances in the study of agenda setting, opinion formation, and media effects. In our view, the reigning consensus has marginalized qualitative methods, resulting in an unnecessary and counterproductive narrowing of our ability to understand central aspects of political communication and how it is changing. Whereas much of the conversation about the state of the field so far has focused on whether new theories are needed (Bennett & Iyengar, 2008; Barnhurst, 2011; Moy et al., 2012), we take a different approach and make a case for a new era of field research, defined broadly to include firsthand observation, participation, and interviewing in the actual contexts where political communication occurs. Field research is particularly well equipped to take on the challenge of theory building and empirical research in a new world. It is a method that, in the words of Herbert J. Gans (1962), "gets the researcher close to the realities of social life" and has helped adjacent fields like journalism studies keep track of often rapidly changing objects of analysis. In our view, political communication should, like journalism studies, become more methodologically diverse and embrace qualitative methods as tools that are just as relevant as quantitative ones when it comes to shaping and addressing the basic questions and theories of the field.

In the pages that follow, we argue that the specific question of method needs to be at the forefront of scholarly debate about political communication. First, we outline the form political communication research took with the institutionalization of the field in the United States in the 1970s, and identify an older tradition of interdisciplinary and mixed-methods work on political communication, originating in the 1930s, that was submerged under the quantitative consensus in the process. Second, we examine some key examples of how researchers working out of this tradition—including Gladys Engel Lang and Kurt Lang as well as, perhaps more surprisingly to present-day readers, Paul Lazarsfeld—used fieldwork in the 1940s and 1950s as an integral part of their empirical and theoretical work. Third, we outline a few ways in which this older tradition of mixed-methods research could guide a new era of fieldwork on political communication, supplement the currently dominant methods, and perhaps help move the field past the impasse identified by Bennett and Iyengar.

THE FIELD AS WE KNOW IT—AND WHAT WENT BEFORE

The basic institutional structure of political communication research as (1) built across the disciplines of communication and political science, (2) recognized as a distinct field within each, (3) particularly strongly anchored in American academic circles, and (4) oriented to a considerable degree toward a single shared journal, *Political Communication*, originates with the International Communication Association's (ICA) recognition of the Political Communication Division (PCD) in 1973. The division, first headed by Keith R. Sanders, started publishing the annual *Political Communication Review* in 1975, providing the first formal forum dedicated to academic research specifically on political communication. Since 1991, the PCD has published *Political Communication* jointly with its sister division, the American Political Science Association.[2]

Since its institutionalization in its current form, the field has continuously presented itself as interdisciplinary and based on multiple methods (Nimmo & Sanders, 1981; Swanson & Nimmo, 1990). The ritual reference to interdisciplinary work and methodological diversity, however, rests uneasily with the de facto dominance of quantitative methods. For example, we have performed a content analysis of the 188 articles published by the *Political Communication* over the last 10 years, from volume 20(1), 2003, onward. We coded as "qualitative" those articles based primarily on interpretative, historical, critical, and rhetorical analyses, as well as those based on interviews or fieldwork. Only 38 out of 188 (20%) articles are qualitative. Of these, only 18 articles (9.6%) present primary data produced through interviews and fieldwork. Even more striking given how much work in the field is focused on and originates in the

United States, only 2 of these 18 articles deal with political communication in the United States.

One reason for this disjuncture between mixed-methods aspirations and actual monocultural practice lies in the particular disciplinary traditions and methodological orientations of the scholars who founded the field as we know it today. In his history of political communication research in the United States, David Ryfe (2001) has shown how the generation that established the PCD drew in particular on three academic disciplines—social psychology, political science, and mass communication research as these were practiced in the United States in the 1960s—much influenced in all three cases by the broader behaviorist movement.[3] From social psychology came a focus on the attitudes and opinions of individuals and an emphasis on experimental and survey methods. From political science came a focus on politics understood primarily as a question of elections and formal political processes, skepticism toward qualitative research and broader sociologically inspired theories, and an orientation toward quantification. From mass communication research came the language of "effects" and "influence," a particular interest in those effects that took the form of short-term observable behavioral change, a legacy interest in politicians' rhetoric, as well as the drive of academics in search of a safe and accepted institutional base for their work.

This particular configuration represents a break with an older tradition of interdisciplinary American research at the intersection between communication and politics that thrived in the 50 years prior to the founding of the PCD in 1973. The 1920s and 1930s saw the publication of a number of important studies that are part of the heritage of political communication research and draw on both qualitative and quantitative methods. To name just a few highlights, consider journalist and political commentator Walter Lippmann's book, *Public Opinion*, published in 1922; Robert E. Park, one of the founders of the Chicago School of Sociology, published *The Immigrant Press and Its Control* the same year; and the polymath political scientist Harold D. Lasswell published *Propaganda Techniques in the World War* in 1927. These men were not political communication researchers as we understand the term today. Only Park and Lasswell spent prolonged periods as university professors, and their work spanned many fields over long and illustrious careers (both served as presidents of their respective scholarly associations, the American Sociological Association and APSA). But all three published serious, analytical work on issues of communication and politics in some of the most prestigious scholarly journals of the time, including the *American Journal of Sociology* (Park), the *Annals of the American Academy of Political and Social Science* (Lasswell and Lippmann), and the *American Political Science Review* (Lasswell). All three drew on the social theory of their day, including psychological theory and philosophical pragmatism (both Lippmann and Park studied with William James at Harvard, Lasswell wrote about James's work and took classes with Park while a student at Chicago). All three used a sometimes eclectic mix of qualitative and quantitative empirical research methods—and sometimes plenty of anecdotal evidence and assertion, to boot.

THE FORGOTTEN ROLE OF FIELDWORK IN THE 1940s AND 1950s

Because it is sometimes forgotten, it is worth highlighting the role of fieldwork in some of the best work on political communication published in the United States in this period, specifically Paul Lazarsfeld's *The People's Choice* (1968/1944), written with Bernard Berelson and Hazel Gaudet, and the work of Gladys Engels Lang and Kurt Lang.

Political communication scholars remember and cite *The People's Choice* to this day for its early argument about the role of personal influence in shaping media effects (Shoemaker & Reese, 1996) and for contributions to political psychology (Iyengar & Kinder, 1987). More generally, scholars remember Lazarsfeld as the father of survey methodology. And yet, Lazarsfeld's writings on method and approach to research were far more varied than is conventionally recognized (for a similar point, see Morrison, 1998). It may be surprising to contemporary eyes and memories that Lazarsfeld was well aware of the analytical power of qualitative research. Two of the central theoretical insights developed by Lazarsfeld and his collaborators—the two-step flow and opinion leaders—emerged during observational fieldwork while researching *The People's Choice*. In his 1972 book, *Qualitative Analysis: Historical and Critical Essays*, Lazarsfeld tells us:

> In one case, such a qualitative analysis of mine had considerable consequences. *The People's Choice*, a study of the role of mass media in the presidential campaign of 1940, made me feel that personal influence played a great role in the way people make up their minds how to vote. Not having anticipated this issue I had no data to pursue it quantitatively. I therefore attached to our book a chapter on "The Nature of Personal Influence" which was based only on a few qualitative observations. Some of the concepts I derived—the two-step flow of communication and the idea of horizontal opinion leaders—have since entered the sociological general literature. (p. xiii)

The passage is remarkable on a number of levels, in particular given that it illustrates how *The People's Choice* was as much a qualitative as a quantitative research project. Lazarsfeld was writing in a different time, before our methodological orthodoxies took root, when he modestly characterized the book as containing a "few qualitative observations." In actuality, *The People's Choice* was what contemporary scholars would call a mixed-methods panel study throughout the entire research project. The authors conducted a panel study, surveying a random sample of

3,000 people, from which a research team interviewed a main sample of 600 individuals seven times from May through November 1940. (The other individuals were grouped into stratified samples to serve as controls.) When an individual changed his vote intention, he was interviewed in an open-ended fashion as to why. As Lazarsfeld, Berelson, and Gaudet (1968) write:

> The repeated interviews made it possible to secure voluminous information about each respondent's personal characteristics, social philosophy, political history, personality traits, relationships with other people, opinions on issues related to the election—in short, information on anything which might contribute to our knowledge of the formation of his political preferences. (p. 5)

In addition, the authors provide narratives from open-ended question responses as evidence of many of their conclusions, and they conducted follow-up, open-ended "special interviews" with voters who changed their votes (the "changers") to explore their responses further (pp. 126–129).

If anything, as the preface to the second edition and the notes to the text make clear, Lazarsfeld, Berelson, and Gaudet regret that the study *did not generate more qualitative field data* (no doubt this was precipitated by the failure to find the strong media effects they were anticipating). At various points, the authors regret not "studying the whole community" and not conducting more interviews (p. xxxix); not developing a more "sophisticated case study approach" and not generating "more descriptive material on a local campaign as a whole," including the "way that local political committees spent money and behavior at public meetings" (p. 160); and the authors even regret not "showing people pictures and allowing them to free associate" (p. 162).

What is striking here is that Lazarsfeld and his collaborators both allowed themselves to be surprised by their findings *and* had observational qualitative fieldwork data that permitted inductive theory building. Unlike much of contemporary political communication research, which reifies its object of analysis through deductive designs that proceed from assumed, stable categories of social life, *The People's Choice* gets close to the realities of political communication processes and the self-perceptions of those involved. In the process, these scholars were able to generate entirely new categories of media influence and interpersonal dynamics that remain influential to this day. As Lazarsfeld makes clear in his 1972 volume, *The People's Choice* had built-in qualitative field research components that permitted the researchers to discover new analytical categories, which were necessary given that the survey research did not yield the results expected from existing theory. The inclusion of open-ended survey data and field observation permitted the researchers to go beyond filling predefined holes in the literature and generate new analytical categories and frame new questions. It was the observation of "personal influence" in the field that led Lazarsfeld to investigate other disciplinary literatures that spoke to the phenomenon and return to the field to explore it empirically in *Personal Influence*.

Writing contemporaneously with Lazarsfeld, Gladys Engel Lang and Kurt Lang were producing classic fieldwork studies. The Langs, like Lazarsfeld, were professional sociologists, trained as graduate students in the Chicago School of Sociology, and drew on a mix of social theory including the philosophical pragmatism of James, Dewey, and Cooley. They worked on communication and politics in a remarkably interdisciplinary fashion. And although their methodological orientation differs from Lazarsfeld's, across the Langs' foundational body of work there is a similar approach to crafting research designs that allow for inductive theory building. For example, in their classic MacArthur Day study, reprinted in *Politics and Television* (1968), the Langs write that they originally set out to do a:

> systematic study of crowd behavior and of the role of the media of mass communication, particularly television, in this kind of event. Our main goal was stymied. The air of curiosity and casualness exhibited by most members of the crowd was a surprise to every observer reporting from the scene. (p. 23)

The Langs, like Lazarsfeld and his collaborators, were writing at a time of unsettled analytical categories. Indeed, the MacArthur Day study was the first to directly compare in-person spectatorship with the mediated coverage of a political event, as well as analyze the ways the latter shaped the understandings of participants witnessing the live event. To do so, their MacArthur Day study "was, by design, open-ended in an effort to 'explore' rather than test specific propositions" (Lang & Lang, 1968/1953, p. 39). This approach to research design ran throughout their body of qualitative fieldwork. For example, the Langs conducted field observations—including what contemporary scholars now call "media ethnography"—and qualitative interviewing at "critical political events" such as the 1952 conventions and analyzed cases such as Watergate (Lang & Lang, 1968, 1983). If they had a methodological and analytical precept, it was a "concern with images of politics, of politicians, and of political moods" (p. 32) whose import could be analyzed and discovered inductively:

> We naturally assume that every event has some kind of effect; our idea is to so conduct the study of any event that, once it is over, we can depict and analyze in some detail *whatever* effects turn up. This often takes us in new and sometimes unanticipated directions. Insights obtained from these attempts to assess and understand the impact of the events in question then become the starting points for entirely new lines of inquiry. (p. 33)

This approach proved extraordinarily productive for the generation of theory and yielded a number of startling insights into political communication. In their remarkable body of work published before 1968 and collected in *Politics and Television*, the Langs prefigured 30 years of subsequent theoretical developments in the field. They open their book with a critique of the "limited effects" model, laying out many themes contained in Todd Gitlin's famous critique of "the dominant paradigm," written 10 years later. Even more, the introduction and collected chapters of *Politics and Television* advance an account of political communication processes as interactions between media, political elites, and citizens that anticipates much of Timothy Cook's (1998) influential new institutional account published 30 years later.

A NEW ERA OF FIELD RESEARCH IN POLITICAL COMMUNICATION?

Despite this tradition of mixed methods and interdisciplinary work on political communication, the center of gravity shifted by the 1960s as the field was institutionalized. From the late 1950s onward, a narrower group of political scientists, social psychologists, and mass communication researchers working out of political science and newly established mass communication departments began to dominate the discussion about communication and politics.[4] Sociologists increasingly turned away from the study of political communication. As Jefferson Pooley and Elihu Katz argue, on the one hand, Lazarsfeld and his associates seemed to show that media content ultimately did not matter as much as some had thought it did. Lazarsfeld's increasingly survey-based research aimed at identifying what influenced individual short-term behavior such as voting and shopping (done in a range of studies conducted in collaboration with Berelson, Katz, Allport, Cantril, and Merton)—what eventually came to be called the "Columbia School"—and arrived at conclusions that seemed to suggest that mass media and other forms of communication were less powerful than those who feared the power of propaganda in the 1930s and 1940s had thought. Implicitly, this made it less important to study. On the other hand, the same group established a paradigm for studying communication that over time became relatively inhospitable to sociological methods and thinking, especially of a more qualitative bent. This paradigm entailed (1) short-run studies of persuasion campaigns, (2) individuals and aggregated public opinion as objects of analysis instead of groups and communities, and (3) analytical interest in "media events" as opposed to more long-run processes of socialization and the consequences of living with media (Pooley & Katz, 2008; Katz, 2009).

While Lazarsfeld (1948) himself acknowledged that immediate behavioral response and short-term effects on individuals are only narrow permutations of the different possible (long-term/institutional, general/structural) effects of communication, the broader sociological sensibilities of the Langs and the Chicago School more generally were, in Pooley and Katz's analysis, displaced by those of the increasingly behaviorally and psychologically oriented Columbia School (just as the qualitative methods associated with Chicago gave way to the quantitative methods associated with Columbia). And the latter provided few reasons for a continued emphasis on studying the intersection between communication and politics. Indeed, after the two landmark books, *The People's Choice* and *Personal Influence*, Lazarsfeld's third and last community study, *Voting* (Berelson et al., 1954), did not pay particular attention to media and communication in its focus on the role of social institutions and salient issues in determining electoral outcomes. It was more concerned with politics than with political communication.

This was the context within which a generation of young American scholars created an institutional space for political communication research with the founding of the PCD in 1973. As a consequence, the new field relegated questions concerning broader issues of organizational, social, and technological change, as well as the qualitative methods that were integral to how pioneers of the field had worked to understand such changes, to the margins of the study of political communication. During a period in which the broader discipline of communication included both quantitative and qualitative work, drawing theoretical inspiration from many different disciplines and intellectual currents—even as scholars argued vigorously over how these elements could be combined—political communication research became increasingly homogenous. The particular set of methods that have occupied the center of political communication since then—in particular, content analysis, surveys, and experiments—are well suited to refining our understanding of established concepts in a relatively static communication landscape, but seems to have been less useful in terms of generating new analytical categories to keep pace with changes in media and social structure. The currently dominant methodological consensus has done little to advance, for example, our understanding of political actors and their work, the growing layer of organizations mediating between politicians and the public in new ways, citizens' social and symbolic construction of their relationships to politics and the news, or how any of these have changed over time.

The challenges for researchers are not limited to the rapid rise of new digital and networked communication technologies and the social practices associated with them, but this particularly spectacular change in the substantive nature of political communication is useful for arguing a broader point about how current methodological approaches risk failing the field when used on their own. Inherited assumptions about political actors, news media organizations, and even citizens themselves may be becoming rapidly obsolete. What *is* a political campaign at a time when outside actors such as newly formed "Super PACs" sometimes spend more money than candidates and parties, and are directed by consultants who, until recently, worked for those with whom they are legally prohibited from coordinating? What *is* a media organization in a time of widespread social media use, group blogs such as DailyKos that have more Web traffic than many professional outlets, and multiplatform media celebrities like Glenn Beck? What *is* an interest group at a time of "Astroturf" groups, Internet-assisted advocacy with loose membership requirements, and the president's Organizing for Action (OFA) pushing the legal boundaries of not-for-profits? What *is* the Internet as a medium when it is evolving continually and rapidly, from the AOL-dominant years of dial-up access to the increasingly ubiquitous and always-on broadband access of today?

These are just the tip of the iceberg. Taking the case of the United States, political scientists, media scholars, sociologists, and economic historians are increasingly arguing that the last 40 years represent a period of rapid and often profound change in the very nature of political parties, campaign organizations, interest groups, social movements, news media institutions, work, leisure, and family life, as well as the basic dynamics of the economy (e.g., Giddens, 1990; Neuman, 1991; Castells, 2000). Few of these changes have registered with the mainstream of political communication research, a field that often seems to operate in a sort of ahistorical generalized present. For example, while the recently published *Sourcebook for Political Communication Research* (Bucy & Holbert, 2011) explicitly recognizes that the field needs to keep up with a changing political communication environment, the vast majority of the theories and methods discussed in the book derive from the same tradition of social psychological, political science, and mass communication research based on surveys, experiments, and content analysis that Bennett and Iyengar (2008) so forcefully argue have proven themselves inadequate on their own to understand the present.

Normal scientific paradigms base their progress in part on the stabilization of certain analytical categories that then are taken for granted and used continually over time. And yet, social scientists face the problem that the very nature of what they study changes, leaving basic categories unsettled. Field research in particular, and many qualitative methods more generally, excels precisely where surveys and experiments are limited: in the inductive examination of social phenomena to generate new theory. As examples of how to do this, the submerged tradition of qualitative field research (like the Langs') and mixed-methods studies (like Lazarsfeld's) holds renewed relevance for the future. Whether pursued alone in free-standing qualitative case studies or as part of mixed-methods designs combining qualitative and quantitative elements, scholars have shown that field research is particularly well suited for getting close to the realities of social life, especially the workings of the otherwise half-secluded social worlds inhabited by political operatives (Howard, 2006), journalists and political publicists (Gershon, 2012; Herbst, 1998), and the information scientists, programmers, and Web developers who are becoming increasingly integral to more or less professionalized processes of political communication (Kreiss, 2012). Field research can provide insight into the everyday operations of mediating institutions including political campaigns (Nielsen, 2012) and parties, news media organizations (Anderson, 2013), and new types of digitally enabled political organizations (Karpf, 2012). It offers a powerful way to discover the realities of the everyday lives of ordinary people, the contexts in which political communication emanating from elites is received, and the setting in which citizens themselves engage with public affairs (Eliasoph, 1998; Walsh, 2004).

Following Lazarsfeld on the role of methodological writings, we do not see it as our task to tell political communication scholars what they *should* do but to highlight what they *might* do, including:

- Supplement existing studies of campaign communication with field research examining the inner workings of campaigns and the relations between the different professional communities and organizations that collaborate formally or informally to get candidates elected or advance a cause.
- Complement existing studies of media agendas and media content with field research examining news production processes that straddles distinctions between online and offline media and details the interactions among reporters, their sources, and a growing number of other actors (including various media-like organizations, groups, and companies) in an ever-faster information cycle.
- Pursue field research among the interest groups, social movements, and new types of sometimes loosely connected political groups appearing in a changing political and technological context.
- Design new studies of citizens' political behavior and media habits with closer, qualitative examination of the everyday life contexts of political action and media use related to public affairs.
- Conduct mediated field observations focused on the hidden objects that shape media production and dissemination but leave no obvious traces, including the proprietary algorithms that determine Facebook and Google content priority, as well as various forms of intranets and other backchannels that support semi-formal elite communication.

Parallel with such work, we need to generate a body of endemic methodological writings related to qualitative field research in political communication that draws on work in other closely related disciplines, such as sociology and anthropology, as well as science studies and media and communications research more broadly. This can help us (1) conceptualize the "fields" and "sites" of politics, (2) develop tools for observation of sociotechnical and distributed practices, (3) address ethical debates over issues like the use of pseudonyms in research, (4) develop guidelines for training young scholars in conducting field research, and (5) address debates over the criteria used to evaluate qualitative research.[5] Such collaborations should also involve forging new interdisciplinary relationships with related disciplines, such as information studies, and a new definition of "methodological pluralism," which includes not only surveys, experiments, and fieldwork, but also approaches to "big data" and field experiments that are now thriving outside the field.

CONCLUSION

In our view, a new era of field research in political communication would, at the very least, represent a valuable addition to our empirical understanding of processes of political communication. At its best, it would help the field move past our current theoretical impasse. It would be a *new* era, because it would be a return to an older tradition of interdisciplinary and mixed-methods research that was submerged when the field as we know it was institutionalized in the United States in the early 1970s around a narrow, more methodologically monocultural set of concerns. This dominant methodological consensus is reflected today in the pages of our leading journal, *Political Communication*, the makeup of PCD panels at APSA and ICA conferences, and in the methodological training offered in leading graduate programs. It has served us well in many respects (Holbert, Garrett, & Gleason, 2010), but it also seems to have run up against its limits in some ways. We believe the future of our discipline lies beyond this consensus, in a fuller embrace of the discipline's past. We believe that responding to the challenge laid out by Bennett and Iyengar (2008) and others requires a reassessment and expansion of our methodological toolkits, as well as our theories and concepts. And we believe now is a particularly appropriate time to pursue more inductive, fieldwork-based, and collaborative work.

As made clear from the start, our call for a new era of qualitative political communication field research does not imply a rejection of traditional quantitative techniques, nor a claim that the field of political communication ever fully excluded qualitative methods. PCD awards have been given to several scholars who have never counted words, conducted an experiment, administered a survey, or run a regression analysis, and some qualitative work is widely respected. Our position is simply that to advance beyond the impasse identified by Iyengar and Bennett (2008), the field needs to reclaim its interdisciplinary heritage and become again, in practice, genuinely mixed-methods (like neighboring fields such as journalism studies). Political communication researchers should not leave it to sociologists (let alone journalists!) to ask the hard, timely, and necessary questions about how processes of political communication actually operate today, how elites communicate among themselves, how political and media actors are changing, and how people relate to them. We think we need to supplement our existing quantitative methods with both old and new qualitative tools and heed Robert E. Park's old call to "go get our pants dirty" doing field research to advance our understanding of political communication and develop new theories fit for a changing world.

NOTES

1. In this chapter, we are primarily concerned with political communication research as it is practiced in the United States. Other traditions of political communication research exist and, while many are influenced (often heavily) by American research, they also differ in important ways both methodologically and theoretically.
2. The very coupling of the ICA and American Political Science Association (APSA) suggests the special role U.S.-based research plays in the field.
3. Political scientists often distinguish between "behaviorism" (the study of individuals' observable behavior), a term used widely in psychology, and so forth, and "behavioralism," which was an attempt to apply the epistemology and methodologies associated with the natural sciences to the study of political life.
4. It is interesting to compare the trajectory of political communication research with that of the adjacent and overlapping field of journalism studies. Whereas the Chicago School largely disappears from political communication and often is overlooked in the broader field's historical self-understanding (Wahl-Jorgensen, 2004), it provided powerful inspiration for journalism studies, directly influencing key works by Gaye Tuchman, Herbert J. Gans, James W. Carey, and many others.
5. Here the field can draw on the intense debates waged over the last decade over the role of qualitative research in political science, starting with the so-called Perestroika movement, calls for more problem-oriented and less methods-driven research, and debates over the design of mixed-methods social inquiry (e.g., see Shapiro, Smith, & Masoud, 2004, and Brady & Collier, 2010).

BIBLIOGRAPHY

Anderson, C. W. (2013). *Rebuilding the news: Metropolitan journalism in the digital age*. Philadelphia, PA: Temple University Press.

Barnhurst, K. G. (2011). The new "media affect" and the crisis of representation for political communication. *International Journal of Press/Politics, 16*(4), 573–593. doi:10.1177/1940161211415666

Bennett, W. L., & Iyengar, S. (2008). A new era of minimal effects? The changing foundations of political communication. *Journal of Communication, 58*(4), 707–731.

Berelson, B., Lazarsfeld, P. F., & McPhee, W. N. (1954). *Voting*. Chicago, IL: University of Chicago Press.

Brady, H. E., & Collier, D. (Eds.). (2010). *Rethinking social inquiry: Diverse tools, shared standards* (2nd ed.). Lanham, MD: Rowman & Littlefield.

Bucy, E. P., & Holbert, R. L. (Eds.). (2011). *Sourcebook for political communication research: Methods, measures, and analytical techniques*. New York, NY: Routledge.

Castells, M. (2000). *The rise of the network society* (2nd ed.). Oxford, England: Blackwell.

Chaffee, S. H., & Metzger, M. J. (2001). The end of mass communication? *Mass Communication and Society, 4*(4), 365–379. doi:10.1207/S15327825MCS0404_3

Cook, T. E. (1998). *Governing with the news: The news media as a political institution*. Chicago, IL: University of Chicago Press.

Eliasoph, N. (1998). *Avoiding politics: How Americans produce apathy in everyday life*. Cambridge, England: Cambridge University Press.

Gans, H. J. (1962). *The urban villagers.* New York, NY: Free Press.

Gershon, S. A. (2012). Press secretaries, journalists, and editors: Shaping local congressional news coverage. *Political Communication, 29*(2), 160–183. doi:10.1080/10584609.2012.671230

Giddens, A. (1990). *The consequences of modernity.* Stanford, CA: Stanford University Press.

Gitlin, T. (1978). Media sociology: The dominant paradigm. *Theory and Society, 6*(2), 205–253.

Herbst, S. (1998). *Reading public opinion: How political actors view the democratic process.* Chicago, IL; London, England: University of Chicago Press.

Holbert, R. L., Garrett, R. K., & Gleason, L. S. (2010). A new era of minimal effects? A response to Bennett and Iyengar. *Journal of Communication, 60*(1), 15–34. doi:10.1111/j.1460-2466.2009.01470.x

Howard, P. N. (2006). *New media campaigns and the managed citizen.* Cambridge, England: Cambridge University Press.

Iyengar, S., & Kinder, D. R. (1987). *News that matters: Television and American opinion.* Chicago, IL: University of Chicago Press.

Karpf, D. (2012). *The MoveOn effect: The unexpected transformation of American political advocacy.* New York, NY: Oxford University Press.

Katz, E. (2009). Why sociology abandoned communication. *American Sociologist, 40*(3), 167–174. doi:10.1007/s12108-009-9077-y

Kreiss, D. (2012). *Taking our country back: The crafting of networked politics from Howard Dean to Barack Obama.* New York, NY: Oxford University Press.

Lang, G. E., & Lang, K. (1983). *The battle for public opinion: The president, the press, and the polls during Watergate.* New York, NY: Columbia University Press.

Lang, K., & Lang, G. E. (1968/1953). *Politics and television.* Chicago, IL: Quadrangle.

Lasswell, H. D. (1971/1927). *Propaganda Techniques in the World War.* Cambridge, MA; London, England: MIT Press.

Lazarsfeld, P. F. (1948). Communication research and the social psychologist. In W. Dennis (Ed.), *Current trends in social psychology* (pp. 218–273). Pittsburgh, PA: University of Pittsburgh Press.

Lazarsfeld, P. F. (1972). *Qualitative analysis: Historical and critical essays.* Boston, MA: Allyn & Bacon.

Lazarsfeld, P. F., Berelson, B., & Gaudet, H. (1968/1944). *The people's choice: How the voter makes up his mind in a presidential campaign* (3rd ed.). New York, NY: Columbia University Press.

Lazarsfeld, P. F., & Rosenberg, M. (Eds.). (1955). *The language of social research.* New York, NY: Free Press.

Lippmann, W. (1997/1922). *Public opinion.* New Brunswick, NJ: Transaction.

Morrison, D. E. (1998). *The search for a method: Focus groups and the development of mass communication research.* Luton, England: University of Luton Press.

Moy, P., Bimber, B., Rojecki, A., Xenos, M., & Iyengar, S. (2012). Transnational connections: Shifting contours in political communication research. *International Journal of Communication, 6,* 247–254.

Neuman, W. R. (1991). *The future of the mass audience.* Cambridge, England: Cambridge University Press.

Nielsen, R. K. (2012). *Ground wars: Personalized communication in political campaigns.* Princeton, NJ: Princeton University Press.

Nimmo, D. D., & Sanders, K. R. (Eds.). (1981). *Handbook of political communication.* Beverly Hills, CA: Sage.

Park, R. E. (1922). *The immigrant press and its control.* New York, NY; London, England: Harper & Brothers.

Pooley, J., & Katz, E. (2008). Further notes on why American sociology abandoned mass communication research. *Journal of Communication, 58*(4), 767–786. doi:10.1111/j.1460-2466.2008.00413.x

Ryfe, D. M. (2001). History and political communication. *Political Communication, 18*(4), 407–420.

Shapiro, I., Smith, R. M., & Masoud, T. E. (Eds.). (2004). *Problems and methods in the study of politics.* Cambridge, England; New York, NY: Cambridge University Press.

Shoemaker, P., & Reese, S. (1996). *Mediating the message: Theories of influences on mass media content* (2nd ed.). White Plains, NY: Longman.

Swanson, D., & Nimmo, D. (Eds.). (1990). *New directions in political communication research.* Newbury Park, CA: Sage.

Wahl-Jorgensen, K. (2004). How not to found a field: New evidence on the origins of mass communication research. *Journal of Communication, 54*(3), 547–564. doi:10.1111/j.1460-2466.2004.tb02644.x

Walsh, K. C. (2004). *Talking about politics: Informal groups and social identity in American life.* Chicago, IL: University of Chicago Press.

PART TWO

Challenging Discourses, Public and Personal

CHAPTER FOUR

Normative Europe AND THE Roma Issue IN THE Romanian AND Bulgarian Press

ALEX BALCH, EKATERINA BALABANOVA, AND
RUXANDRA TRANDAFOIU

For Bulgaria and Romania the emigration of significant numbers of their citizens to other parts of Europe following European Union (EU) membership in 2007 was to be expected. For those living in these relatively small states in the southeast of Europe—struggling to grow their economies after ridding themselves of Communism—opportunities lying elsewhere acted as a magnet. Predictably, talk of an "invasion" or "flood" of immigrants from Eastern Europe dominated the public debates in the countries that received them—such as France, Germany, and the United Kingdom. Less obvious or easy to predict was the impact on public debates in those countries from which they came. Even more uncertain was how the EU institutions would react to any suspicion of discrimination, as well as at what point and to what extent the rights of European citizenship would be defended.

This chapter uses the high-profile expulsion of Roma communities from France in the summer of 2010 as an opportunity to examine these uncertainties. The events created waves in Europe and beyond, leading many to ask what this meant for "normative Europe" (Severance, 2010)—the idea that the EU possesses real power through shared ideas and values (Manners, 2002). As we shall see, there was (eventually) an intervention by the European Commission (EC) to defend the core European norms of free movement and nondiscrimination, but with mixed results. The case, of course, highlights the problem of a lack of societal integration of Europe's Roma communities, moving this issue to the center of the European stage. On the one hand, the immigration of minority groups defined and disadvantaged by their ethnicity strikes at the very liberal heart of the European project. On the other hand it potentially reopens and reconfigures debates about these questions, along with national identity and modes of incorporation and societal inclusion, in Europe's new periphery.

The role of the media is central to this Europeanization of public debates. Ideas, opinions, and debates now move about in Europe almost as freely as goods, capital, services, and people. Discussion about Eastern European migration in receiving countries is almost instantly recycled, reproduced, and reinterpreted in sending countries (Balabanova & Balch, 2010). However variable and uneven European integration is, there are growing institutional, political, economic, social, and cultural linkages among European countries. Comments by a politician in one EU member-state about the citizens of another have great potential to shock and scandalize. These chain reactions allow us to explore evolving perceptions of what Europe is, and what it is becoming.

THE ROMA AND EUROPE: A BRIEF HISTORY

This chapter aims to show how the process of Europeanization and the idea of normative Europe shaped and reconfigured public debates over France's expulsion of the Roma. It does this through analysis of political discourse and press coverage of the scandal in Bulgaria and Romania. Before this, however, it is useful to provide a brief background to Europe's most numerous and transnational minority, and to sketch out some key points regarding the scandal that erupted following former French president Nicolas Sarkozy's actions in the summer of 2010.

The Roma are a population of Indian origin whose presence in the Balkan area has been attested since the fourteenth century (Achim, 2004). Their numbers are estimated at up to 2.5 million in Romania and 700,000 in Bulgaria, although statistics are unreliable due to self-identification and identity assignation difficulties (Csepeli & Simon, 2007, p. 132). Policies directed at the Roma varied until the nineteenth century, depending on whether they were under Hapsburg rule (Transylvania), Ottoman rule (Bulgaria), or in the Romanian Principalities (Csepeli & Simon, p. 130).[1]

The contemporary era is framed by three key policies toward the Roma in the twentieth century: deportations in the 1940s under the Fascist regimes in Hungary and Romania, forced sedentarization and assimilation during the Communist regimes in most Eastern European countries,[2] and the idea of the Roma as a "problem without solution" during the post-Communist transitions. Throughout, marginality has defined the Roma, irrespective of historical period, nation-state or political regime (Barany, 1994).

In the post-Communist transitions, the Roma provided a useful distraction from other social and political conflicts (Fonseca, 1996, p. 143; see also Woodcock,

2007).[3] The burning of Roma settlements and their eviction in some parts of Eastern Europe, all encouraged by the local media, were the precursors of similar incidents in Italy[4] and France almost two decades later. As a result of historical discrimination, public and media discourses in both Romania and Bulgaria are dominated by hate speech, inability to address the Roma in politically correct terms, and widespread "myths." These include, for example, the belief that the image of both countries has been tainted in the West by Roma emigration and subsequent delinquency (Csepeli & Simon, 2007, pp. 133–134). As Rövid (2011, p. 1) argues, the EU's dilemma vis-à-vis the Roma includes whether universal individual rights or group minority rights are appropriate. If it is the latter, the questions of whether general or specific minority rights should be applied, as well as whether the Roma should be treated as a "national minority or a "non-territorial nation" arise. This is further complicated by the fact that outsiders perceive the Roma as a homogeneous group defined by certain (largely negative or romanticized) traits, while the Roma see themselves as heterogeneous, geographically dispersed, and of different religions and cultural traditions (Csepeli & Simon, 2007; McGarry, 2011).

The Roma became "an issue" for the EU during its enlargement toward the East and the accession talks concerning countries like Romania and Bulgaria. Following a 2003 conference, the "Decade of Roma Inclusion 2005–2015" was launched, bringing together several signatory states demanding EU support.[5] The European Social Fund supports, among other things, the social integration of the Roma (Rövid, 2011, pp. 3–4), but despite the EU discourse of inclusion and equality of opportunity (and the availability of resources to back this up), a gap remains between rhetoric and reality, maintaining incentives for Roma to emigrate (McGarry, 2011, p. 129).

In April 2011, the European Commission adopted the EU Framework for National Roma Integration Strategies,[6] which contains a number of initiatives to tackle employment, housing, and education challenges for the Roma. However, this was quickly criticized for failing to provide solutions for widespread anti-Gypsyism and discrimination. Moreover, by asking national governments to take responsibility for implementation, the EU has been criticized for its failure to take a more active role (McGarry, 2011, p. 133).

FRANCE, THE "ROMA AFFAIR," AND THE EU AS DEFENDER OF EUROPEAN NORMS

Policy announcements by Nicolas Sarkozy in July 2010 promising the dismantling of camps and mass deportations of those guilty of public order offenses were at first mainly of interest to the French domestic audience and the international human rights community. However, they would lead to escalating political conflict between France and the EU (Nacu, 2012).[7] The political fallout grew significantly following the emergence of a *circulaire*,[8] which proved that there had been targeting of Roma as a particular ethnic group in the deportations—something consistently denied by the government. This initiated a more intense European dimension to the debate and an intervention by EU Commissioner Viviane Reding, who connected the actions to the horrors (genocides) of World War II—where Roma were killed alongside Jews by the Nazis. This prompted a series of personal attacks on Reding by Sarkozy. The affair peaked during a European summit, according to reports of dramatic scenes between Sarkozy and Jose-Manuel Barroso, president of the EC. Following this, the French government eventually negotiated to neutralize the threat of EU enforcement action and called a truce.

The EC position was to protect antidiscrimination and free movement rules—the latter considered foundational to the process of European integration itself.[9] Historically, the reality has been significant restrictions on the scope of this right (i.e., only enjoyed by workers or those economically active). However, through the development of European citizenship, created following the Treaty of Maastricht in 1992, and a proactive pro-mobility agenda at the EU level, including judgments made by the European Court of Justice, the right has progressively been extended to cover more citizens of member-states. The EU has formally adopted the principle of nondiscrimination, chiefly as a means with which to enable free movement and the single market.[10]

The politicization of France's expulsions of European citizens can be traced to a number of tensions between regional integration and national sovereignty, particularly over the rights of states to control immigration but also on how to address minority questions. Communitarian liberals tend to argue that the deportation of foreign nationals is justifiable on the basis of the principle of sovereignty—in other words, the state has the right to exclude nonmembers on the basis of a political community's right to self-determination (Walzer, 1983). However, the EU's treaty structure affects the ability of states to expel foreign nationals from any other member-state. Various rules limit the conditions by which this can take place—there usually must be justification on the grounds of public security or public health (Guild, 2009).

The question of minority rights is something contested in the EU—not formally enshrined in treaty arrangements (Wiener & Schwellnus, 2004) and undermined by fundamental disagreements about definitions and solutions. However, the EU has made moves in this area, partly due to the argument—following the fall of Communism in 1989—that policies on minorities in post-Communist regimes needed to be addressed (Kymlicka, 2008, pp. 36–37). Recognition of minority rights has thus been part of the enlargement processes, but only since criteria were laid out in an agreement reached in Copenhagen in 1993. What this means is that the EU's impact in this area is variable, depending on the timing of the membership process (Grigoriadis, 2008). The results have predictably been mixed: incremental change but little real transformation of living standards for the Roma in Europe (Ram, 2007). The EU's role in protecting minority rights is, therefore, patchy and partial (Naxidou, 2012).

CASE STUDIES: BULGARIA AND ROMANIA

Bulgaria and Romania are often cited as cases where the EU's power to influence domestic policy was reduced dramatically once the conditionality of the membership process was concluded. However, the EU can be considered as a series of concentric circles where membership is only the start. The next European "clubs" to join are the European Monetary Union (EMU), which produces the European single currency, and "Schengen," the agreement on border controls allowing passport-free movement between European countries.

We would, therefore, expect the magnetic power of Europe to shape the public debates, but the question of minorities remains highly sensitive. Post-Communist countries are often accused of simply paying lip service to minority rights (Dovile & Vilana, 2009). In both Bulgaria and Romania there remains a deep ambivalence toward the issue—some formal recognition of multiculturalism that is weakly enforced. In Bulgaria, the 1991 constitution guarantees freedom of conscience and religion, as well as the right to ethnic self-identification, but the actual existence of minorities is not explicitly stated. Expressions such as "citizens whose mother tongue is not Bulgarian" or who have a diverging "ethnic identification" are used as a substitute for the term "minorities" (State Gazette articles 36.2 and 54.1, cited in Rechel, 2008, p. 222). In addition, minority rights are restricted by two other provisions: the prohibition of regional autonomy according to ethnic differentiation and the formation of parties on exclusively ethnic or religious lines (Bell, 1999, p. 255).[11] Despite its strong influence on Romania's electoral and judicial systems, the French Republican model of governance did not extend its influence to minority policy. The Romanian constitution explicitly recognizes the collective rights of national minorities (Article 4), even if it has demonstrated a reluctance to enforce or protect them (Iordachi, 2010).

Given this apparent conflict between the desire for greater inclusion within the European community of states and a reluctance to deal with minority inclusion, France's Roma affair becomes a window through which to explore the power of European norms, the Europeanization of the Roma as a policy problem, and the role of the EU as defender of European values. The next sections present empirical material showing how the story unfolded in the Bulgarian and Romanian press. This is the result of a detailed examination of key political statements, the reactions of both government and opposition, and the framing of this debate in mainstream press coverage. For the purposes of this investigation, *Dnevnik* and *Adevărul* were selected as key newspapers for each country.[12]

BULGARIA: SCHENGEN AT ALL COSTS

The Bulgarian government initially followed the official French position but the scandal proved to be too tempting an opportunity for opposition politicians. In July 2010, joint operations with Romania were announced to receive those Roma guilty of "public order offences." The foreign minister reassured the public that free movement would not be restricted for Bulgarians. The underlying notion (stressed in public) was that this was a domestic issue for France: a social, rather than a political, problem. In the words of Bulgarian foreign minister Nikolaj Mladenov, "all Bulgarian citizens abroad have to follow the laws of that country and the European requirements."[13] Prime Minister Bojko Borisov went further, declaring there was no Roma issue at all.[14] Support for the French government was also provided by claims there was no evidence of discrimination on the basis of ethnic or group belonging—that returnees were of varied ethnic origin,[15] with no complaints received about human rights violations.

The official discourse can be summarized as an attempt to draw the political heat from the affair. Government estimates were that only 150 Bulgarian citizens would be returned; there was every attempt to explain there should be no link between France's Roma policy and Bulgaria's entry into Schengen. The point that Schengen entry depended entirely only on Bulgaria was made very often by all government officials. Overall, the government was trying to steer clear of arguments between Romania, France, and the EU to avoid affecting its Schengen entry. However, while the EC agreed with this argument, French politicians made a direct association, suggesting Romania must integrate its Roma better before entering Schengen (without mentioning Bulgaria). A final aspect of the official government discourse was the concession that integration of Roma in Bulgaria should be improved, with the help of funds already provided by the EU for this purpose.

In contrast to the government position, oppositional parties along with then-president Georgi Parvanov—elected with the support of the largest oppositional party, the Bulgarian Socialist Party (BSP)—saw an opportunity to put pressure on the government and ask whether European norms were being contravened. The BSP challenged the French policy and demanded reasons for each expulsion. The issue was used to criticize existing programs and advocate a new European conversation about Roma integration with Bulgaria playing a strong role. However, the BSP concurred with the government that the issue should not be linked to Schengen membership. For many commentators, the Roma expulsions seemed to represent a chance for the BSP to flex its muscles.

President Parvanov, in opposition to the government, argued that the expulsion of Roma was against European values and rules established before Bulgaria joined in 2007, particularly the attribution of guilt on the basis of ethnicity.[16] He also declared his position against the link between the Roma issue and Bulgaria's entry into Schengen and the view that the problem was European as it affected European citizens from a particular ethnicity. The opposition party Movement for Rights and Freedoms demanded a parliamentary declaration condemning the expulsions as a violent restriction of freedom of movement in the EU, breaking international legal norms.[17]

The question of European norms was often brought to the fore with non-government voices. *Dnevnik* reported the comments of sociologist Kolyo Kolev, who claimed that the act of expulsion was anti-European. For him, the right of free movement did not seem to apply equally, showing that Europe was not ready to follow its own directives.[18] Public opinion was reported as agreeing that the fundamental European right to free movement was being violated by France. It is interesting that there was also the feeling that those who break the law in France should face justice in France, rather than being "exported" back to Bulgaria or Romania.

Despite the government's desire to keep a low profile, there were spontaneous public protests over the issue—demanding recognition of human rights and European citizenship—in front of the French Embassy in Sofia by Bulgarian Roma and supported by other Bulgarians. A letter to the French ambassador stressed that Bulgarian Roma are European citizens and their human and civil rights have to be respected by France the way the country respects the rights of French citizens. They demanded that the French government apologize to the deported people.

The role of the EU in the affair had little impact on the public debate in Bulgaria. While the involvement of the commission and parliament were reported, there was no public reaction from government officials or opposition parties. The only clear link between the discussions at the European and national levels was the involvement of Bulgarian and Romanian members of the European Parliament (MEPs) in the debates taking place in the European Parliament. However, this MEP involvement has been characterized as inconsequential.

In one sense, the government approach was successful: A link was barely made between minority rights and deeper public policy problems relating to the Roma issue in Bulgaria. This was helped by the way the issue was reported in the press: reactions and opinions of other countries and international organizations were covered as foreign news, with little reaction from the government or from the journalists themselves. This included the scandal over Commissioner Reding's comments. Accusations around racism, discrimination, and minority rights were present in the reporting of the issue, but nearly always in reference to international actors.

A good example is the intervention of George Soros, prominent philanthropist and commentator. *Dnevnik* reported his denouncement of French actions for their violation of French and European laws, and the accompanying discourse focused on solving the integration of Roma in Europe with an appeal to the EU to deal with the issue.[19] The voluntary nature of the returns was repeated in *Dnevnik's* reporting, using government officials and the Bulgarian ambassador to France as sources. The arrival of every group of Bulgarian citizens led to occasional interviews with people claiming they were fairly treated and statistics demonstrating Bulgaria's returnees were small in number compared to Romania. Rather than a problem for Bulgaria, the policy was presented as provoking considerable debates in France and the EU.

Another argument that cropped up regularly in the public debate was the distinction between Bulgaria and Romania. The rhetoric of most actors focused on Romania and Romanian Roma, and in *Dnevnik* there was reference to the differing reactions of the two countries: Bulgaria cooperating with France, while Romania criticized French actions. The press reported on criticisms of Bulgaria made by the French ambassador to Bulgaria, saying there was talk but no action on the Roma, and arguing it was not clear where money for integration of Roma is going.

ROMANIA: EUROPEAN, RATHER THAN NATIONAL, PROBLEM

As with Bulgaria, the Romanian government was initially silent on the scandal in France: press releases were left to the Romanian Embassy in Paris. The tenor of the debate soon moved in an altogether more defensive and critical direction, however, and led to more soul-searching on the issue of Roma integration. The Romanian Ministry for Foreign Affairs at first described the expulsions as "voluntary repatriations" and there was even veiled sympathy for France's problems with Roma criminals.[20] Concerns were soon expressed, however, about the Western confusion between Roma and Romanians.[21] In the same way as we saw in Bulgaria, there was a strategy of distancing, leaving the Roma in an ambiguous position in the EU: a European minority, but under the protection of individual nation-states. However, by the September 2010 EU summit, the Romanian government was prepared to be more vocal, seeing an opportunity to attract more EU money for Roma integration projects.

Public opinion was that the West had lost its democratic credentials, since there was clear evidence of discrimination against a certain category of EU citizens.[22] Free movement in the EU, perceived as a hard fought right, was considered under threat. In Romania, the public debate showed greater intolerance of the Roma minority—described as "unmanageable," or a "problem without solution."[23] Some commentators even felt vindicated that the Roma were as difficult to "manage" abroad as in Romania, particularly as Romania had been criticized repeatedly for its treatment of the minority.[24] The responsibility of the EU was central to the public debate in Romania. *Adevărul* backed the government position that the EU has "a duty of care," despite the commission's initial insistence that the issue was a national one, better left to France and Romania to solve. It should be mentioned that the historical friendship with France is important for many in Romania—the dispute between the two countries led to much lamenting in the Romanian press about the meaning for this "special relationship."[25]

After the first repatriation flights began to arrive, *Adevărul* provided readers with vibrant investigations about the lives and adventures of the returnees, and the term "Eurogypsy" entered everyday vocabulary.[26] The minority was almost romanticized by these depictions, which fell in line with the positive stereotypes about the Roma: Roma as fun and life-loving rogues. Interestingly, compared to the Bulgarian case, Roma stereotypes and voices are given more space in the public debate—even when reported as complaining over double standards in the EU's attitude. "We are not treated as human beings" becomes a commonly echoed claim.[27] Despite this relative tolerance, however, negative stereotypes flourished. The Roma were presented as a security issue and criminalized in a language dominated by words such as "thieves," "vandals," "beggars," and "criminals" (though some of these terms were reproduced from the French press and the discourse of French politicians).[28]

As a result, the public debate in Romania was dominated by two dilemmas. The first concerned whether the removals should be seen as a purely national issue, which seemed to be the initial reading of the EU or, rather, a European one. While the Romanian government aimed to frame the issue around a "European responsibility," France looked for European allies in its attempt to push for new legislation that would aid and justify its policies against the Roma. The consequence was that the EU was forced to enter the arena as referee and also to clarify its normative duty as "defender of the treaties." While Romania emphasized freedom of movement and France lauded state sovereignty, the EU preferred to talk about nondiscrimination and minority rights. The prevailing discourse of the Romanian press thus began to revolve around double standards: Easterners versus Westerners and Roma versus other EU citizens. Romanian journalists also deplored the apparent lack of adequate EU legal instruments.[29]

A dilemma between taking the stand of the victim to protect the rights of Romanian citizens, on the one hand, and indulging in institutionalized racism, on the other, put the plight of the Roma at the center of domestic debate (unlike in Bulgaria where the issue remains largely one of international affairs). For instance, *Adevărul* Editor in Chief Grigore Cartianu, known for his colorful vocabulary vis-à-vis the Roma, was forced to respond to a piece that sparked a racist feast among online readers.[30] Racist remarks were tolerated in opinion pieces, but as the affair developed, more substantial investigation features began to contextualize the plight of the Roma, culturally and historically.

There was a willingness to attack the French position, which is not seen in the Bulgarian case. As the son of a Hungarian immigrant,[31] President Sarkozy's own family pedigree was raised (to attack the French government's attempt to define a new French national identity through anti-immigration policies). There was less awareness, however, about the way the Romanian government was also being instrumental in milking the EU for more Roma integration funds. Another distinction between Bulgaria and Romania is that Schengen membership only played a marginal role in the latter's public debate. This may be due to some myopia about the importance of Roma integration for the decision, although France's warning over future Schengen membership and 2013 EU funding renegotiations were linked to solving the Roma issue.

A number of articles in *Adevărul* recalled the Roma expulsion and segregation strategies deployed by the Italian government in 2007–2008, which showed the formation of a policy continuum of exclusion. Like Italy, France had called for Romanian police officers to help with the removals, but the Romanian authorities claimed that none of those deported in the summer of 2010 from France had committed illegal acts.[32] They argued, instead, that France had bypassed normative EU frameworks, leading some Romanian commentators to fear for the collapse of the entire European project.

Double standards on policies regarding the Roma are not only the preserve of Romania, however. When Sweden's European Affairs Minister Birgitta Ohlsson called for France to be sanctioned, the Swedish opposition quickly reminded her of the July 2010 expulsion of 50 Romanian and Bulgarian Roma caught begging on the underground.[33] Ultimately, there remain unresolved questions: To whom do the Roma belong? Who speaks or should speak for them? In the Romanian public debate there is irritation that neither EU member-states nor EU institutions seem to agree about these questions or suggest any practical answers.

CONCLUSION

In the middle of the Roma affair, the *EU Observer* accused the Romanian and Bulgarian public of displaying indifference toward France's expulsion of their fellow citizens.[34] The evidence here is that the events did have a significant impact on the public debate, but in very distinct ways. European migration provoked the return of old debates about Roma integration, but the discourse is now refracted and filtered through the prism of the EU. National differences persist over the significance of European norms, and this is reflected in how they are framed by political elites and the role assigned to Europe and the EU.

As expected, the "European-ness" of the main issues in the affair was prominent. Political actors in both countries emphasized the European dimension of the issue and the principle of solidarity between member-states—but for ulterior motives. This was a particular type of Europeanization, where domestic political factors were considered in light of questions relating to European integration and appealing to Europe was a political strategy. The calculations for both Bulgarian and Romanian governments clearly were informed by self-interest. This confirms what has been said about the dangers of an EU-wide policy directed at the Roma—transferring national responsibility for minority policy to a European level absolves governments already tempted to claim that the Roma are a European problem and creates further difficulties for the EU (McGarry, 2011, p. 128).

In terms of common European values, the norm of free movement was center stage in both nations, but the role of the EU became more politicized in the Romanian case. There was a crescendo in Romanian newspaper coverage and a corresponding shift from mere objective reporting to emotive and colorful language. Both Romanian politicians and the press embarked on a journey of initial indifference mixed with racism that slowly transformed into an analysis of normative issues and a general assessment of the state of the EU's legal instruments. The prominence of the EU in the debate reflects the central role played by European integration in the post-Communist constitutional processes, but the notion of European values appeared to have more weight in the Romanian debate.

An interesting finding in the public debate in Bulgaria is the relative absence of normative discussions, when compared with Romania. This is most likely due to the relatively fewer numbers of Bulgarian citizens directly affected by the expulsions. However, as with Romania, the Bulgarian government was quick to go along with the official French discourse. The difference here is that this was maintained throughout, and no attempt at the official level was made to engage with the notions of antidiscrimination, minority rights, or freedom of movement. The government was keen to support the sovereignty of France to deal with the issue. Bulgaria's primary foreign policy priority—entry into Schengen—dominated discussions.

The reaction to the expulsion of Roma was not aided by the general policy and attitudes toward the Roma community within Bulgaria, especially when the interior minister was quoted in the national press as saying that the Roma community generates criminal activity. The debate demonstrated clear evidence of instrumental thinking on the part of the Bulgarian government at the expense of any normative and value-driven considerations.

This chapter has explored the repercussions of the Roma affair in two of Europe's new member-states to provide a snapshot of the development of a Europe of rights. What can the findings tell us about the power of European norms and values in public debates in Bulgaria and Romania? Not pretending to provide the whole answer, the examination at least begins to explain some of the ways in which norms are affected by the dynamics of Europeanization. Their EU membership meant that the French government's targeting of Bulgarian and Romanian nationals produced an irresistible and inexorable Europeanization of the issue of Roma integration, driven by national interests. Although a distancing strategy by government emerged in both countries, this was more successfully achieved in Bulgaria than in Romania. The reasons behind this—perhaps relating to the development of liberal values, political culture, or the quality of the public sphere—deserve further investigation. Future research could, for example, examine how levels of pluralism in the political system or different types of media structure affect the framing of European news events such as the Roma affair.

NOTES

1. In the Romanian Principalities, those known as "Gypsies" were enslaved until their legal emancipation in 1856. In Bulgaria, deracination, denial, and self-misrepresentation defined the Gypsies, who, for opportunistic reasons under Ottoman rule, but also due to genuine assimilation, would often remain undifferentiated from the larger Turkish minority (Fonseca, 1996, p. 120).
2. Bulgaria constitutes one of the more striking cases of assimilation. The status of national minority and use of own language guaranteed by the 1947 Constitution were withdrawn in 1971. As in the case of the Turks, Gypsy names were Bulgarianized and the use of Romani language and the wearing of "folkloric" clothes were banned (Fonseca, 1996, p. 116).
3. Shortly after the 1989 anti-Communist revolutions, ethnic conflicts emerged, notably the 1993 pogrom against the Roma in the Romanian village of Hădăreni (retrieved from http://www.errc.org/cikk.php?cikk=3581), which was nevertheless preceded by the burning of Gypsy houses in other parts of Romania (Gheorghe, 1991, p. 833).
4. An important precedent to the French case occurred in Italy in 2007–2008, when the government instigated removals on the basis of a possible "social threat" and "inability to integrate" and implemented the mass fingerprinting of Roma (including children). The EU showed concern, but Italy was allowed to carry out its "program" unimpeded (see Sigona, 2005; Fekete, 2009).
5. See http://www.romadecade.org/index, accessed August 9, 2013.
6. *Communication from the Commission to the European Parliament, the Council, the European Economic and Social Committee and the Committee of the Regions: An EU Framework for National Roma Integration Strategies up to 2020.* Retrieved from http://ec.europa.eu/justice/policies/discrimination/docs/com_2011_173_en.pdf
7. See, for example, the September 2012 special issue of the *Journal of Ethnic and Migration Studies.*
8. The circulaire was dated August 5, and signed by Michel Bart, Minister for the Interior.
9. The free movement of workers was one of the four fundamental "freedoms" (the others being goods, services, and capital) mentioned in the founding agreements of European integration (e.g., the Treaty of Rome, 1958).
10. For example, Article 21 of the 2000 Charter of Fundamental Rights of the European Union and the Racial Equality Directive 2000/43/EC—the key EU legislation combating discrimination "on grounds of race or ethnic origin."

11. This prohibition was not strictly followed. In 1990 an ethnic Turk founded the Movement for Rights and Freedoms (MRF), which came to play a significant role in Bulgarian political life.
12. *Dnevnik* is a Bulgarian daily broadsheet with a circulation of 30,000 known for its independent editorial line and professional reporting standards. *Adevărul* is one of the oldest Romanian newspapers and the top-selling broadsheet, with an average circulation (at the time of the Roma affair) of 82,000 and a left-of-center political position.
13. *Dnevnik.* (2010, August 25). "Николай Младенов: Ситуацията с ромите не се представя правилно от медиите." Retrieved from http://www.dnevnik.bg/bulgaria/2010/08/25/950994_nikolai_mladenov_situaciiata_s_romite_ne_se_predstavia/
14. Ирина Новакова. (2010, September 16). Dnevnik: "Борисов: Наложи се мнението, че ромите са номади, на които трябва да им се даде възможност да обикалят из Европа." Retrieved from http://www.dnevnik.bg/evropa/novini_ot_es/2010/09/16/961652_borisov_naloji_se_mnenieto_che_romite_sa_nomadi_na/
15. This particular fact is not surprising as traditionally some Roma identify themselves as Roma, while others tick the box "Bulgarian."
16. *Dnevnik.* (2010, September 15). "Първанов за диалога си с премиера: Това е конструктивно напрежение." Retrieved from http://www.dnevnik.bg/bulgaria/2010/09/15/960971_purvanov_za_dialoga_si_s_premiera_tova_e_konstruktivno/
17. *Dnevnik.* (2010, October 15). "ДПС иска парламентът да гласува декларация срещу депортирането на роми от Франция." Retrieved from http://www.dnevnik.bg/bulgaria/2010/10/13/976158_dps_iska_parlamentut_da_glasuva_deklaraciia_sreshtu/
18. *Dnevnik.* (2010, August 18). "МВР: Не се очаква депортация на български роми от Франция." Retrieved from http://www.dnevnik.bg/sviat/2010/08/18/948422_mvr_ne_se_ochakva_deportaciia_na_bulgarski_romi_ot/
19. *Dnevnik.* (2010, August 25). "Европа не може да загуби още едно поколение роми, смята Джордж Сорос." Retrieved from http://www.dnevnik.bg/evropa/novini_ot_es/2010/08/25/951261_evropa_ne_moje_da_zagubi_oshte_edno_pokolenie_romi/
20. Ghica, S. (2010, August 20). "S-au întors euroţiganii." *Adevărul.* Retrieved from http://www.adevarul.ro/actualitate/eveniment/S-au_intors_eurotiganii_0_319768635.html
21. Marin, V. (2010, July 30). "Nicolas Sarkozy ne trimite ţiganii înapoi la pachet." *Adevarul.* Retrieved from http://www.adevarul.ro/international/Nicolas_Sarkozy_ne_trimite_tiganii_inapoi_la_pachet_0_307169866.html#
22. *Adevărul.* (2010, July 28). "Ţiganii noştri sunt şi ai lor!" Retrieved from http://www.adevarul.ro/adrian_halpert_-_editorial/Tiganii_nostri_sunt_si_ai_lor_7_306639341.html
23. *Adevărul.* (2010, July 12). "VIDEO Cum au blocat hoții români în Franța 120 de TGV-uri." Retrieved from http://www.adevarul.ro/actualitate/eveniment/Hoti_romani_mai_rapizi_decat_TGV_0_296370743.html
24. Iaru, F. (2010, August 7). "Mica ţiganiadă europeană." *Adevarul.* Retrieved from http://www.adevarul.ro/florin_iaru_-_opinii/Mica_tiganiada_europeana_7_312638736.html
25. Cartianu, G. (2010, September 13). "De laAllez, allez!" la "Ales bules." *Adevărul.* Retrieved from http://www.adevarul.ro/grigore_cartianu/De_la_-Allez-allez-_la_-Ales_bules_7_334836515.html
26. *Adevărul* (2010, August 20). "„Euroțiganii" din Bihor au fost repatriați joi din Franța, fiind așteptați în localitățile natale." Retrieved from http://www.adevarul.ro/locale/oradea/Eurotiganii-Bihor-repatriati-autoritatile-intoarcerii_0_320368162.html

27. Ghica, S. (2010, August 20). "S-au întors euroţiganii." *Adevărul*. Retrieved from http://www.adevarul.ro/actualitate/eveniment/S-au_intors_eurotiganii_0_319768635.html
28. *Adevărul*. (2010, July 12). 'VIDEO Cum au blocat hoţii români în Franţa 120 de TGV-uri' Retrieved from http://www.adevarul.ro/actualitate/eveniment/Hoti_romani_mai_rapizi_decat_TGV_0_296370743.html#
29. Vasilescu, M. (2010, September 14). "Bâlbâială pe franţuzeşte." *Adevărul*. Retrieved from http://www.adevarul.ro/mircea_vasilescu/Balbaiala_pe_frantuzeste_7_335436454.html
30. Cartianu, G. (2010, August 23). "Am întâlnit şi ţigani cinstiţi." *Adevărul*. Retrieved from http://www.adevarul.ro/grigore_cartianu/Am_intalnit_si_tigani_cinstiti_7_322237778.html
31. *Adevărul*. (2010, August 19). "Francezul Sarkozy şi ţiganil Sarközi." Retrieved from http://www.adevarul.ro/international/Francezul_Sarkozy_si_tiganul_Sarkozi_0_319768606.html
32. *Adevărul*. (2010, September 1). "Europa, la vânătoare de ţigani. La propriu." Retrieved from http://www.adevarul.ro/international/Europa-la_vanatoare_de_tigani-_La_propriu_0_326967895.html
33. *Adevărul*. (2010, August 21). "Ministru suedez: Franţa trebuie sancţionată financiar pentru expulzarea rromilor." Retrieved from http://www.adevarul.ro/international/europa/Ministru_suedez-_Franta_trebuie_sanctionata_financiar_pentru_expulzarea_romilor_0_320968061.html
34. *Adevărul*. (2010, August 26). "Expulzarea ţiganilor români, partea a doua: Alţi 230 de romi trimiţi joi înapoi în România." Retrieved from http://www.adevarul.ro/international/europa/Expulzarea_tiganilor_romani-partea_a_doua-_Alti_230_de_tigani_trimisi_joi_inapoi_in_Romania_0_323967952.html

BIBLIOGRAPHY

Achim, V. (2004). *The Roma in Romanian history*. Budapest, Hungary: Central European University Press.

Balabanova, E., & Balch, A. (2010). Sending and receiving: The ethical framing of free movement in the EU. *European Journal of Communication, 25*(4), 382–397.

Barany, Z. D. (1994). Living on the edge: The East European Roma in postcommunist politics and societies. *Slavic Review, 53*(2), 321–344.

Bell, J. D. (1999). The "revival process": The Turkish and Pomak minorities in Bulgarian politics. In T. Sfikas & C. Williams (Eds.), *Ethnicity and nationalism in East Central Europe and the Balkans* (pp. 237–268). Aldershot, England: Ashgate.

Csepeli, G., & Simon, D. (2004). Construction of Roma identity in Eastern and Central Europe: Perception and self-identification. *Journal of Ethnic and Migration Studies, 30*(1), 129–150.

Dovile, B., & Vilana, P. S. (2009). European norms, local interpretations: Minority rights issues and related discourses in Lithuania after EU expansion. In E. Prugl & M. Thiel (Eds.), *Diversity in the European Union* (pp. 221–236). New York, NY: Palgrave.

Fekete, L. (2009). *A suitable enemy: Racism, migration and Islamophobia in Europe*. London, England: Pluto.

Fonseca, I. (1996). *Bury me standing: The Gypsies and their journey*. London, England: Vintage.

Gheorghe, N. (1991). Roma-Gypsy ethnicity in Eastern Europe. *Social Research, 58*(4), 829–844.

Grigoriadis, I. (2008). On the Europeanisation of minority rights protection: Comparing the cases of Greece and Turkey. *Mediterranean Politics, 13*(1), 23–41.

Guild, E. (2009). *Security and migration in the 21st century*. Cambridge, England: Cambridge University Press.

Iordachi, C. (2010). *Country report: Romania.* Florence, Italy: EUDO Citizenship Observatory, European University Institute, Robert Schuman Centre for Advanced Studies.
Kymlicka, W. (2008). The evolving basis of European norms of minority rights: Rights to culture, participation and autonomy. In M. Weller, D. Blacklock, & K. Nobbs (Eds.), *Protection of minorities in the wider Europe* [Palgrave Studies in European Union Politics Series] (pp. 11–41). Basingstoke, England: Palgrave.
Manners, I. (2002). Normative power Europe: A contradiction in terms? *Journal of Common Market Studies, 40*(2), 235–258.
McGarry, A. (2011). The dilemma of the European Union's Roma policy. *Critical Social Policy, 32*(1), 126–136.
Nacu, A. (2012). From silent marginality to spotlight scapegoating? A brief case study of France's policy towards the Roma. *Journal of Ethnic and Migration Studies, 38*(8), 1323–1328.
Naxidou, E. (2012). Nationalism versus multiculturalism: The minority issue in twenty-first-century Bulgaria. *Nationalities Papers: The Journal of Nationalism and Ethnicity, 40*(1), 85–105.
Pogány, I. (2006). Minority rights and the Roma of Central and Eastern Europe. *Human Rights Law Review, 6*(1), 1–25.
Ram, M. H. (2010). Interests, norms and advocacy: Explaining the emergence of the Roma onto the EU's agenda. *Ethnopolitics, 9*(2), 197–217.
Rechel, B. (2008). *The long way back to Europe: Minority protection in Bulgaria.* Stuttgart, Germany: Ibidem.
Rövid, M. (2011). One-size-fits-all Roma? On the normative dilemmas of the emerging European Roma policy. *Romani Studies 5, 21*(1), 1–22.
Severance, K. (2010). France's expulsion of Roma migrants: A test case for Europe. *Migration Information Source.* Retrieved from http://www.migrationinformation.org/Feature/display.cfm?ID=803
Sigona, N. (2005). Locating the Gypsy problem: The Roma in Italy: Stereotyping, labeling and nomad camps. *Journal of Ethnic and Migration Studies, 31*(4), 741–756.
Walzer, M. (1983). *Spheres of justice: A defense of pluralism and equality.* New York, NY: Basic Books.
Wiener, A., & Schwellnus, G. (2004). *Contested norms in the process of EU enlargement: Non-discrimination and minority rights* (No. p0009). Bath, England: Department of European Studies and Modern Languages, University of Bath.
Woodcock, S. (2007). Romania and Europe: Roma, Roma and Ţigani as sites for the contestation of ethno-national identities. *Patterns of Prejudice, 41*(5), 493–515.

CHAPTER FIVE

Would Jürgen Habermas Enjoy *The Daily Show*?

Entertainment Media and the Normative Presuppositions of the Political Public Sphere

UDO GÖTTLICH AND MARTIN ROLF HERBERS

The theories of democracy might differ in certain aspects, but they all feature a core element: political power and legitimation are derived from the citizens and are distributed through electoral processes. The freedom of the citizens to vote for their own leaders and to raise their voices in favor of or against certain issues is both a blessing and a curse. On the normative level, democracy demands participation but has no means to enforce it. Thus, politically attentive citizens bear the same weight as inattentive citizens, which can result in problems for the democratic process. Nevertheless, political participation is easy. Kaase (1992, p. 340) lists several possible forms of political participation, including the use of political media. This is congruent with another normative presumption of democratic theory: "Democracy functions best when its citizens are politically informed" (Delli Carpini & Keeter, 1996, p. 1).

If informed citizenship is at the heart of democracy, the means by which this information is provided is crucial to the democratic process. The distribution of political information takes place in the political public sphere. This normative theoretical concept has been described from many different points of view. Keeping the informed citizenship in mind, we turn to Jürgen Habermas's works on the political public sphere that put the communicative processes leading to an informed citizenship at the center of his thought. Habermas (1992, p. 436) describes the public sphere as a network of communications, consisting of a variety of issues and opinions. Those streams of communications are filtered and synthesized and form thematic strands of public opinions. The communications that constitute the public sphere adhere to certain normative rules. They have to (1) provide orientation in the world of politics and put the citizens in the position to participate politically; (2) create transparency by highlighting issues and problems that have to be solved collectively, making society in itself and for itself observable; and (3) establish validity by providing means of deliberation for the issues at hand (Donges & Imhof, 2010, p. 186). Habermas places special emphasis on the normative aspects of transparency and validity. He furthermore defines transparency as the fundamental right of every citizen to participate in the public sphere and adds that no one should be excluded from the public sphere *eo ipso* (Habermas, 1990, p. 156). With regard to validity, he demands that all deliberation on public issues should result in a consensus, resulting in non-emotional reasoning and exchange of arguments (Donges & Imhof, p. 193).

Additionally, the communications that constitute the public sphere can take place in three separate, but interconnected, arenas. The first and basic arena takes place in everyday life and consists of social interactions between partners with equal rights to talk and listen. On a spatial level, this arena is very small and allows the partners to observe each other. The second arena consists mainly of an assembly of different individuals, discussing a certain political issue. Here, the partaking individuals can be divided into speaker and audience, resulting in an unequal relation between the partners: the speaker has the right to talk; the audience merely has the right to listen and seldom talks back (Peters, 2008, p. 77). Spatially, in this assembly-based arena the individuals still have the possibility to observe each other. This is not possible in the third arena, where means of mass media are the dominant form of communication. In this case, the distinction between speaker and audience becomes even more solidified, as the audience has little means to talk back to the speaker and is scattered spatially. Presently, this is the dominant arena of the public sphere (Donges & Imhof, 2010).

This ideal type of the public sphere is currently undergoing processes of transformation. Habermas (1990) identifies two processes that alter the ideal type of the public sphere and challenge its normative prerequisites. The (1) changing social structure of the public sphere is based on Habermas's assumptions that the ideal public sphere formerly consisted mainly of bourgeois citizens, who were highly educated and discussed politics rationally. Since the late nineteenth century, this social structure has changed with the omission of class barriers, resulting in a loss of the bourgeois way of thinking about and discussing politics. Following this transformation, the public sphere is undergoing further change processes. The bourgeois public sphere turned to journalistic news media that adhered to their rational demands, such as quality newspapers that discuss politics critically. With the advent of media that follow an economic logic rather than adhering to the ideals of the process of enlightenment, Habermas notices (2) a political transformation of the public sphere, as it turns from the rational discussion of politics by a critical audience to an audience that is manipulated by economically driven mass media. The audience is turning from reasoning about politics to consuming politics (Habermas, 1990; Donges & Imhof, 2010, pp. 199–201).

Both processes of transformation lead to challenges of the normative assumptions of the public sphere. As the media start to follow economic principles rather than sticking to the ideals of enlightenment, they start to produce content that does not necessarily follow the above-mentioned normative assumptions of the public sphere. As the structural transformation of the public sphere results in an audience, which consists of bourgeois-type individuals as well as individuals who are not interested in politics, the public sphere becomes fragmented (Habermas, 2006). Entertainment media, in particular, are assumed to be key drivers of this transformation of the public sphere because they are economically successful and appeal to a large audience, resulting in a marginalization of political content. Entertainment is regarded widely to be the antithesis of a serious occupation with politics. As a consequence of entertainment media's role in the transformation of the public sphere, the normatively required informed citizenship that enables democratic society can be regarded as endangered.

THE HYBRIDIZATION OF ENTERTAINMENT MEDIA AND POLITICS

This rather pessimistic view of the consequences of the structural transformation of the public sphere leads to many "apocalyptic" (Eco, 1989) views on the relationship between politics and entertainment media (e.g., Postman, 1987). Nevertheless, other voices are raised that challenge this bleak outlook. As far as television is concerned, the distinction between programs with an explicitly political content and entertainment programs is obvious, but on closer look, it is possible to find certain programs that combine these apparently incompatible forms of content.

These new and hybrid forms of television programs that merge political content with entertainment programs have been given many names. Among these denotations are terms like "infotainment," "politainment" (Dörner, 2001), and "politicotainment" (Riegert, 2007). Dörner's politainment promotes two opposing views on this phenomenon. On the one hand, television programs take up political issues as a storytelling device, for example, a soap opera that deals with political issues like unemployment or ecological questions. On the other hand, political actors can make use of the entertainment industry's symbolic repertoires in order to make their own images or public appearances more appealing to the general public—for example, posing with movie stars or performing publicity stunts (Dörner, 2001, p. 37).

Although these new forms of television programs sometimes "crash-merge" (Hartley, 2007, p. 21) politics and entertainment rather violently, they often serve as the primary source of political information for many citizens and their everyday political life (van Zoonen, 2005). As already mentioned, the political public sphere is conceptually based on rational, journalistic media (e.g., newspapers or television news) and most of the time political scientists who seek answers to questions of political information or participation turn to this "ideal type" of political coverage (Hartley, 2007, p. 23).

Though Delli Carpini and Keeter (1996, pp. 182–184) have shown that watching television has no significant effect on political information, they do not reject the idea that "viewers learn nothing from it" (p. 185). To prove this position, we have to take a closer look at the aforementioned recent forms of political entertainment television that place political issues in fictional contexts and evoke certain effects. As Matthew Baum points out, this rather pessimistic view on the interplay between politics and entertainment can be turned into an analytical, more differentiated one. Through the combination of political content and entertainment, it is possible to bring political issues to the attention of citizens who would otherwise systematically avoid political content on television. Through this piggyback type (Baum, 2002, p. 96) of presentation of political information, it is possible to meet the normative postulation of an informed citizenship through entertainment media. Politically inattentive citizens, therefore, have the opportunity (by purposely avoiding serious political content) to engage with political information and can contribute to the democratic process as well as informed citizens (Baum, 2002).

THE CONTRIBUTION OF ENTERTAINMENT MEDIA TO THE PUBLIC SPHERE

Although the normative stipulation of an informed citizenship as a requirement of the democratic process seems to be achieved by these forms of entertainment, some other questions with regard to the public sphere remain unanswered. Focusing on Habermas's normative assumptions of *transparency*, *validity*, and *orientation*, little is known about the contributions of political entertainment media to these prerequisites. Citizens learn about political issues from entertainment media, but are they put into a position to discuss the issues in order to reach a consensus? Is the information skewed or biased? Can anybody participate? As Göttlich (2009, p. 212) points out, it is necessary to analyze the normative assumptions of transparency, validity, and orientation against the background of entertainment media in order to evaluate their contribution to the political public sphere. Further questions, derived from the social transformation of the public sphere, have to be taken into account as well to evaluate the role of entertainment media for the political public sphere: Which role does the stratification of audiences in different milieus play in choosing and using certain entertainment formats? The aforementioned differentiation of the communication process into speakers and audiences also must be challenged, as it is insufficient to describe the complexity of entertainment communication, which has no clear role of a speaker and no clear role of an addressed audience, either. Are there asymmetries deriving from social strata and milieus that play a role in fulfilling these functions? To address these issues, the following research questions are posed: To what extent do political entertainment media fulfill the normative assumptions of the political public sphere, oriented to the role of the audiences that consist of members of different milieus, as well as oriented to the quality of entertainment itself?

Entertainment media come in numerous forms. In order to evaluate the contribution of entertainment media for the political public sphere, it is necessary to differentiate them from other media. As mentioned above, the political public sphere is based on certain media effects, such as reasoning, persuasion, or cognitive processes like learning. Therefore, these cognitive effects have to be achieved by entertainment media as well, in order to fulfill the assumed contribution to the political public sphere. Hence, as far as the content of these types of media is concerned, there has to be at least some kind of political information on these programs (Holbert, 2005, p. 443). Furthermore, entertainment media have to be entertaining. This is by no means a trivial assumption as media—and communication science—is still seeking a valid answer to the question of the properties of entertainment (Bosshart & Macconi, 1998). With regard to the question of the normative contributions of entertainment media to the political public sphere, it is necessary to find a working definition of entertainment that covers both the elements of content and the psychological phenomenon based on the reception of the content. Furthermore, from a cultural studies perspective, entertaining texts are polysemantic and, therefore, have to be interpreted by the audience. Thus, a single text can offer different meanings and can be encoded differently.

Current research on media entertainment as a psychological phenomenon emphasizes two distinct psychological processes: enjoyment and entertainment. Enjoyment is the presumption for entertainment. As Oliver and Bartsch (2011, p. 29) point out, enjoyment can be defined—on a basic level—as a positively valenced psychological response to a (media) stimulus. More recently, this definition has been broadened to include other forms of stimuli that do not result in a positive effect and affect but are, nevertheless, described as enjoyable. Enjoyment, there fore, is not only based on the valence of an experience but also can be described as the fulfillment of certain psychological needs. Taking this into consideration, enjoyment can result from the reception of entertainment media as well as journalistic media as they fulfill certain needs, such as the need for information, cognitive stability, or escapism. In this case, enjoyment is a psychological phenomenon based on the experiences of the audience. This is not sufficient for a definition of entertainment. As mentioned above, there has to be at least some extent some kind of content that allows the audience to judge whether the reception of a certain program will result in enjoyment or not (Holbert, 2005, p. 443). Based on this, Hans-Otto Hügel points out that entertainment can only be derived from a certain aesthetic stimulus, the so-called equivocalness of *Unterhaltung* (entertainment). This double entendre of "stimulus," in combination with the psychological process of enjoyment, can result in the experience of entertainment (Hügel, 2007, pp. 36–37) as an interpretation of the given text.

Thus, entertainment is based on two elements: (1) the psychological process of enjoyment that is derived from the fulfillment of needs and (2) certain aspects of the media stimuli and their specific values as aesthetic equivocal stimuli. With regard to the research question of the contribution of entertainment media to the political public sphere, we have to look for television programs that provide not only enjoyment but also entertainment—in combination with political content. Based on these assumptions, it is possible to identify certain types of entertainment media that fall under this definition. Holbert (2005) provides a concise overview of entertainment programs that fall under this definition. His typology is based on two dichotomic axes. He points out that the entertainment programs differ in the importance that is placed on the political content. Some programs regard politics as primary (e.g., a fictional political drama that takes place in the White House), while in some programs the political content serves only secondary functions (e.g., an entertainment television program like *Who Wants To Be a Millionaire?* that poses questions on political affairs, among others). Furthermore, Holbert draws a distinction between explicit and implicit political content. Some programs mention politics directly (e.g., a soft news program that gives a report on a current political event), while in some programs, political content is only mentioned as an aside (e.g., satirical situation comedies that deal with a certain political issue but never address it directly) (Holbert, 2005, pp. 443–444).

As Holbert's typology shows, the notion of "entertainment media" is not complex enough and has to be broken down to certain distinct programs of political entertainment media in order to assess their contributions to the political public sphere. For an initial analysis and assessment of political entertainment media it is best to place focus on those programs that emphasize politics and regard it as primary content, as well as those programs that deal with politics explicitly. We can assume that these kinds of programs can be seen as a major contribution to the public sphere, as they follow the underlying normative assumptions of the ideal public sphere quite closely. Holbert proposes that entertaining talk shows meet both of these criteria, with fictional political dramas and traditional satire next to them. In order to get a valid impression of the contribution of these programs to the political public sphere, it would be best to analyze them all. Current research on these programs places special emphasis on entertaining talk shows and traditional satire and their political effects and provides a substantial body of literature that can be used to answer the underlying research question. Through this analysis of secondary literature it is possible to relate these findings to the broader questions of normativity, which most of these analyses omit. To answer the underlying research question, special emphasis is placed on the findings on the political talk and satire show *The Daily Show with Jon Stewart.* Not only does this show meet two of the three requirements for a program that places political content as primary—host Jon Stewart presides over a talk segment and then a satire segment that mocks current political affairs in a fake news style—but also it is regarded widely as a new form of journalism providing political information to those citizens who would normally bypass traditionally presented political content (Baym, 2005).

THE DAILY SHOW—FINDINGS AND NORMATIVE IMPLICATIONS

At this point, we proceed with a review of secondary literature on *The Daily Show* as a kind of case study in order to evaluate the normative implications postulated by Habermas with regard to research on entertainment media.

The first normative demand proposed by Habermas is that communication in the political public sphere should provide orientation. Hence, there is the need to turn to findings that place emphasis on the content, its valence, and the psychological effects that constitute public opinion. Baumgartner and Morris (2006) analyzed jokes about George W. Bush and John Kerry and found that after hearing these jokes the audience rated both politicians negatively. Furthermore, the authors found an increase in cynicism toward the American electoral system as well as the media itself. On the other hand, their findings show that the audience developed an increasing confidence in their understanding of the complicated world of politics. The work of Cao (2010) shows that by watching *The Daily Show*, the audience learned a great deal about the topics and issues, which were covered frequently (e.g., the war in Afghanistan). Nevertheless, a positive relation toward these issues decreased. With regard to the topics of *The Daily Show*, a study conducted by Fox, Koloen, and Sahin (2007) compares the amount of "substantial news" presented in *The Daily Show* with broadcast news. They find little difference in the substance of the information that is given, concluding the show is at least as substantive as traditional news sources. Additionally, through the frequent watching of *The Daily Show*, less attentive audiences show an increased attentiveness to politics and turn to other, more traditional, sources of political information. Although the entertainment program serves as a gateway to other sources of information, this does not necessarily lead to an increased level of knowledge of the issues that raised that interest in the first place (Xenos & Becker, 2009). Furthermore, Holbert, Lambe, Dudo, and Carlton (2007) point out that through watching *The Daily Show*, audiences get political gratifications, such as the impression of being well informed. These gratifications increase in association with the viewing of television news through a primacy effect and have a positive influence on political self-efficacy, especially on those audiences who are usually politically inattentive.

In order to find a consensus through political communication, the content of these communications should provide arguments and counterarguments to ensure deliberation. Many of the communications in *The Daily Show* do not meet this criterion. Baumgartner and Morris (2006) show that jokes about George W. Bush and John Kerry portray them in a rather skewed and unbalanced way, focusing on their flaws and personality traits. With regard to the presentation style of these communications, Fox, Koloen, and Sahin (2007) showed that *The Daily Show* uses humor as the primary mode of presentation, regardless of the issue.

No group of citizens should be excluded from participating in the public sphere. It follows, then, that diversity—of participants, as well as of audiences from different milieus—is key for a functioning democratic process. This normative implication usually is challenged by a fragmented audience that is split into politically inattentive citizens and political information junkies (Peters, 2008, p. 89). These are the individuals who Habermas kept in mind as he formulated the ideal type of a political public sphere. Many studies analyze the effects of *The Daily Show* on two groups that are not at the heart of Habermas's understanding of the public sphere. These are young people (Baumgartner & Morris, 2006; Feldman, 2008) and politically inattentive individuals (Cao, 2010; Holbert et al., 2007; Xenos & Becker, 2009).

These findings present an ambiguous picture of the contribution of entertainment media to the political public sphere. The strongest contributions of entertainment media can be found with regard to transparency. Through these, it is possible for politically inattentive audiences to get in touch with political information on current issues and participate in the democratic process. Furthermore, young audiences whose political socialization is still underway can get in touch with a lighthearted, understandable presentation of the political world. Thus, entertainment media increase the diversity of audiences and can reduce fragmentation of the public sphere.

These audiences also receive orientation in the political world as they learn about ongoing political issues and increase their knowledge of these topics. Furthermore, their political confidence and self-efficacy is increased, which results in greater general attention to politics. This leads to an increased use of traditional news sources on political issues, thus placing these audiences back into the center of the political public sphere. Entertainment media, therefore, provide a valuable contribution to the political orientation of the audience by enhancing knowledge and serving as a gateway to further information.

As the exemplary discussion has shown, the increased transparency and orientation provided by entertainment media can be seen as a valuable addition to the political public sphere. Thus, the "apocalyptic" view that entertainment media eventually might destroy the political public sphere has to be reconsidered. Only validation seems to be a critical point, since *The Daily Show* focuses on a humorous—and therefore inherently biased—mode of presentation. Therefore, we propose that Habermas might enjoy *The Daily Show* since it fulfills some normative presuppositions of the theory of the public sphere, but he likely would keep a keen eye on the show's limitations.

NEWS AND ENTERTAINMENT—IS THERE STILL A NEED FOR THIS DISTINCTION?

Nevertheless, the theoretical assumptions of the public sphere have to be reconsidered, as well as the role of journalistic media as the primary distributor of political communication. We begin with Habermas's rationality assumption.

For his outline of the political public sphere, Habermas assumed a rational audience that exchanges arguments in favor of or against a certain political issue, shunning any emotions that might accompany this issue. Through a course of deliberation, a consensus is formed. Entertainment media challenge this rational-critical form of argumentation insofar as they do not need to adhere to this strict form of discourse since they use humor, satire, and other stylistic devices, which are irrational by definition. The application of humor to discourse about serious issues creates a new form of political communication. By combining rational discourse with nonrational techniques of presentation, the audience is actively involved as it needs to dissimilate the political content from the mere form. This is a nontrivial cognitive task, which is based on at least a certain amount of precursory knowledge of politics in order to get the joke. Thus, this form of political communication not only facilitates learning (as shown above), it also provides emotional relief as well. The nonrational forms of political communication might lead to political cynicism or distrust, but this can also be viewed as a new form of a critical audience that challenges its political system and leaders by publicly mocking them instead of following them blindly (Paletz, 1990). This carnivalization of politics (Bakhtin, 1995) is as old as politics itself and has always been a part of political (media) culture and the political public sphere. Therefore, it should not be excluded from the theoretical assumptions of the political public sphere, as it is an important part not only of everyday political life but also a part of political communication itself.

If entertainment media are placed as contributors to the public sphere, this challenges the dominant position of traditional journalism. As mentioned above, studies found no major differences in the substance of the political content of *The Daily Show* and broadcast news, although a different mode of framing (Entman, 1993) is employed. With regard to the normative aspects of orientation, validation, and transparency, journalism and entertainment seem to serve the same purpose. Therefore, Baym (2005) argues that *The Daily Show* should be seen as a new form of political journalism that surpasses the traditional boundaries of reporting in favor of a postmodern style of presentation that corresponds to the audience's viewing habits. However, this claim goes too far as entertainment media do not fall under the normative role of journalism as fourth estate and, hence, do not fall under its constitutional protection. Furthermore, entertainment media and journalism adhere to different modes of production as they select, interpret, and present topics and issues differently. Therefore, journalism still remains a major contributor to the public sphere, although entertainment media challenge its position. However, through its function as a gateway to traditional news, entertainment media can be seen as a complementary addition not only to the public sphere but also to the marketplace of ideas. By doing so, entertainment media can play out their strengths with regard to transparency and orientation and overcome their flaws in the validation of issues, as this normative demand can be reached through the interplay of journalism and entertainment media on the level of the media system (Wessler, 2008).

ARE SOCIAL STRATA A PREDICTOR FOR INTEREST IN ENTERTAINMENT MEDIA AND POLITICS?

Our previous discussion has shown that the audience of *The Daily Show* consists mainly of young citizens and politically inattentive individuals. Despite the learning effect derived from watching the show in these groups of citizens, from a sociological point of view these findings are relatively coarse. Further differentiation of the audiences is necessary to draw a sharper image of the contribution of entertainment media to the political public sphere. As Neumann (1986) points out, democratic societies can be subdivided into several groups of citizens that differ in their willingness to participate in politics and in their political sophistication. Neumann's findings are consistent with the above-mentioned issues of the political public sphere with regard to participation. As there is a stratum in democratic societies that is inattentive to politics, this imbalance can result in malfunctions of the political process. Nevertheless, this undifferentiated mass public has to be scrutinized as it follows the apocalyptic worldview in which a mass audience uncritically watches television without any political effect. The research on *The Daily Show* presents a different picture: the inattentive mass audience becomes active and even self-reports sophistication in politics through watching this television show. Therefore, the findings of Neumann should be reevaluated with regard to entertainment television, considering that there is insufficient data on how different milieus use and interpret these programs.

Nevertheless, as Bourdieu (1984) has shown, the social stratum of a certain individual member of a society has effects on his or her way of life. Economic, cultural, and social capital can be indicative of distinctions between individuals and groups, which enable these individuals or groups to participate in a certain lifestyle. For example, a wealthy person might enjoy different food than a blue-collar, working-class individual. The social stratum also affects the choice of media: as wealthy individuals might seek to be informed by quality media in order to uphold their social position, blue-collar individuals might seek relaxation from a hard day's work and enjoyment by watching comedy television.

As far as political participation and political information are concerned, the underlying assumption that the public sphere consists mainly of politically interested and politically inattentive citizens cannot be upheld, as the sociological findings draw a far more complex picture. *The Daily Show* serves both functions of information and entertainment provider and, thus, appeals to many groups of citizens. Therefore, the boundaries between social strata and milieus might be blurred through these forms of entertainment media, which can result in positive effects on the political public sphere.

GOOD NEWS, GOOD ENTERTAINMENT, GOOD POLITICS?

Entertainment media can provide an alternative source of political information, as they increase the quantity of channels for mediated political communication. Nevertheless, the question arises whether an increase in quantity is sufficient for a viable contribution to the democratic process. As Zaller (2003) argues with regard to journalism's role in democracy, the political communication should adhere to a certain standard of quality, as well. Focusing on entertainment media, this discussion goes back to early forms of entertaining communication. The critique of entertainment is often apocalyptic (Eco, 1989) and is associated widely with a cultural degeneration, as it prevents individuals from dealing with more important issues. The demarcation of high cultural products (e.g., art and literature) and low cultural products (e.g., television and comic books) is well known and draws canonical distinctions in society. High and low culture, therefore, is associated with different manifest cultural products and different groups of users, as shown above. This essentialist view on cultural products proclaims differences in quality—a painting by Pablo Picasso is better than a television show. Furthermore, materialistic perspectives on culture come to mind: Horkheimer and

Adorno (2003) argue that cultural products meant for entertaining the masses are produced in service and in favor of groups of powerful individuals who control the means of production and seek to uphold this superior position by providing entertainment media that deceive the masses.

Nevertheless, the hybrid forms of television challenge the distinction between high and low culture. By drawing heavily from politics and combining it with elements of popular discourse and culture, *The Daily Show* playfully dissolves this distinction. It mocks politics, toppling it from its throne down to the sphere of the common people, and gives them a chance to ridicule their leaders and issues that are too big to understand (Bakhtin, 1995). Therefore, a third kind of culture is formed—neither high nor low, but a hybrid culture—in which the established forms of political communication converge with the new forms of entertainment (Jenkins, 2008).

It is important to ask whether *The Daily Show* and other forms of politainment provide sufficient enough information to the political public sphere. On the content level, questions of selecting political information and its presentation have to be answered. As our argument has shown, a lot of political information focuses on top-level political actors. The lower ranks, for example, members of the parliament, are seldom mentioned. Nevertheless, they are part of the political process and part of the political public sphere. With regard to political issues, mainly current issues are discussed, thus biasing the content of the program. Basically, political entertainment media have the same problems as journalistic media: an emphasis on current issues and people who attract the attention of the audience. Furthermore, the underlying question of the political public sphere concerning the audience is still without answer: What should citizens know about politics (Delli Carpini & Keeter, 1996, pp. 63–65)? If entertainment media are to provide political information, their contribution has to be judged by the quality of the given information—which is still an unanswered normative question.

Taking everything into consideration, we propose that *The Daily Show* serves as an example of a valuable addition to the political public sphere and fulfills at least to some extent the normative presumptions of transparency, orientation, and—to some degree—validation. It may help citizens to cross the restrictions of social strata and milieus to access news and establishes a new kind of quality for political communication. With the help of entertainment media, citizens from all ways of life can participate in public life by enabling a "public connection" (Couldry, Livingstone, & Markham, 2007, p. 3). The question of how this connection happens is still open.

To analyze this public connection, "we need detailed evidence from people's reflections on their daily lives" (Couldry, Livingstone, & Markham, 2007, p. 16). Since traditional political communication research lacks this perspective, further research on this topic should include social differentiations (as mentioned in the research question). These are the keys to understanding not only divergent interpretations of a given text, but also phenomena (such as fragmentation) of the political public sphere.

BIBLIOGRAPHY

Bakhtin, M. (1995). *Rabelais und seine Welt. Volkskultur als Gegenkultur*. Frankfurt am Main, Germany: Suhrkamp.

Baum, M. A. (2002). Sex, lies, and war: How soft news brings foreign policy to the inattentive public. *American Political Science Review, 96*(1), 91–109. doi:10.1017/S0003055402004252

Baumgartner, J., & Morris, J. S. (2006). *The Daily Show* effect: Candidate evaluations, efficacy, and American youth. *American Politics Research, 34*(3), 341–367. doi:10.1177/1532673X05280074

Baym, G. (2005). *The Daily Show*: Discursive integration and the reinvention of political journalism. *Political Communication, 22*(33), 259–276. doi:10.1080/10584600591006492

Bosshart, L., & Macconi, I. (1998). Media entertainment. *Communication Research Trends, 18*(3), 5–8. Retrieved from http://cscc.scu.edu/trends/v18/v18_3.pdf

Bourdieu, P. (1984). *Distinction: A social critique of the judgment of taste*. Cambridge, MA: Harvard University Press.

Cao, X. (2010). Hearing it from John Stewart: The impact of *The Daily Show* on public attentiveness to politics. *International Journal of Public Opinion Research, 22*(1), 26–46. doi: 10.1093/ijpor/edp043

Couldry, N., Livingstone, S., & Markham, T. (2007). *Media consumption and public engagement: Beyond the presumption of attention*. Basingstoke, England: Palgrave Macmillan.

Delli Carpini, M., & Keeter, S. (1996). *What Americans know about politics and why it matters*. New Haven, CT: Yale University Press.

Donges, P., & Imhof, K. (2010). Öffentlichkeit im Wandel. In H. Bonfadelli, O. Jarren, & G. Siegert (Eds.), *Einführung in die Publizistikwissenschaft* (3rd ed., pp. 183–212). Bern, Switzerland; Stuttgart, Germany; Vienna, Austria: Haupt.

Dörner, A. (2001). *Politainment. Politik in der medialen Erlebnisgesellschaft*. Frankfurt am Main, Germany: Suhrkamp.

Eco, U. (1989). *Apokalyptiker und Integrierte. Zur kritischen Kritik der Massenkultur*. Frankfurt am Main, Germany: Fischer.

Entman, R. (1993). Framing: Toward clarification of a fractured paradigm. *Journal of Communication, 43*(4), 51–58. doi:10.1111/j.1460-2466.1993.tb01304.x

Feldman, L. (2008). The news about comedy: Young audiences, the *Daily Show*, and evolving notions of journalism. *Journalism, 8*(4), 406–427. doi:10.1177/1464884907078655

Fox, J. R., Koloen, G., & Sahin, V. (2007): No joke: A comparison of substance in *The Daily Show with John Stewart* and broadcast network television of the 2004 presidential election campaigns. *Journal of Broadcasting & Electronic Media, 51*(2), 213–227. doi:10.1080/08838150701304621

Göttlich, U. (2009). Auf dem Weg zur Unterhaltungsöffentlichkeit? Aktuelle Herausforderungen des Öffentlichkeitswandels in der Medienkultur. In U. Göttlich & S. Porombka (Eds.), *Die Zweideutigkeit der Unterhaltung. Zugangsweisen zur Populären Kultur* (pp. 202–219). Cologne, Germany: von Halem.

Habermas, J. (1990). *Strukturwandel der Öffentlichkeit. Untersuchungen zu einer Kategorie der bürgerlichen Gesellschaft*. Frankfurt am Main, Germany: Suhrkamp.

Habermas, J. (1992). *Faktizität und Geltung. Beiträge zu einer Diskurstheorie des Rechts.* Frankfurt am Main, Germany: Suhrkamp.

Habermas, J. (2006). Political communication in media society. Does democracy still enjoy an epistemic dimension? The impact of normative theory on empirical research. *Communication Theory, 16*(4), 411–426. doi:10.1111/j.1468-2885.2006.00280.x

Hartley, J. (2007). "Reality" and the plebiscite. In K. Riegert (Ed.), *Politicotainment: Television's take on the real* (pp. 21–58). New York, NY: Peter Lang.

Holbert, L. R. (2005). A typology for the study of entertainment television and politics. *American Behavioral Scientist, 49*(3), 436–453. doi:10.1177/0002764205279419

Holbert, L. R., Lambe, J. L., Dudo, A. D., & Carlton, K. A. (2007). Primacy effect of *The Daily Show* and national TV news viewing: Young viewers, political gratifications, and internal political self-efficacy. *Journal of Broadcasting & Electronic Media, 51*(1), 20–38. doi:10.1080/08838150701308002

Horkheimer, M., & Adorno, T. W. (2003). Dialektik der Aufklärung. In M. Horkheimer (Ed.), *Gesammelte Schriften. Band 5: Dialektik der Aufklärung und Schriften, 1940–1950* (3rd ed., pp. 13–290). Frankfurt am Main, Germany: Fischer.

Hügel, H. (2007). Genau Lektüren. Zu Begriff, Theorie und Geschichte der Unterhaltung. In B. Frizzoni & I. Tomkowiak (Eds.), *Unterhaltung. Konzepte-Formen-Wirkungen* (pp. 31–48). Zurich, Switzerland: Chronos.

Jenkins, H. (2008). *Convergence culture: Where old and new media collide.* New York, NY; London, England: New York University Press.

Kaase, M. (1992). Politische Beteiligung. In M. G. Schmidt (Ed.), *Lexikon der Politik. Band 3: Die westlichen Länder* (pp. 339–346). München, Germany: C. H. Beck.

Neumann, R. W. (1986). *The paradox of mass politics. Knowledge and opinion in the American electorate.* Cambridge, MA; London, England: Harvard University Press.

Oliver, M. B., & Bartsch, A. (2011). Appreciation of entertainment: The importance of meaningfulness via virtue and wisdom. *Journal of Media Psychology, 23*(1), 29–33. doi:10.1027/1864-1105/a000029

Paletz, D. L. (1990). Political humor and authority: From support to subversion. *International Political Science Review, 11*(4), 483–493. doi:10.1177/019251219001100406

Peters, B. (2008). On public deliberation and public culture. In H. Wessler (Ed.), *Public deliberation and public culture: The writings of Bernhard Peters, 1993–2005* (pp. 68–118). Basingstoke, England: Palgrave Macmillan.

Postman, N. (1987). *Amusing ourselves to death: Public discourse in the age of show business.* London, England: Methuen.

Riegert, K. (2007). Introduction. In K. Riegert (Ed.), *Politicotainment: Television's take on the real* (pp. 1–19). New York, NY: Peter Lang.

Van Zoonen, L. (2005). *Entertaining the citizen: When politics and popular culture converge.* Lanham, MD: Rowman & Littlefield.

Wessler, H. (2008). Investigating deliberativeness comparatively. *Political Communication, 25*(1), 1–22. doi:10.1080/10584600701807752

Xenos, M. A., & Becker, A. B. (2009). Moments of Zen: Effects of *The Daily Show* on information seeking and political learning. *Political Communication, 26*(3), 317–332. doi:10.1080/10584600903053569

Zaller, J. (2003). A new standard of news quality: Burglar alarms for the monitorial citizen. *Political Communication, 20*(2), 109–130. doi:10.1080/10584600390211136

CHAPTER SIX

Beyond the Corporate Lens

The Use of Humor in Activist Communication

KATHARINA WOLF

Although not a characteristic that is associated commonly with neither professional communication nor activism in mainstream Western culture, this article demonstrates that humor performs a crucial role in activist communication. Based on in-depth periods of participant observation among one of Australia's most prominent social movements, the West Australian antinuclear movement (WA ANM), I argue that comedy, wit, and hilarity are core components of activist campaigns.

Their communication styles and tools, therefore, set activists apart from their corporate counterparts, among whom humor is not recognized as an element of the strategic communications toolkit. This unfamiliarity and adverse connotations associated with humor in a business context may lead to injudicious misunderstanding or dismissal of activists for seeming unprofessional, amateurish, and attention seeking. Instead, this chapter reveals that humor fulfils a number of vital internal and external functions within the WA ANM network.

Four key themes have emerged from my data: Humorous actions enable activists to create a sense of community by attracting people's attention and drawing in diverse audiences. Humor can be used as an educational tool, making science-based and often confrontational, or even disturbing, information more interesting, digestible, and memorable. However, humor also performs a crucial role within the movement itself, first by ensuring actions and participation are sustainable over a prolonged period and finally by actively shaping the WA ANM's collective identity, hence ensuring its survival over time.

LITERATURE REVIEW

Scholarly research on activism spans more than three decades and represents one of the most prevalent streams in public relations literature. However, despite the strong scholarly interest in activist communication, the public relations research agenda has to date been largely limited to the corporate perspective, motivated by a focus on issues management and damage limitation (e.g., Bunting & Lipski, 2001; Deegan, 2001; L. A. Grunig, 1992; Illia, 2003; John & Thomson, 2003; Turner, 2007; Werder, 2006). In both scholarly works and practitioner literature the focus has been on how opposition and outrage can be detected, managed, and eliminated (e.g., Anderson, 1992; Coombs, 2002; Deegan, 2001; J. E. Grunig & Grunig, 1997), at the expense of insight into public relations' role across all facets of society.

Public relations scholars have focused to date largely on how activists are similar to, rather than different from, corporations and organizational PR departments. As a result, the current PR activism literature is dominated by a focus on established not-for-profit organizations with corporation-like PR departments. Holtzhausen (2007) argues that once organizations become institutionalised, like the Sierra Club, the World Wildlife Fund (WWF), People for the Ethical Treatment of Animals (PETA), or, in fact, most non-profit organizations, they "lose their typical activist attributes" (p. 369). As they grow in size they begin to adopt business principles and become "national or multinational entities with 'brand value,' multi-million dollar budgets, and teams of full time employees" (Jaques, 2006, p. 413). This prevailing focus on large, established, and corporation-like activist groups in PR scholarship may be motivated largely by ease of access and convenience. Smith and Ferguson (2001) acknowledge that the relatively short lifecycle of some issues and dynamic nature of many activist groups may make it challenging to study them. As a result, much of the existing body of knowledge is concerned with how activist groups operate in comparison to corporations or, more specifically, corporations' public relations departments. Scholars have traditionally been outsiders, looking inside activist organizations with no or only limited firsthand activist contact. By researching activist communication through a corporate lens, scholars largely have failed to gain insight into how nontraditional communicators practice public relations or, indeed, if they practice public relations at all, thereby neglecting an opportunity to further inform our knowledge and understanding of activist communication as well as public relations as a discipline. In contrast to corporations' well-funded and deliberate campaigns, grassroots activism materializes in response to situations and issues and, hence, often lacks the benefit of established networks and resources (Demetrious, 2001). This chapter argues that as grassroots and social movement activists may lack the resources and specialist communication training from which their corporate counterparts benefit; they draw on alternative communication tools to increase their share of voice in society. Humor is a unique tool in this context, which offers grassroots activists multiple benefits.

To date the role and function of humor in activism largely has been ignored in public relations and communications research. Notable exceptions are Kay Weaver's (2010) case study on the Mothers Against Genetic Engineering group in New Zealand, in which she positions carnivalesque activism as a public relations genre in its own right, and the multidisciplinary works by Marty Branagan (2005, 2006, 2007a, 2007b, 2010), throughout which he draws on his personal experience as environmental activist in Australia. Humor has, however, attracted much attention in other related disciplines.

Although multidisciplinary by nature, "humorology" has evolved into a field of research in its own right (Hart & Bos, 2007), with dedicated scholarly journals, such as *Humor: The International Journal of Humor Research*, *European Journal of Humor Research*, and *Israeli Journal of Humor Research*. Humor has a long history as a tool to "confront privilege, weaken the power of oppressors and empower resistance" (Branagan, 2007b, p. 470). A classic example is the royal court jester, who could express critical thoughts about policies without fearing punishment (Hart & Bos, 2007). Lievrouw (2011) similarly argues that activists' political and artistic heritage is in Dada and situationism, which leads to the use of irony and humor as a means to confront power, challenge the status quo, and emphasise alternative points of view via, for example, culture jamming, flash mobs, or provocative media artifacts. Scholars, hence, refer to humor as a "powerful communication tool" (Meyer, 2000, p. 328), which is employed frequently as a communication strategy in its own right (Hart & Bos, 2007). Humor complements other forms of activism (Branagan, 2007b), particularly political activism and protest (Bruner, 2005; Hart & Bos, 2007). In this context, Branagan (2007b) highlights the American community organizer Saul Alinsky, author of arguably the most commonly referred to activist text, *Rules for Radicals* (Alinsky, 1971). He argues that humor can be used as a non-alienating, two-way communication tool that undermines and deflates the powerful and exposes the absurdity of a given political situation. In fact, Alinsky refers to satire and ridicule as one of the most potent weapons known to mankind. The importance of humor has been extensively documented in activists' accounts of campaigns, such as the history of the antinuclear movement in Western Australia (Kearns, 2004) and Munro, Scott, and David's (1996) colorful insight into a multitude of Australian campaigns in *How to Make Trouble and Influence People: Australasian Pranks, Hoaxes and Political Mischief Making* (see also later versions by McIntyre, 2009; McIntyre, Sevil, & Smith, 2009). Activist guides and how-to literature similarly touch on the concepts of humor and being unconventional as effective means to attract attention (see, e.g., Alinsky, 1946; Alinsky, 1971).

Humorous protest literature has paid particular attention to the rich history of carnivalesque action (see, e.g., Bruner, 2005; Hart & Bos, 2007; Weaver, 2010), providing insight into situations where political protest was only possible, or nonpunishable, if done in a joking, entertaining manner (Hart, 2007). As the masquerades could hide the identity of participants, members of "lower classes arguably *exploited* these events to express their hostility towards the ruling oligarchy" (Hart, 2007, p. 4). Although both have lost much of their traditional political character, two classical examples are Mardi Gras and Carnaval, which are vibrant street festivals that take place leading up to Lent in various major cities around the world. Both events commenced as colorful, fun, inclusive public performances with a strong political message that tolerated and even enabled the breaking of taboos and the expression of repressed behaviors and social tensions, such as those "suffered by the Brazilian minorities, which are little voiced during the apparent normality of the rest of the year" (Correa, 2012). By means of song, dance, and catchy music they draw audiences in, effectively recruiting them as an extension to the official performers. Hart explains how public parades offer such opportunities to activist minorities like the LGBTQ community: "By inviting the public to laugh *with* them, the participants in these parades aim to establish peaceful change in the existing homophobic discourse" (Hart, 2007, p. 16). Hence, people who are "usually divided by the barriers of caste, property, profession and age" (Bakhtin, 1984, p. 10) are suddenly considered equal and free to participate actively. As such, carnivalesque activism has the potential to communicate a message to a wider audience as it draws on shared human experiences (Bakhtin, 1984). In *Rabelais and His World*, Bakhtin illustrates how carnival used to function as a social institution. Due to the temporary suspension of hierarchies and distinctions, ridicule and the symbolic crowning and subsequent de-crowning of a *mock* king was tolerated. Bakhtin argues that kings permitted and even endorsed carnivalesque action as an outlet for aggression and rebellion against norms, hence protecting their own status in the long term.

PR scholars have increasingly highlighted the need to broaden the PR research agenda by conducting research inside activist organizations, thereby recognizing activists as communication experts in their own right (e.g., Hallahan, Holtzhausen, van Ruler, Vercic, & Sriramesh, 2007; Heath & Palenchar, 2009; Karagianni & Cornelissen, 2006; Smith & Ferguson, 2001). This chapter draws on three phases of data collection as part of a PhD project, which set out to address the current gap in PR activism literature by providing insight into the activist perspective.

METHODOLOGY

This study is of exploratory nature, based on ethnographic research, with the aim of providing emic insights into the antinuclear debate and "thick description"

(Geertz, 1973) of the movement's communication efforts. A grounded theory approach was chosen for this study, as this is considered particularly suitable for the exploration of social organizations from the participants' point of view (Glaser, 1998); in this case, through the eyes of West Australian (WA) antinuclear activists. To overcome the scarcity of existing knowledge and insights (particularly within the WA and antinuclear context), a single case study approach was selected, enabling me "to collect 'rich,' detailed information across a wide range of dimensions" (Daymon & Holloway, 2011, p. 115).

ABOUT THE WA ANM

The Western Australian antinuclear movement (WA ANM) has been a prominent voice in Australian politics and social commentary for more than four decades. Emerging out of the global mass demonstration movement in the 1960s, the WA ANM became particularly prominent in the late 1970s, when the state was positioned as the future nuclear powerhouse of Australia. The WA ANM has remained active ever since, shifting its focus first from nuclear reactors and opposition to nuclear testing, then to demonstrations against nuclear warships, and, today, primarily to uranium mining. However, the movement is aging. Furthermore, a number of opinion polls have indicated that public opposition to uranium mining and nuclear energy is shifting (e.g., Channel 7, 2010), particularly among young Australians (e.g., Painted Dog Research, 2010). As mining companies encounter challenges in other Australian states, the focus has increasingly shifted to pro-mining Western Australia, attracting not only investors but also activists from around the country. Facing what arguably might be their biggest challenge yet (to prevent the mining of uranium in Western Australia), the WA ANM has reformed with new energy, currently representing one of the most visible and outspoken social movements in Australia.

However, despite its experience and existing profile, the WA ANM largely has been ignored by governments and disregarded by the state's major mining companies. I argue that in order to overcome the endemic lack of human and financial resources, activists are taking approaches to communication that are dissimilar to those employed by their corporate counterparts in an effort to ensure that their voice is being heard in the (West) Australian community. Based on primary data collected during interviews with key activists and intensive periods of participant observation over 2.5 years, this chapter demonstrates how satire, hilarity, and wit are used by activists as a unique, memorable communication tool. I identify four core functions of humor in activist communication that not only aid activists in conveying their key messages but also ensure consistency and the long-term survival of the group. Each of these is examined in more detail in the following section.

COMMUNITY-BUILDING CHARACTERISTICS OF HUMOR

Scholars have explored humor primarily as a method to attract support for activist causes by means of creating a stark contrast to the negative didacticism of violent protest as commonly depicted in the mainstream media (Branagan, 2007a; Weaver, 2010). The humorous approach, therefore, particularly suits the WA ANM, a collective that historically has been committed to nonviolent action and peaceful protest. One of the major challenges facing WA antinuclear activists is the size of the state and the fact that the majority of the WA community lives in the state capital, Perth, while uranium operations are located in remote outback locations. As a result, the (West) Australian public is ambivalent about the practice and impacts of uranium mining, due to social and geographical distancing. Being aware of this significant disadvantage in their battle to win over the hearts, minds, and essential support of the community, WA antinuclear activists embarked on a number of publicity stunts, with the aim of raising awareness, engaging citizens, and encouraging discussion.

Humorous actions draw heavily on drama, costuming, and carnivalesque culture, which communicate subject-specific information in an engaging way. WA ANM examples include a small group of "nuclear scientists with yellowcake uranium drums" boarding a commuter train in the central business district during peak hours and the re-creation of a "Nuclear Spill Scenario" on one of the state's most popular beaches among hundreds of early morning swimmers. The harsh disparity between the industrial suits and community members in swimsuits; the rough and dirty drums against the backdrop of the pristine beach on a glorious summer day; as well as the implied danger of the radioactive symbol in contrast to its peaceful, natural environment, lends itself to humor. The surreal, unexpected nature of the scenario prompted walkers to stop, point, laugh, and in many cases to approach the small group, keen to find out what was going on. Not surprising, there was also some exhausted headshaking, but, overall, the reactions were perceived as overwhelmingly positive. As Johno explains:

> Down there at Cottesloe, ... you got types of people that wouldn't really approve of ... anti-government type activity and wouldn't [think about] nuclear, but in fact several of them stopped and asked and had quite a lot of interest. (Personal interview, March 3, 2011)

This response corresponds to Bruner's (2005) claim that humorous activism is often more effective than serious protest. In this example, the nuclear spill scenario provided a hook that encouraged the local community to engage with the nuclear topic. Rather than confront and repel, humorous activism like this example creates common ground that enables further discussion, awareness raising, and direct exchange with bystanders and curious members of the public. As Rachel explains, humorous actions:

> make people laugh ... and not only people who are there [participants & activists], but maybe outside it [bystanders]. You get the message across and they get a laugh out of it. (Personal interview, May 20, 2011)

By creating enjoyable experiences for audiences and bystanders, humor first catches attention and then draws in the audience, effectively inviting it to play an active part in the wider movement (Branagan, 2007a), in this example, by asking questions and taking photos. Other public actions by the WA ANM invite audiences to join in by singing, clapping, and laughing along. Rather than lecturing audiences or building physical barriers between activists and the community through blockading, marching, or angry shouting, humor includes audiences and provides a starting point for dialogue and further engagement (Branagan, 2007b).

The resulting sense of community or collective camaraderie may even extend to law and order representatives (Branagan, 2007b). This was the case in the train action, where police sided with activists rather than an aggressive community member. The toxic spill action unexpectedly created the opportunity to engage with a uranium mining representative, who stopped on his way to work.

Humor is particularly crucial in the context of the WA ANM, which aims to raise awareness about an issue that is complex and, at times, confronting. As Verity explains, "Nuclear apocalypse is really not funny" (personal interview, April 28, 2011). Fear, horror, and the prospect of nuclear war may alarm and repel audiences rather than attract them. Jay made this same point, saying, "People are deterred by too much seriousness in life" (personal interview, May 13, 2011). For Verity, "we need to make it meaningful and hopeful: Humor can turn the horror of nuclear war into hope for preventing it." Jay commented similarly: "It's much more likely you get people thinking than handing out flyers or shouting, simply because it's fun."

HUMOR AS EDUCATIONAL TOOL

Once activists' have attracted and engaged an audience in the "performance," they need to demonstrate that they possess the necessary subject knowledge (i.e., cultural capital) in order to be taken seriously. Antinuclear activists deal with highly complex and technical subject matters, such as fusion, energy production, and the technicalities of mining operations. Furthermore, the potential health and environmental impacts of, for example, a nuclear meltdown may alarm audiences rather than entice them. In this context, humor can be a highly valuable educational tool, helping to communicate complicated and potentially worrisome information in an entertaining but memorable way.

First, humor effectively lowers an audience's defenses and, hence, makes it more open to new perspectives (Meyer, 2000). Even if bystanders and activists do not share the same point of view, humor establishes a common ground that allows further exploration or discussion by drawing on "shared values rather than dualistic opposites" (Branagan, 2007b, p. 473).

> I think that it gets people thinking. People aren't going to engage in something that they don't want to see, but if you can add a bit of satire to something … if we can give people a laugh you will get them thinking … so it's definitely not meant to downplay the seriousness of uranium mining or nuclear power, but it's just more effective I think. (Jay, personal interview, May 13, 2011)

Antinuclear activists' mission is to educate the community about what essentially are highly alarming, if not terrifying, potential consequences associated with the nuclear circle. Radiation, nuclear warfare, and health risks associated with uranium mining arguably may be more suitable themes for a Hollywood science fiction movie than a community-friendly information event in the West Australian tourist down of Fremantle, which frequently hosts national and international uranium mining conferences. Activists protesting outside these conferences are highly conscious of the potential risk to alarm, distress, and ultimately alienate their audiences. Disillusionment and despair are widely documented emotional states within the activism context (see, e.g., Barker, Martin, & Zournazi, 2008; Cox, 2009; Hoare, 1998; La Rocca, 2004; Macy, 1983; Moyer, McAllister, Finley, & Soifer, 2001). However, the nuclear industry appears to evoke particularly strong emotions, to the extent that some key organizers within the WA ANM admitted deliberately avoiding involvement over a prolonged period.

Humor-inspired street theater, songs, dance, and other types of creative performances are, therefore, tools of political education, which are favored within the antinuclear context. These performances enable activists to challenge openly science- and economics-based discourses, evaluate their own positions and knowledge, take in new perspectives and information, and engage with the nuclear debate. The familiarity of popular songs, the playfulness of actors, and the colors of activists' costumes attract the audience. More important, by embedding serious, often confronting, messages within well-known lyrics, satirical poems, and playful performances, activists are able to retain audiences and communicate key messages within an enjoyable and entertaining context. The memorable nature of these fun activities ensures the "stickiness" of the message well beyond the actual performance.

Moreover, humor enables activists to communicate about weighty and complex topics (Branagan, 2007a), such as the scientific concepts behind the generation of nuclear energy, thereby making them accessible and memorable. For example, the proposal of a nuclear waste disposal site in the Australian outback reemerged during the course of this study. There is no need for audience members to gain in-depth knowledge about logistics, soil samples, and detailed health implications. Instead, street performances lend themselves to communicate core messages and the essence of the WA ANM's arguments. By exaggerating and humouring the pro-nuclear lobby's claims, activists effectively turn the corporate sales pitch for the project into a farce—a comedy so far exaggerated that audiences are left asking themselves, "Can they possibly be serious about this?" They may laugh at the actors, shake their heads at the preposterous nature of the proposal, and leave motivated to find out more. However, most significant, through the audience's engagement, a business proposal for a remote location in the Australian outback essentially is repositioned as a health hazard in "our backyard" that concerns everyone. In Verity's words: "If you've made a joke and you've connected with someone ... you've made a thousand arguments. You don't need to bore the hell out of them" (personal interview, April 28, 2011).

By providing alternative information about uranium mining and nuclear energy, activists like Verity educate audiences in a fun and engaging way, simultaneously challenging existing perceptions and what they refer to as the "of courseness" of the nuclear industry's role in combatting global warming.

HUMOR AS A SUSTAINABILITY TOOL

Humor historically has been "an essential ingredient" (Joy, e-mail conversation, May 10, 2011) of WA-based antinuclear action, as documented in activist publications such as Kearn's (2004) *Stepping out for Peace*, a history of the WA ANM based on interviews with key antinuclear activists. Much of the WA ANM's humor originates out of the inherent adversity—even absurdity and sheer hopelessness—of the activists' situation: A collective of poorly resourced volunteers is attempting to prevent multibillion-dollar international mining companies, with full federal and state government support, from ultimately generating more wealth for their shareholders, at a time when, in West Australia, mining companies are largely perceived to be crucial to the country's economy. By antinuclear activists boldly positioning themselves as the counter-voice and challengers of the status quo, humor arises naturally.

The enormity of the challenge activists face eventually may lead to resentment, frustration, anger, and other emotions that undermine and erode activists' abilities and long-term success. Despair, disillusionment, and burnout are well documented in activist and social movement literature and widely acknowledged by grassroots activists. WA ANM activists acknowledge how relevant emotion is, particularly within the antinuclear context, as they struggle on a personal level with the severity of the potential health and environmental effects of the nuclear cycle:

> The despair that people often feel when you face up to this issue is kind of profound and devastating and if you don't provide hope and humor you will just drown in the horror of it. It's overwhelming and terrifying. (Verity, personal interview, April 28, 2011)

In contrast to corporate communication professionals, activists invest their own time and energy outside work, study, and family commitments. Consequently, they are more vulnerable to exhaustion, stress, and health issues, particularly when considering the level of personal, emotional investment in the antinuclear issue. The risk of activism fatigue and burnout emphasizes the crucial role humor can play as, in contrast to anger, it allows activists to release emotions, such as rage and frustration, while simultaneously providing positive, enjoyable experiences for their audiences (Branagan, 2007b). In particular, humor is valuable for the sustainability of individual activists. Through the creation of rewarding, relaxing, empowering, and reenergizing experiences, activists gain new perspective and hope, avoiding burnout and the need to take prolonged breaks away from the movement. Humorous actions may also act as a reward in themselves, by creating positive experiences to compensate for the time, energy, and personal resources that have been invested in the movement, balancing out negative emotions and incidences. These initiatives include colorful publicity stunts, street theater and costumes, poems and musical performances by the Raging Grannies, and public dance routines, such as one inspired by the U.S. singer Britney Spears's song, "Toxic."

> Having fun, for me it's even more important because I spend my days working and studying in something quite serious: policy and politics. And then sometimes I just want to wear a funny outfit and do something fun. But that still is in the vein of what I have been doing [campaigning against uranium mining]. (Alice, personal interview, June 6, 2011)

Hence, the fun factor of individual actions and benefits to individual activists' well-being appears to override, or at least overshadow, strategic communication decisions concerning audiences' needs and preferences. "It's more about me. It's self-indulgent, yes," is how Alice explains the rationale behind a number of humorous and creative initiatives. In the planning sessions I participated in, corporate audiences and their communication styles rarely were considered. Arguably, this is due largely to the dual role humor fulfills: On one hand, it attracts community members and aids in the conveying of complex messages; on the other hand, it is crucial to ensure the long-term survival of the movement itself, by acting both as a creative outlet and as a reenergizing means.

THE ROLE OF HUMOR IN CREATING A COLLECTIVE IDENTITY

Humor and laughter traditionally have served as powerful tools in social protest, by constructing a strong sense of unity (Hart, 2007). This is illustrated in Kearn's (2004) historic account of the WA ANM, which depicts a wide range of humorous campaign examples and initiatives, as well as other forms of creative expression, that have shaped and strengthened the identity of the movement over time. The enjoyable, invigorating, and often healing experience of humorous activism enables the development of a strong bond within the group or movement, and even beyond, by drawing on common experiences across affinity groups (Branagan, 2007a).

However, humor is particularly effective in creating intra-group or intra-movement *bonding social capital*. Bonding social capital is what Putnam (2000) refers to as the sociological super glue of society. It brings people who already know each other even closer together (Putnam, 1998). Humor actively shapes and strengthens the WA ANM's collective identity through "mutual identification and clarification of positions and values" (Meyer, 2000, p. 310). As such, a relatively short-term experience, such as participation in the nuclear spill action, can have a long-term binding effect, resulting in feelings of affection, solidarity, and loyalty among activists (Hart & Bos, 2007). This closeness and shared experience develops trust, cooperation, and reciprocity (Kagan, Lawthom, Knowles, & Burton, 2000), which ultimately help movements to get by on a daily basis (Putnam, 2002), as well as survive in the long term.

Another example within the context of the WA ANM is the Stop the Nuclear Madness Radioactive Tea Party, a themed float that participated in the 2010 Fremantle Street Carnival. Although weeks of planning and a number of evening workshops went into the building and decoration of the float, the actual parade through the city took less than an hour. However, the carnival experience, intensified via the humorous interaction with fellow activists and curious community members along the way, had a long-lasting binding effect. Although the float had community building and educational features, as well as aiding individual activists in recharging their own energy and motivational levels, arguably its major contribution to the WA ANM was the shaping and strengthening of the movement's collective identity. More than six months after the carnival, at least half of the central activists in the parade continued to use a close-up photo of their characters as their profile pictures on the social media site Facebook.

In her case study of anticapitalist activism in Madrid, Flesher Fominaya (2007) highlights the crucial role humor plays, particularly for resource-poor autonomous movements, in terms of building and sustaining the movement over time. By nature, movements like the WA ANM are heterogeneous groups, bringing together people of various backgrounds, experiences, and social classes. Flesher Fominaya argues that in the absence of a common product–based identity or shared ideology, humor "can serve as a crucial resource in the process of collective identity formation" (Flesher Fominaya, 2007, p. 257). The resulting bond shapes and further reinforces key WA ANM values such as a deeply ingrained commitment to collective decision making, nonviolent direct action, and civil disobedience.

CONCLUSION

To conclude, although humor may not be a characteristic that the average citizen associates with activism, I argue that action-embedded comedy, absurdity, and hilarity provide activists with valuable capital and, hence, a greater share of power. Humor fulfils a number of important roles for the WA ANM. First, in contrast to violent outbursts or aggressive protests, humorous actions draw in the community and affinity groups, thereby enabling the WA ANM to build and expand bridging social capital, that is, to enlarge its networks and support structures. Second, humor is recognized as an effective means to share and strengthen knowledge. By publicly challenging the status quo, as well as sharing subject-specific expertise externally and reinforcing it internally, the WA ANM builds its cultural capital. However, although humorous action can be seen as a communication strategy in itself, the key benefit is for the survival of the movement by building and strengthening bonding social capital. Humor can achieve this by reenergizing individual activists via participation in fun and enjoyable acts of civil disobedience that provide a clear break from traditional activist activities and day-to-day responsibilities and limit the need for recovery breaks. Furthermore, humor helps develop and strengthen the WA ANM's collective identity. The WA ANM has traditionally been characterized by a deeply ingrained commitment to collective decision making, nonviolent direct action, and civil disobedience. Humorous actions can aid in reinforcing these core values and beliefs among what is essentially a heterogeneous group of people of various backgrounds, experiences, and social classes. I, therefore, argue that humor positively impacts the sustainability of the movement over time and aids activists in securing valuable cultural and social capital.

The concept of humor is largely misunderstood and underutilized within the corporate context, which can lead to underestimating or even dismissing activists' capabilities. This illustrates how the prevailing corporate perspective in PR scholarship is insufficient when aiming to gain an understanding of activist communication. The existing focus on corporation-like activist groups has been to the detriment of grassroots community and social movement activists, who operate without the benefit of paid PR consultants and highly qualified in-house teams and may have different needs, priorities, and objectives. Hence, more research is needed into activism from the activist perspective to ensure public relations scholarship is moving beyond its function as industry-serving discipline, toward a field that aims to understand communication across all facets of society.

BIBLIOGRAPHY

Alinsky, S. D. (1946). *Reveille for radicals: A practical primer for realistic radicals.* New York: Vintage Books.

Alinsky, S. D. (1971). *Rules for radicals: A practical primer for realistic radicals*: New York: Random House.

Anderson, D. S. (1992). Identifying and responding to activist publics: A case study. *Journal of Public Relations Research, 4*(3), 151–165.

Bakhtin, M. M. (1984). *Rabelais and his world* (H. Iswolsky, Trans.). Bloomington: Indiana University Press.

Barker, C., Martin, B., & Zournazi, M. (2008). Emotional self-management for activists. *Reflective Practice, 9*(4), 423–435.

Branagan, M. (2005). Environmental education, activism and the arts. *Convergence, 38*(4), 33–50.

Branagan, M. (2006). *Art alone will move us: Nonviolence developments in the australian eco-pax movement 1982-2003.* Doctor of Philosophy, University of New England, Armidale.

Branagan, M. (2007a). Activism and the power of humour. *Australian Journal of Communication 34*(1), 41–54.

Branagan, M. (2007b). The last laugh: humour in community activism. *Community Development Journal, 42*(4), 470–481.

Branagan, M. (2010). *Communicating a nonviolent paradigm through the arts and humour.* Paper presented at the International Peace Research Association Conference, Sydney.

Bruner, M. L. (2005). Carnivalesque protest and the humorless state. *Text and Performance Quarterly, 25*(2), 136–155.

Bunting, M., & Lipski, R. (2001). Drowned out? Rethinking corporate reputation management for the Internet. *Journal of Communication Management, 5*(2), 170–178.

Channel 7 (Writer). (2010). Sunrise interview and phone poll: "Should Australia use nuclear power?" 18 February [TV]. Australia.

Coombs, W. T. (2002). Assessing online issue threats: Issue contagions and their effect on issue prioritisation. *Journal of Public Affairs, 2*(4), 215–229.

Correa, R. (2012). *Carnival as a ghetto of homosexual behaviour.* Retrieved March 12th, from http://www.brazilianartists.net/exhibition/homosexualism.htm

Cox, L. (2009). "Hearts with one purpose alone"? Thinking personal sustainability in social movements. *Emotion, Space and Society, 2*(1), 52–61.

Daymon, C., & Holloway, I. (2011). *Qualitative research methods in public relations and marketing communications* (2nd ed.). Abingdon, England: Routledge.

Deegan, D. (2001). *Managing activism: A guide to dealing with activists and pressure groups.* London, England: Kogan Page.

Demetrious, K. (2001). People, power and public relations. *Asia Pacific Public Relations Journal, 3*(2), 109–120.

Flesher Fominaya, C. (2007). The role of humour in the process of collective identity formation in autonomous social movement groups in contemporary Madrid. *International Review of Social History, 52*(S15), 243–258.

Geertz, C. (1973). *Thick description: Toward an interpretive theory of culture in the interpretation of cultures: Selected essays.* New York: Basic Books.

Glaser, B. G. (1998). *Doing grounded theory: Issues and discussions.* Mill Valley, CA: Sociology Press.

Grunig, J. E., & Grunig, L. A. (1997). *Review of a program of research on activism: Incidence in four countries, activist publics, strategies of activist groups and organisational responses to activism.* Paper presented at the Fourth Public Relations Research Symposium, Managing Environmental Issues, Lake Bled, Slovenia, July 11–13.

Grunig, L. A. (1992). Activism: How it limits the effectiveness of organizations and how excellent public relations departments respond. In *Excellence in public relations and communication management* (pp. 503–530). Hillsdale, NJ: Lawrence Erlbaum.

Hallahan, K., Holtzhausen, D., van Ruler, B., Vercic, D., & Sriramesh, K. (2007). Defining strategic communication. *International Journal of Strategic Communication, 1*(1), 3–35.

Hart, M. (2007). Humour and social protest: An introduction. In M. Hart & D. Bos (Eds.), *Humour and social protest* (Vol. 15, pp. 1-20). Cambridge, England: Press Syndicate of the University of Cambridge.

Hart, M., & Bos, D. (Eds.). (2007). *Humour and social protest* (Vol. 15). Cambridge, England: Cambridge University Press.

Heath, R. L., & Palenchar, M. J. (2009). *Strategic issues management* (2 ed.). Thousand Oaks, CA: Sage Publications.

Hoare, B. (1998). A passion for protest: An insider's view. In *Protest! Environmental activism in NSW 1968–1998* (pp. 19–26). Sydney, Australia: Public Houses Trust of New South Wales.

Holtzhausen, D. R. (2007). Activism. In E. L. Toth (Ed.), *The future of excellence in public relations and communication management: Challenges for the next generation* (pp. 357–379). Mahwah, NJ: Erlbaum.

Illia, L. (2003). Passage to cyberactivism: How dynamics of activism change. *Journal of Public Affairs, 3*(4), 326–337.

Jaques, T. (2006). Activist "rules" and the convergence with issue management. *Journal of Communication Management, 10*(4), 407–420.

John, S., & Thomson, S. (2003). *New activism and the corporate response.* London, England: Palgrave Macmillan.

Kagan, C., Lawthom, R., Knowles, K., & Burton, M. (2000). *Community activism, participation and social capital on a peripheral housing estate.*

Karagianni, K. S., & Cornelissen, J. (2006). Anti-corporate movements and public relations. *Public Relations Review, 32*(2), 168–170.

Kearns, B. (2004). *Stepping out for peace - A history of CANE and PND (WA).* Perth, Australia: People for Nuclear Disarmament.

La Rocca, S. (2004). *Making a difference: Factors that influence participation in grassroots environmental activism in Australia.* Bachelor of Science in Australian Environmental Studies with Honours, Griffith University, Nathan, Queensland.

Lievrouw, L. A. (2011). *Alternative and activist new media.* Cambridge, England: Polity Press.

Macy, J. (1983). *Despair and personal power in the nuclear age.* Philadelphia, PA: New Society Publishers.

McIntyre, I. (2009). How to make trouble and influence people: Anti-nuclear action, 1958-2006. *Chain Reaction*(107), 32.

McIntyre, I., Sevil, T., & Smith, L. (2009). *How to make trouble and influence people: Pranks, hoaxes, graffiti and political mischief making from across Australia.* Carlton, Australia: Breakdown Press.

Meyer, J. C. (2000). Humor as a double-edged sword: Four functions of humor in communication. *Communication Theory, 10*(3), 310–331.

Moyer, B., McAllister, J., Finley, M. L., & Soifer, S. (2001). *Doing democracy: The MAP model for organizing social movements.* Gabriola Island, BC: New Society Publishers.

Munro, M., Scott, B., & David, G. (1996). *How to make trouble and influence people: Australasian pranks, hoaxes and political mischief making.* Sydney, Australia: Political Hooligan Publications.

Painted Dog Research. (2010). I Generation Research: Conducted on behalf of HBF and The West Australian.

Putnam, R. D. (1998). Foreword. *Housing Policy Debate, 9*(1), v–viii.

Putnam, R. D. (2000). *Bowling alone: The collapse and revival of American community.* New York: Simon & Schuster.

Putnam, R. D. (Ed.). (2002). *Democracies in flux: The evolution of social capital in contemporary society.* New York: Oxford University Press.

Smith, M. F., & Ferguson, D. P. (2001). Activism. In L. H. Robert (Ed.), *Handbook of public relations* (pp. 291–300). Thousand Oaks, CA: Sage.

Turner, M. M. (2007). Using emotion in risk communication: The anger activism model. *Public Relations Review, 33*(2), 114–119.

Weaver, C. K. (2010). Carnivalesque activism as a public relations genre: A case study of the New Zealand group Mothers Against Genetic Engineering. *Public Relations Review, 36*(1), 35–41.

Werder, K. P. (2006). Responding to activism: An experimental analysis of public relations strategy influence on attributes of publics. *Journal of Public Relations Research, 18*(4), 335–356.

CHAPTER SEVEN

Representation Matters(?)

When, How, and If Representation Matters to Marginalized Game Audiences

ADRIENNE SHAW

Why does representation matter? I begin many a class discussion on media diversity with that question. Most of my students give answers that imply some sort of media effect: "bad" representation, representation that casts a group in a negative light or makes people biased toward marginalized groups. "Good" representation, that which helps normalize marginalized groups, provides evidence for equality. Students working in areas of media production argue that it is important to represent groups well so that they will watch/listen/read/play/buy a product. Occasionally, someone will also say that representation matters so that children can grow up and have positive self-images, something that can only happen if they see "good" media representation of people like them. In nearly all cases, my students only talk about these effects in terms of other people, rarely connecting it to their own media consumption practices or experiences unless directly prompted.

My students' responses jibe well with the long history of research on media representation. Jessica Davis and Oscar Gandy (1999) assert, "Media representations play an important role in informing the ways in which we understand social, cultural, ethnic, and racial differences" (p. 367). Julie D'Acci (2004) demonstrates the ways that "television representations of gender … have very profound effects on very real human bodies, societies, and economics" (p. 376). Film scholar Richard Dyer (2002) argues that "how we are seen determines in part how we are treated; how we treat others is based on how we see them; such seeing comes from representation" (p. 1). Similar arguments are made about representations of marginalized groups in video games, as well (Cassell & Jenkins, 2000; King & Krzywinska, 2006; Leonard, 2006; Shaw, 2009; Sisler, 2006).

Media scholars argue that representations have beneficial or negative social implications for a given group (reviewed in Gross, 2001). Some authors argue that it is important for individuals, minorities in particular, to see themselves reflected in the media. This is often discussed in relation to social identity theory (Blumler, Rosengren, Wenner, & Palmgreen, 1985; Harwood, 1999). Alternatively, researchers argue that *good* representation of marginal groups is important because it can combat negative stereotypes and bigotry in dominant groups, or, conversely, *bad* representations can encourage negative stereotypes (Gorham, 1999). As Gross (2001) asserts, "The media are likely to be most powerful in cultivating images of events and groups about which we have little firsthand opportunity for learning" (p. 11). Even if we approach the problem through critical cultural theory, the literature is clear that representation matters in how groups are imagined (Hall, 1985).

Something that is often difficult to explain to my students is that the very idea we can describe representations of specific identifiers as good or bad implies a stability of meaning of those identifiers that simply does not hold up to scrutiny, as D'Acci (2004) describes. Further, what is beneficial or negative depends on one's point of view and politics (Gross & Woods, 1999, p. 20). When one looks at a medium that is built on interactivity, like a video game, the implications of representation are further complicated. How can we think about how audiences interact with representation in particular media and how representation comes to matter in a way that can account for intersectional or hybrid identities? How might an argument for representation take into account the macro-level media sphere and the micro-level of individual engagement with media texts?

By using video games as an entry point, in the study described here I spoke with dozens of people who identified as marginalized from the construction of the mainstream video game audience along the axes of race, gender, and sexuality. I did this because in previous research I had conducted on marginalized gamer communities, whenever I got to the question of representation many interviewees were very ambivalent about the importance of representation. In part, this was explained by individual political differences and an overwhelming presence of market logic that a group will be targeted for marketing if a game company deems it profitable. There was also a sense that representation matters at some times, in some texts, and in some genres or media more than others. Representation was not as much an issue for video games, many argued, as it was in other media. In the project described here, I wanted to unpack this ambivalence about representation rather than merely dismiss it as a form of "false consciousness." As James Carey puts it in an interview with Larry Grossberg (2006), "Whether consciousness is true or false, it's the only consciousness we have, and you have to deal with it" (p. 220). To take this ambivalence seriously—to understand what it is and why it is expressed in this way—is important in thinking about what arguments for representation look like in an era of interactive media.

In addition, I was concerned that in past research I focused too much on recruiting people on the basis of identity categories. This put, I suspect, interviewees in a marginalized position feeling pressure to, and resisting the call to, answer as members of those specific groups. To correct for this, in this study I used an online survey to recruit game players of all types and then selected from those people interviewees who identified outside the white, male, heterosexual, U.S. gamer construction. By using sexuality, gender, and race as starting points for selecting interviewees, I do not mean to imply that these categories matter to the interviewees' relationship with gaming. Rather, these are categories that popular and academic discourses about gaming foreground as being underrepresented and particularly concerned with representation. The challenge this study poses, however, is in leaving them as starting points, not deterministic lenses through which to interpret results. In addition, as my focus was people who play video games, rather than gamers per se, interviewees varied in types of games, platforms, and amount of playing time. Over the course of two interviews, the second being a gaming interview during which they played a game while I watched and asked questions, I spoke to them about games, as well as other media, to help unpack the different ways representation matters across media. In concluding, I demonstrate the ways this repositioning of the discussion on *how* rather than *that* representation matters offers a new way to argue for the importance of diversity in media representation, particularly when looking at interactive media.

TO WHOM IT MATTERS

Given the stakes of representation described above, it would be logical to assume that members of marginalized groups are particularly attuned to or care about representation of people "like them," leaving "like them" open to encompass a variety of identifications. In my research with members of marginalized groups, however, this is not always the case. Contrasting two pairs of interviewees, however, offers another perspective from which to view this issue.

Rusty identifies[1] as a heterosexual, white male[2] in his late 30s, who grew up in the Chicago suburbs, and currently lives with his partner, Tanner,[3] in a Philadelphia suburb. Gregory, in contrast, identifies as a black, gay man in his early 30s, who was born and raised in a middle-working-class family in North Philadelphia. Rusty asserted that he does not think much about whether he identifies with characters or about representation: "I just kind of know who I am, and that's the only thinking I do about that." In part, he ties this to the fact that he sees himself as boring and views games as a way to escape, rather than find, himself. "I'm white; I'm boring (laughs). I want to be that Orc that could rip a car in half with my hands, or, you know, blasting cities from orbit." In contrast, representation is important to Gregory. He stated very specifically that seeing people like him in media "shows that I'm being heard and seen and I'm being acknowledged and I'm here." Though it is rhetorically useful for me to contrast Rusty and Gregory based on their social demographics, to rely on those as the explanatory factors for their differing opinions is overly simplistic. It is more than their demographic differences that explain their divergent takes on the importance of representation, which can be seen by looking at a counter-example.

Kat, identified as a white woman in her early 20s, did not disclose her sexuality, and was raised in what she called the "WASPy" suburbs of Atlanta. I contrast her answers here with Julia, who was in her late 30s and identified as an African American, gay woman from Northwest Philadelphia. Julia does not feel strongly about representation. She argued, however, that this was because she does not identify with the signifiers that typically signal "blackness." Her partner, Elise,[4] who took part in the first interview, made a similar comment about queer identity and representation. An excerpt of their interview:

Julia: All I'm saying is that, not to generalize … I don't identify with those people, even though they are black. We have nothing in common whatsoever. So I don't, for me, [representation is] not important at all.

[later in the discussion]

Elise: Being gay is this much of my life [holds up thumb and forefinger slightly parted] … I mean we tend to hang out with gay people, just, I think, by virtue of being into the same stuff, but I don't think I would specifically watch a show, like we never watched *Queer Eye* or the *L Word* or anything. … It wasn't like, "Oh my God there's a queer person!" You know what I mean?

Julia also believed that lack of representation in video games is not an issue because they are "just games." For Kat, however, representation is very important, even in video games. Due to this, when she discussed the importance of seeing people like her in media, she felt that it is important, but that diversity in media in general is important and this tempered her need to see people specifically "like her":

> It's important to me. … I'm definitely more prone to go see a movie if I see someone who looks like me and who has encountered situations like me, rather than someone else. But at the same time, I definitely value diversity. I mean, as a white American girl, I wouldn't be offended if they put more diversity in there. Because I think that's beneficial. I don't think that our media needs more white American girls, you know?

Tying these two comparisons together, we can see that the importance of representation is not tied specifically to the marginalized identifiers most research tends to emphasize. That is not to say that people did not stress these marginalized identities when they described representation, but that there is not an inherent connection between marginalization and feeling that representation is important. Rather, there is an approach to media evident in these four interviewees' comments that cannot be reduced to social demographics. Moreover, regardless of whether interviewees thought representation was important to them, the power of media was largely described in terms of escapism and imaginative power. Representation can help audiences imagine what might be possible, which is in many ways a counter-narrative to much previous research that talks about representation in terms of realism. To say representation is important implies either that (1) media must be realistic (something Rusty pushed back against) or (2) one is making allegiances to a specific group identity (something Julia and Elise rejected). Certainly, diversity was important to interviewees in a general sense because it demonstrates what types of being are possible (as both Kat and Gregory argued). The "what might be" importance representation, thus, was significant to interviewees whether they felt representation had an important effect.

I am not arguing that representation is not important, and thus textual analyses that form the backbone of much of representation studies is passé. Rather, in finding the ways it is not inherently important, taking at face value that it does not always matter to audiences, we can begin to unpack how representation matters. Focusing on the specific moments in which it comes to matter, according to interviewees, I found that it became relevant in relation to an individual's connection to specific identities, the text itself, and the context in which a text was used.

IDENTITY MATTERS

For some interviewees the representation of certain identifiers was extremely important, though not always. Gregory explicated the nuances and complications of representation, specifically in relation to his sexual and racial identities:

> I used to watch *Queer as Folk* all the time, and I was like this is the only fucking town where there is no gay black people! (laughs) *[later in the discussion]* You ever see that show called *The Wire*? ... I never watched it. But, they said it's a good show. I don't know. I mean, that might depict something, but everybody in the hood ain't a drug dealer.

In discussing two shows that purportedly include characters like him, Gregory offered an exemplar for the issue that is at the core of this analysis. Focusing on single identifiers in discussing representation, even focusing on intersectional identities, is far too limited to capture the essence of why representation matters.

He critiqued representation by discussing the ways texts closed down options for being, particularly as they connect with the entirety of the media sphere where such images dominate.

Interviewees made connections between how they identify themselves and the importance they give to seeing people like them, but not in the way usually assumed. This was evident in Julia and Elise's exchange, above. Seeing people like them was largely immaterial to their media consumption. This was not, as assumed in the SIT literature, because these identities were less salient for them but rather that the typical articulation of those identifiers does not correlate with their experiences. Evan, having struggled with his own identity over time, and because he tends to identify with heroic characters, stated: "I don't think I identify with people like me. … I'm a transman … they're not really depicted in movies and if they are they're not really heroic per se." In another interview he referenced *Queer as Folk* and the *L Word* as texts that, by all accounts, should have resonated with him as an early 30s, white, middle-class, bisexual transman. He stated, "It was like queer content that was very specifically something that had to do with me and my lifestyle, and you want to talk about underrepresented—I had no interest." Both shows have characters that represent a variety of identities with which he might, in theory, connect. For Evan and other interviewees, however, seeing people like them was just not a driving factor for their media consumption—at least not always. Often this was because they do not identify with the way their many identities typically are portrayed, particularly in a way that honors the intersectionality of their identities.

In addition, interviewees were cognizant of the problems of representation; they recognize that tokenization and stereotyping are dangers of demanding diversity in representation, as Chuck pointed out:

> When I think of diversity, how it's done in the media—do you remember … the [Burger King Kids Club] where it would be like the kid in the wheelchair who's named Wheels, and there's like the one black kid, the one Asian girl. That stuff always drives me insane.

Largely those problems stem from a focus on specific identifiers without the acknowledgment that identities are not reducible to individual signifiers. Yes, group differences exist. However, the ways these differences are marked in media often oversimplify these differences.

Some interviewees argued that games could be uniquely suited to overcoming such problems of representation. Character creation tools were seen as a way for players to have the option of playing as people like them without feeling limited by producers' construction of their "group." Speaking of race, Sasha said, for example, that avatar customization allows players more choices, "like Nintendo Wii, they have like all shades. You can, like, customize a shade. Because everybody comes in different colors. You know all black people aren't dark skinned. All Caucasian people aren't pale." Other interviewees discussed the moral choices or dialog options of some games as offering them a chance to express their personalities. In these ways games were seen to offer nuances not available in other media.

Avatar creation tools and character options make video games more readily suited to providing audiences with the opportunity to create more diverse visual representations than other media, but the options are limited. T. L. Taylor (2006) points out that in Everquest, for example, "some bodies are ascribed legitimacy and some are not" (p. 117). A few interviewees discussed this in relation to creating avatars that end up being the "skinny" version of the player, as avatar creation tools do not include a variety of body type options. Kat also points out that while making Miis during her gaming interview, "It was interesting to see the things that weren't there. Like, there were no dreadlocks, there were no weaves. I don't know. It was interesting." Making exact replications of oneself is not always the goal in using these tools. Several interviewees described making characters that were attractive or created aspirational versions of themselves. Certain types of game spaces and texts, however, encourage self-representation as I discuss below, and even in the ones that do not researchers can still be critical of the limits placed on avatar creation. When the choices included in those spaces limit the types of "selves" that can be represented, audiences notice the absence.

In addition, representation as an option marks particular identities as the exception to the norm of heterosexual, white, and male, as Janet describes:

> I guess I'm very aware of the extent to which white male is seen as like the default, and so like these are all regular people plus one black person—black people aren't regular people? Or like, these are all regular drivers but we'll show one female driver. She's not a regular driver. She's a female driver.

Not only should researchers be critical of what representations exist, they should also pay attention to when they are made available. Zahriel, for example, said that in games like Zelda and Halo, gender does not matter to the game and yet the protagonists are still male. "Where it's painfully obvious that they could have used a woman if they wanted to, that really annoys me. ... You could just make a person who is very androgynous, who could go either way, and leave it at that. But they just default to men." In games where there are choices of avatars, she felt that games tend to make room for a gender choice, though these are only choices of binary gender. The problem with which she took issue is not just the lack of choice but also the overall resistance to use female, or even androgynous, as a default. Video games do not offer players infinite options. Games are structured in ways that encourage and value certain types of play over others. In terms of representation, different identities make sense in some games in ways they do not in others, which we can also see when looking at how representation is made relevant in specific kinds of texts.

TEXTUAL MATTERS

How identities are signaled is important, but why is crucial as well. Representations of identifiers become relevant, salient, and are experienced in relation to specific moments of articulation. They are also related to the individual's reason for engaging with the text. As Janet points out, "I guess it depends on what I'm getting out of it." Using a non-game example, she discussed the types of people and bodies represented in the yoga DVDs she gets from Netflix: "I'm like, oh man they should totally make a yoga DVD with somebody who's like kinda old and has bad knees like me. That would be great." In the context of other genres of shows, however, that kind of representation was less important: "I don't require like, somebody on a cooking show to be old and have bad knees because that's not really relevant to the product that I'm consuming." In video games, similarly, Janet discusses the ways game mechanics shape the relative importance of representation:

> I guess it would depend on how important that was in the game. Like if I'm playing *The Sims* I want to play someone who looks like me because why should I have to play a character who doesn't look anything like me? … If I was playing a fighting game, I wouldn't want a character who looked like me (laughs) because I would be terrible at it. I understand that I'm not particularly suited for some modes (laughing).

Sometimes the ludic elements of games matter more to players than representation, as explored by some games theorists (Aarseth, 2004; Newman, 2002). In games, representation does not always matter, and yet this is the very reason one might expect more diversity in games. If players truly are unconcerned, or not always concerned, with the figure that represents them on the screen, then why do we not see more diversity in what comprises that image?

Representation matters more in some games than it does in others of course. Interviewees stressed, for example, connections between game mechanics and how they approach avatar creation. Cody, who identifies as a heterosexual, African American male in his mid-20s, said that how he chooses a character depends on the type of game. When he plays EverQuest or World of Warcraft (WoW),[5] he does not care what his character looks like. He picks the one that has the abilities he needs to do well in the game. When he plays sports games, he picks the professional athletes he most identifies with, being an athlete himself. When playing a realistic skateboarding game like Tony Hawk, he picks an African American avatar if available, but he was ambivalent about its importance.

In the gaming interview, there was some evidence that, when given the option, Cody would choose to represent his race and gender, but not necessarily to represent himself. He showed me the avatar he created for the wrestling game he played during the gaming interview. It did not look like him as the wrestler had dreadlocks (which Cody did not), was covered in tattoos (which Cody did not visibly have), and wore a gas mask and leather cape (which Cody seemed unlikely to wear). It did have Cody's skin tone and a similar name, but he did not feel the character reflected him. According to Cody, "I just wanted to make the guy as nuts as I could. No real reflection of me." In contrast, when creating an avatar on Xbox Live he said he made it look as much like him as possible because it was meant to be a representation of himself to his friends.

In an interactive medium like games, the relative importance of representation can be traced through the ways players make decisions about their characters. This is not, however, because researchers can decipher a player's identity from their avatar design. Rather it is because the process of making those decisions illuminates when, how, and if self-representation is important to them. Players work with the game world, because they have to if they want to play (Taylor, 2006). According to Hayes (2007), players' use of a game involves an interplay between their own dispositions and the game's mechanics. They balance what they enjoy doing in the game with what will make them successful in the game. Knowing this allows researchers to analyze the way game designers limit player's choices in some game texts but expand upon them in others. We can also look at how decisions are made in relation to the context in which the game is played.

CONTEXT MATTERS

Countering prevailing discourses that embodied identities like gender and race disappear online, there is plenty of evidence that this is not the case (Haggin, 2009; Nakamura, 2002). When social identifiers are considered unimportant in online spaces, it is through the pretense that everyone is the same. Usually the assumption is that everyone is heterosexual, white or Anglo, and male. During their[6] gaming interview, Pouncy described this in relation to an online version of Settlers of Catan: "Unless someone has an overtly feminine sounding name in their screen name, everyone assumes that everyone is male. Well, I don't (laughs) but most people." How players can and do represent themselves online affects the game space and other players' experiences with the space.

Related to this, the relative importance of what avatars players choose can shift if they play online or offline. In the game Diablo II, for example, Malcolm explains: "If you choose one class you're playing a male character, if you choose another class you're playing a female character." He played as both a male and female avatar during the gaming interview.[7] On the other hand, when he plays WoW he does not play as a female character, because even if other players "know psychologically that 90% of the people that play these games are male, they are still going to, you know, hope that that's a female and try to interact with you in that way." Playing in an online environment changes the types of and implications of choices players make. In online spaces, people represent themselves to an audience who will make assumptions about them based on the aesthetic and ludic choices they make. The interpretations of those choices are shaped by the way those games spaces are designed. If, for example, everyone in WoW had to play as an androgynous or even female character, it would alter the implications of playing as a female *toon*—the term for the player's in-game WoW character.

Speaking of context more broadly, many interviewees said that representation is socially important, even if it is not important to them. It is not merely important for individuals to see themselves reflected in a mediated mirror. Representation also is important because it is an external acknowledgment of one's existence. This is intertwined with Gregory's assertion that people want representation because they want people like them to be seen. The interviewees who felt they were mainstream—regardless of whether they may be seen as marginalized in some way—did not think they needed, or in some cases had the right, to say that representation of their group is important.

Regardless of whether people feel that it is important for them to see people like themselves in media, everyone believes that it is important for other people. In some cases they display what communication scholars call a "third-person effect" (Davison, 1983). They assume that others do not usually get to see themselves and, thus, for them representation is important.

> Renee: That's really funny because I don't really think it's important to me. But I think it's important to other people, to see people that look like them. Like I see people that look like me all the time and so I don't think of it as that important but I think that if I didn't see people that looked like me all the time I would think that I would think that it's important. But that's a lot of "I would thinks."

Part of this stems from the idea that individuals, as Renee describes, feel that they do get to see themselves represented in some aspects of their identities. Pouncy makes this point, for example:

> I feel like the media is full of representations of people who look like me in terms of skin color and—well, I don't feel like my gender is represented very often in terms of gender not being a binary, which is not a way that a lot of people look at that—but more in terms of characters that think like me and have my values.

People can think of themselves, and sometimes even their group, in a nuanced and inclusive manner. When they talk about other groups, however, they tend to view them as static and cohesive. This is, in fact, the very trouble of representation. Part of the problem of saying that media makers should offer diverse representations is that when producers try to represent groups, they tend to think narrowly about what membership in those groups entails.

Interviewees were hesitant, however, to say that representation should matter to other people. Janet, for example, acknowledges that her own position on representation being important could be potentially proscriptive:

> I don't always think it's a bad thing. If you're going into a gaming environment as a bespectacled Asian dude and you want to play a gigantic blonde Amazon, like it's no skin off my ass. I don't think you should have to sit down with a therapist and fill in a form, like whether it's okay for you to do that (chuckles). Whether it's culturally acceptable.

Moreover, as Anya points out, to some extent the emphasis on representation may be a form of hegemonic discourse: "It's supposed to be important and society and media tells you that it's supposed to be important so that's why people argue for it. But I don't know how many people really stop and think about whether it's important." Nick Couldry (2003) discusses this in terms of the "myth of the mediated center," the assumption that "'the media' has a privileged relationship to that 'centre,' as a highly centralized system of symbolic production whose 'natural' role is to represent or frame that 'centre'" (p. 45). The very notion that media representation is important is tied to assumptions about social power. The media are assumed to be the primary site at which we can make sense of social reality. This, in turn, is why people think that media representation signals or is the path to social equality. Media become the target for treatment, when it is only a symptom of inequality.

This focus on media derives from assumptions about media effects. As Gregory points out, however, in an excerpt that seems to represent a quick history of social and communication theory: "Some people are influenced in so many different ways … you learn from all different places. You can learn from friends, you can learn from reading a magazine … you could have ten people play this game and they all take something different from it." Here we see incidental references to active audiences (Fiske, 1989), polysemy (Hebdige, 1979), and personal influence (Katz & Lazarsfeld, 2006). The assumption that representation matters is disentangled rarely from how and why it matters. It matters if, as some scholars suggest, media help shape our world views (Gerbner, Gross, Moran, Signorielli, & Shanahan, 2002). As Gregory suggests, however, this is not a deterministic process. Arguments for the importance of representation cannot ignore the active meaning-making process, nor can they focus too specifically on the individual, marginalized audience member as the primary target for media representation.

CONCLUSION

Returning to the initial question: Why is representation important? When interviewees asserted that representation is important to them, it was largely through critiquing what representations exist or do not exist in relation to realism. In this and in my previous research, interviewees did not necessarily say that they always sought out representation. This is because, as Taylor describes, "People may not know what they *could* enjoy" (2006, p. 102). Wanting representation, the act of desiring it, is a very different issue from critiquing portrayals that exist. The reason representation matters to some people is because they see the under- or misrepresentation of certain groups as unrealistic.

Overall, interviewees were aware of the arguments for the importance of representation. However, they dubbed representation as unimportant in texts they used for escapism or they view as primarily fantasy. The goal of researchers and activists must be to deal with the fact that for those who think that video games' main purpose is not to reflect reality, the argument that games are misrepresenting reality holds little value. The paradox those dealing with issues of representation in fiction must face is arguing for the seriousness of fantasy without diminishing enjoyment of the fictional.

Interviewees felt they could see themselves represented, or represent themselves, in many media texts regardless of their membership in marginalized identity categories. If games are to be play spaces, we can be critical of the limits placed on identity play. In research, we must also be careful about making assumptions about those with whom audiences are willing to identify. Being sensitive to identity is not the same as using identity as an analytic category through which to analyze data. How representation matters exists at the nexus of several factors: a given audience member's reasons for using a text; how individual players-viewers understand their identities; how and if the representation is made relevant in a given text; the context in which the text is consumed; and the social sphere in which those texts are created and consumed. That representation does not always matter frees us to focus on those times in which it does matter. Specifically, it is imperative that media offer a diverse view of the world that exists and a world that might be across texts.

NOTES

1. All descriptions of interviewees' identifiers are a combination of survey and interview data.
2. Although the main focus of this project was marginalized gamers, I had the opportunity to speak to Rusty and Chuck, who were partners of Tanner and Carol, respectively. As mainstream gamers they provided useful points of contrast and connection with other interviewees.
3. Tanner identifies as a heterosexual, white/Arab/Arab American female in her late 30s from the New Jersey Shore area.
4. Elise did not fill out the survey, so I do not know how she identifies. She appeared to be white/Anglo and a woman, however, and called herself queer in the course of the interview.
5. These are both massive multiplayer online role-playing games.
6. This is Pouncy's preferred pronoun.
7. He had played this game on previous occasions and had played as all of the characters at some point.

BIBLIOGRAPHY

Aarseth, E. (2004). Genre trouble: Narrativism and the art of simulation. In P. Harrigan & N. Wardrip-Fruin (Eds.), *First person* (pp. 45–55). Cambridge, MA: MIT Press.
Blumler, J. G., Rosengren, K. E., Wenner, W. A., & Palmgreen, P. (1985). The social character of media gratifications. In K. E. Rosengren, L. A. Wenner, & P. Palmgreen (Eds.), *Media gratifications research: Current perspectives* (pp. 41–59). Beverly Hills, CA: Sage.
Cassell, J., & Jenkins, H. (2000). *From Barbie to Mortal Kombat: Gender and computer games.* Cambridge, MA: MIT Press.
Couldry, N. (2003). *Media rituals: A critical approach.* London, England; New York, NY: Routledge.
D'Acci, J. (2004). Television, representation and gender. In R. C. Allen & A. Hill (Eds.), *The television studies reader.* New York, NY: Routledge.
Davis, J. L., & Gandy, O. H. (1999). Racial identity and media orientation: Exploring the nature of constraint. *Journal of Black Studies, 29*(3), 367–397.
Davison, W. P. (1983). The third-person effect in communication. *Public Opinion Quarterly, 47*(1), 1–15.
Dyer, R. (2002). *The matter of images: Essays on representation* (2nd ed.). London, England; New York, NY: Routledge.
Fiske, J. (1989). *Understanding popular culture.* Boston, MA: Unwin Hyman.
Gerbner, G., Gross, L., Moran, M., Signorielli, N., & Shanahan, J. (2002). Growing up with television: Cultivation processes. In J. Bryant & D. Zillmann (Eds.), *Media effects: Advances in theory and research* (2nd ed., pp. 43-67). Mahwah, NJ: Lawrence Erlbaum.
Gorham, B. W. (1999). Stereotypes in the media: So what? *Howard Journal of Communications, 10*(4), 229–247.
Gross, L. P. (2001). *Up from invisibility: Lesbians, gay men, and the media in America.* New York, NY: Columbia University Press.
Gross, L. P., & Woods, J. D. (1999). *The Columbia reader on lesbians and gay men in media, society, and politics.* New York, NY: Columbia University Press.
Grossberg, L. (2006). Configurations of culture, history and politics. James Carey in conversation with Lawrence Grossberg, Part 2. In J. Packer & C. Robertson (Eds.), *Thinking with James Carey: Essays on communications, transportation, history* (pp. 199–225). New York, NY: Peter Lang.
Haggin, T. (2009). Blackless fantasy: The disapperance of race in massively multiplayer online role-playing games. *Games and Culture, 4*(3), 3–26.
Hall, S. (1985). Signification, representation, ideology: Althusser and the post-structuralist debates. *Critical Studies in Mass Communication, 2*(2), 91–114.
Harwood, J. (1999). Age identification, social identity gratifications, and television viewing. *Journal of Broadcasting and Electronic Media, 43*(1), 123–136.
Hayes, E. (2007). Gendered identities at play: Case studies of two women playing Morrowind. *Games and Culture, 2*(1), 23–48.
Hebdige, D. (1979). *Subculture: The meaning of style.* London, England: Methuen.
Katz, E., & Lazarsfeld, P. F. (2006). *Personal influence: The part played by people in the flow of mass communications* (2nd ed.). New Brunswick, NJ: Transaction.
King, G., & Krzywinska, T. (2006). *Tomb Raiders & Space Invaders: Videogame forms & contexts.* New York, NY: I. B. Tauris.
Leonard, D. J. (2006). Not a hater, just keepin' it real: The importance of race- and gender-based game studies. *Games and Culture, 1*(1), 83–88. doi:10.1177/1555412005281403

Nakamura, L. (2002). *Cybertypes: Race, ethnicity, and identity on the Internet*. New York, NY: Routledge.
Newman, J. (2002). The myth of the ergodic videogame: Some thoughts on player-character relationships in videogames. *Game Studies, 2*(1). http://www.gamestudies.org/0102/newman/
Shaw, A. (2009). Putting the gay in game: Cultural production and GLBT content in video games. *Games and Culture, 4*, 228–253.
Sisler, V. (2006). Representation and self-representation: Arabs and Muslims in digital games. In M. Santoineous & N. Dimitriadi (Eds.), *Gaming realities: A challenge for digital culture* (pp. 85–92). Athens, GA: Fournos.
Taylor, T. L. (2006). *Play between worlds: Exploring online game culture*. Cambridge, MA: MIT Press.

PART THREE

Challenging Communicative Action and Agency

CHAPTER EIGHT

Uncommon Knowledge

Testing Persistent Beliefs about Configurable Culture and Society

ARAM SINNREICH AND MARK LATONERO[1]

Since the turn of the century, the rapid coevolution of networked digital media platforms and the cultural forms and practices that rely upon them has blurred the lines that previously divided opposing social categories, such as production versus consumption, professional versus amateur, and public versus private (Aufderheide & Jaszi, 2011; Bruns, 2008; Deuze, 2007; Gunderson, 2004; Jenkins, 2006; Lowood, 2006; Ondrejka, 2004; Shiga, 2007; Sinnreich, 2010; Sinnreich, Latonero, & Gluck, 2009; Taylor, 2006). Individuals and communities operating in digital, networked, and mobile environments are able to create, copy, appropriate, manipulate, edit, distribute, and consume audio and visual content in a multitude of new ways. The affordances of the personal computer, digital content, editing software, and Internet technologies have contributed to an ever-expanding number of emergent cultural forms; mash-ups, remixes, machinima, software add-ons, video game mods, and photoshopping are just a few examples.

Because of the ontological blurriness they engender, many of these technologies and practices do not fit neatly into—and often come into direct conflict with—the existing social institutions that regulate cultural creation and exchange. Recent battles over cultural authorship and ownership have become a familiar manifestation of this tension (Elkin-Koren, 1996; Kim, 2007; Lessig, 2004, 2008; McLeod, 2007; Ondrejka, 2004; Ross, 2006; Shiga, 2007; Vaidhyanathan, 2001; Wagner, 2003). Increasingly, individuals find source material for cultural expression within their mediated environment. Television programs, recorded music, film, video games, news media, political speeches, and advertising images—once considered "content" for the purpose of consumption via mass media—are now routinely appropriated, reconfigured, mashed up, and redistributed to others within the networked mediascape—rarely with the permission of the owners of said content.

This chapter uses a framework we outlined in previous publications (Latonero & Sinnreich, 2013; Sinnreich, 2010; Sinnreich & Latonero, forthcoming; Sinnreich, Latonero, & Gluck, 2009), employing the term "configurable culture" to describe a range of cultural practices that have emerged in the wake of the mainstream adoption of digital media technologies. These practices are configurable in two ways. First, cultural information, once digitized, can serve equally well as any link in the traditional value chain of cultural production, from source material to finished product. Second, an infinitely broad range of modifiers and algorithms (in the form of "effects," "plugins," "add-ons," and so forth) can be applied to mediated expression itself as a form of second-order expression.

The central purpose of this chapter is to leverage communication research to explore—and challenge—several widely held beliefs surrounding digital culture that inform both scholarly and popular debate. Specifically, we aim to examine through empirical analysis of survey data the implications of configurable cultural practices with respect to consumption, production, copyright, access, participation, and privacy, addressing related questions and assumptions that appear in relevant literature.

For example, copyright has emerged as a crucial subject in recent years, as the music, television, radio, and film conglomerates of legacy media industries have relied increasingly on intellectual property law to secure their market dominance, thereby maintaining their positions as informatic gatekeepers and arbiters of "legitimate" cultural exchange (Denegri-Knott, 2006; Sinnreich, 2013). Historically, complex and capital-intensive production and distribution technologies and processes served as effective barriers to entry against unaffiliated individuals seeking to enter into the cultural marketplace in roles other than as consumers. Recently, however, access to widespread, affordable digital technologies has enabled users to appropriate and manipulate commercial content on a massive and unprecedented global scale. To what extent are individuals participating in these practices taking on the role of producers in addition to (or instead of) consumers? And can we understand any intermediate degree of cultural engagement as an exemplar of a third category of content interaction (e.g., "produsage," as Bruns [2008] suggests), or is a more fluid cultural spectrum emerging between the traditional poles of "pure" consumption and production?

In an effort to reconcile the disparities between network-era cultural behaviors and copyright laws still mired in the assumptions of the mass media era, activists and scholars such as Richard M. Stallman (Stallman & Gay, 2009) and Lawrence Lessig (2004) have proposed alternatives to the dominant copyright regime, introducing "free" and "open" frameworks, such as the General Public License and Creative Commons licenses, which appropriate the power of copyright opportunistically to affirm users' rights to reconfigure and redistribute protected works. These solutions are designed to enable, rather than inhibit, emerging models of production, which commonly is held to have a broadly democratizing effect on cultural participation. Although the use of Creative Commons and free software licenses has increased measurably over the past decade, there is a paucity of research on the aggregate makeup of these users (Kim, 2007). Who uses these licenses, who does not use them, and what can we infer about their democratizing potential from these data?

Other scholars have proposed additional frameworks for discussing the social consequences of digital culture. Notable examples include "participatory culture" (Jenkins, Clinton, Purushotma, Robison, & Weigel, 2009), a term that highlights the democratizing implications of users entering into the realm of cultural production, and "convergence culture" (Jenkins, 2006), which emphasizes the tension between old and new media configurations and identifies opportunities for reconciliation. Contrarian arguments include lamentations that professional and expert cultural production has become overrun by debased amateurism (Keen, 2007), alarms about devastating economic consequences for legacy media industries (Levine, 2011) and dire warnings that humanity's very soul risks dissolution in the acid bath of digital collectivism (Lanier, 2010). Some negative reactions within the academy simply reassert the validity of traditional cultural power dynamics. For instance, a recent study of copy culture (Karaganis, 2011) employs the language of piracy, theft, authority, and copyright enforcement to discuss practices of digital appropriation.

We challenge the premises that these changes are inherently democratizing and solely inherent to the consumer experience. While most of these new cultural ideas are "bottom up," emerging from collaborative digital environments, they have also been employed strategically by the culture industries to extend their hegemonic positions. And while they offer participants the opportunity to stake new social positions and forge new political alliances, they also have the capacity to reproduce traditional biases and power dynamics, widening, rather than narrowing, the gulf between the haves and have-nots.

Finally, we aim to examine commonly held beliefs about the role of age in shaping people's attitudes toward configurable culture, as well as their levels of concern and expertise when it comes to privacy online. Previous research has examined young people's engagement with emerging digital cultural forms (Burwell, 2013; Jocson, 2013; Serazio, 2008), and the extent to which older people may be included or excluded from participation (Brenner & Smith, 2013; Xie, Watkins, Golbeck, & Huang, 2012). Other scholars have contrasted the role of age with factors such as income and education (Hargittai, 2010; Hargittai

& Hsieh, 2010; Hargittai & Shafer, 2006; Hargittai & Walejko, 2008). Additionally, following on the work of boyd and Hargittai (2010) and Lenhart, Madden, Smith, Purcell, Zickuhr, and Rainie (2011), this study seeks to measure the degree to which privacy concerns contribute to proactive engagement with information disclosure. Ultimately, we aim to question two propositions related to this field of research. The first proposition is that younger people care less about their online privacy than their elders, or, as Jeffrey I. Cole concluded after a recent USC Annenberg survey, "Online privacy is dead—Millennials understand that, while older users have not adapted" (Hill, 2013). The second proposition is that younger people who have grown up as "digital natives" (Palfrey & Gasser, 2008) have a fundamentally different attitude toward configurable culture than their elders do, conferring a degree of cultural legitimacy on cutting, pasting, mixing, and mashing, while these practices remain anathema to older generations. As we argue below, neither of these propositions is as simple or as easily demonstrable as common knowledge would have it.

METHODOLOGY

We fielded a survey (completed by 1,779 respondents) in July 2006, gauging the awareness, behaviors, and opinions of U.S. adults with regard to configurable cultural practices across a range of media, including mash-ups, remixes (music and video), machinima (fan movies made with video games), and mods (fan-created video game modifications). In November and December of 2010, a largely identical survey was administered to adults in the United States and around the globe,[2] adding some additional questions on subjects including privacy, news, and advertising.

Respondents for both surveys were members of a larger panel previously recruited online by a California-based market research firm called Intellisurvey.[3] The survey was programmed, hosted, and administered online. Respondents were invited to participate in the Web-based survey via email, which may present some challenges in terms of generalizability. Email recruitment from an existing panel clearly limits the sampling frame, for example, those who have access to email and who regularly use the Internet/Web. However, given the costs of random digit dialing in the domestic and (especially) the international contexts, these methods proved to be the best available option to recruit large numbers of respondents.

The 2010 completed survey sample consisted of 3,055 adult, English-speaking respondents from dozens of countries, including the United States (36%), India (11%), Turkey (10%), Canada (5%), South Africa (5%), and the Philippines (5%). Respondents represented a diverse range of ages (41% aged 18–34 years, 43% aged 35–54 years, and 17% aged 55 years and older), near parity between genders (44% male, 56% female), and a diverse range of income levels (52% below $40,000 per year, 25% between $40,000 and $80,000 per year, and 11% more than $80,000 per year; the remaining 12% opted not to report their income). We gathered such demographic information not only to gauge the generalizability of our sample but also for the purposes of performing cross-tabulation and other statistical analyses by age, gender, income, geography, and education level.

The 2006 survey data were weighted by age and gender to reflect distributions reported in the 2000 U.S. Census. Due to the 2010 U.S. sample's close similarity in age[4] and gender distribution to 2010 census data, and the lack of readily available census data for the other countries represented, we opted not to weight the 2010 data. Despite the evident imperfections in online sampling methodologies, the similarity of our respondent demographics to census data and the consistency between our 2006 and 2010 surveys both offer promising indications that our data are representative of the larger population under study.

Respondents were informed of the purpose of the study prior to taking the survey and signed informed consent forms per institutional review board (IRB) protocols. Respondents were offered incentive to participate by being entered into a lottery to win one of four $50 gift cards for an online retailer. No personally identifiable information was collected from any human subject by the research team. Respondents had the opportunity to abandon the survey at any time, as well as the choice not to answer any given question.

RESULTS

Because configurable culture by definition undermines the practical distinctions between traditional categories of production and consumption, we designed and analyzed our survey in a way that would be attuned to these differences without overdetermining them. Thus, we developed a schema that divided respondents' relationship to cultural forms and behaviors into three broad categories: awareness, usage, and engagement. *Awareness* means that a respondent has heard of a given practice, such as mashing and remixing (exemplified by the survey question, "Which of the following practices have you heard about before?"). *Usage* suggests that the respondent has accessed the products of configurable practices, such as mash-ups and remixes, in the context of traditional consumption (exemplified by the survey question, "Have you used or consumed the following in the last year?"). Finally, *engagement* means that the respondent has entered into the gray area between production and consumption, by altering or interacting with cultural information to some degree (exemplified by survey questions such as, "In the past year, which of the following *music-related activities* have you engaged in?").

When it comes to engagement, our data suggest that not only has the gray area between production and consumption been populated with a broad range of new cultural forms and behaviors, but that these behaviors fall along a spectrum. The more prevalent configurable cultural practices tend to be those that are "consumption-adjacent," or more similar to traditional consumption, while those that are "production-adjacent" are far less common.[5] Those engaging in production-adjacent activities tend to be people with access to what one might call "the means of configuration," comprising the requisite tools, expertise, cultural capital, and social networks to reappropriate and redistribute culture digitally. On the other end of the spectrum, those engaging in consumption-adjacent practices also have access to digital-networked environments; however, they lack the ability or the desire to participate at a deeper level. This very distinction challenges overly optimistic assumptions and hyperbole about the necessarily transformative qualities of a monolithic participatory culture.

Additionally, our 2010 survey results indicate that engagement levels for the vast majority of configurable cultural practices are considerably higher for English-speaking respondents who were citizens of countries outside of the United States than for Americans. Based on our data, we identify three basic tiers of prevalence: *marginal* (0%–14.9%), *emerging* (15%–34.9%), and *mainstream* (35% and greater). Although there are some examples of research attempting to measure mainstream versus marginal culture (Doran & Littrell, 2012; Huq, 2003), the literature does not suggest widely agreed upon statistics in this area. Thus, these threshold percentages are based on emergent trends in the data rather than on an existing theoretical framework, and we use them primarily in order to benchmark longitudinal and geographic differences in levels of awareness and usage.

In the case of music, accessing songs via video streaming sites (41.4% U.S., 58.9% non-U.S.), customizing a playlist (34.8% U.S., 51.6% non-U.S.; 21.6% in 2006), burning a CD (33.3% U.S., 58.7% non-U.S.), and ripping a CD (27.3% U.S., 42.9% non-U.S.) are mainstream behaviors outside the United States and mainstream or emerging domestically. Using a music recommendation engine (17.9% U.S., 30.1% non-U.S.) is an emerging practice in the United States and elsewhere. Practices such as sharing a playlist with others (13.5% U.S., 30.8% non-U.S.; 8.3% in 2006), sharing music files (11.8% U.S., 29.1 % non-U.S.; 9.8% in 2006), using software or mobile applications to identify a song (8.7% U.S., 16.7% non-U.S.) and karaoke (9.3% U.S., 24.4% non-U.S.; 12.4% in 2006) are marginal behaviors in the United States and emerging elsewhere in the world. Finally, practices such as making sample-based music (3.3% U.S., 8.5% non-U.S.; 3.2% in 2006) and deejaying a set (2.4% U.S., 5.3% non-U.S.) are marginal practices in every region. As figure 8.1 illustrates, these practices align clearly along a spectrum from production-adjacent (lower-left quadrant) to consumption-adjacent (upper-right quadrant). Similar trends (reported in Sinnreich & Latonero, 2013) emerged from our data on configurable practices in video, games, images, software, social media, news, and politics.

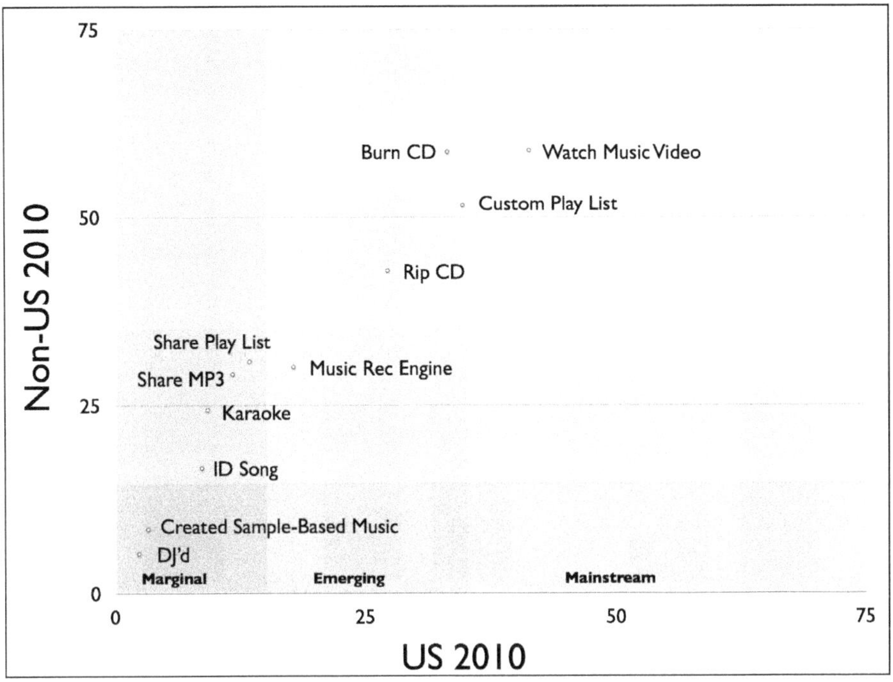

Fig. 8.1: Engagement with configurable music practices, U.S. and non-U.S., 2010.

In both our 2006 and 2010 surveys, respondents in different age groups tended to report differing levels of awareness, usage, and engagement with configurable cultural practices, as well as differing opinions regarding the validity of these practices. Specifically, younger people are generally more aware, more engaged, and more likely to see mash-ups and remixes as "original" than their elders.

We gauged opinion in part by asking the question, "To what extent do you consider mash-ups and remixes 'original'?" Younger respondents were far more likely to say that some or all uses were original than were older respondents. In our 2006 survey, for instance (see Figure 8.2), almost four-fifths of respondents aged 18–25 years conceded that appropriation-based cultural products can be original, while nearly half of respondents 55 years and older rejected any possibility of originality.

It would be natural to infer from these data that either (1) younger people are more accepting of change or ambivalence than their elders, and therefore less resistant to configurable culture, or (2) the younger cohort, having been raised as "digital natives" (Palfrey & Gasser, 2008), are, and will remain, more receptive to these practices. However, the reality appears to be a bit more interesting.

In our 2010 survey, we gave respondents the ability to select "prefer not to answer" as an alternative to the other three responses. Judging by comparison

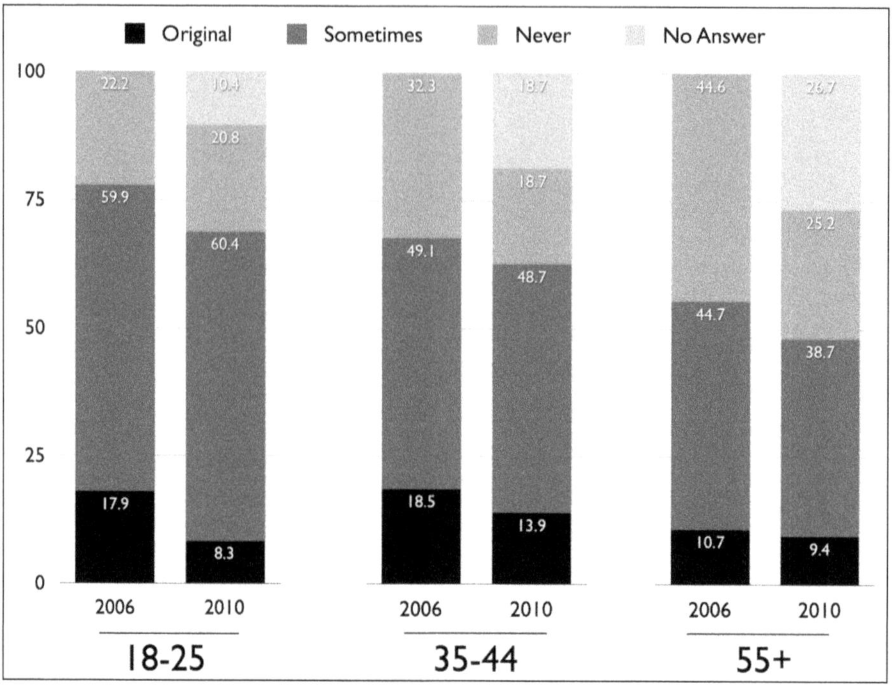

Fig. 8.2: Opinions about configurable culture by age, 2006 and 2010.

between the 2006 and 2010 data sets, most of the younger respondents who opted not to answer in the latter year appear to be those who would have opted for "original" in the earlier survey, while among the older respondents, the "prefer not to answer" response appears to have cannibalized the "never" responses. We interpret this to mean that younger respondents, forced to render a judgment regarding cultural practices about which they are unfamiliar, will most likely give it the benefit of the doubt, while older respondents in the same situation will reject the unfamiliar cultural practice. This is significant; due to the fact that older people tend to be less familiar with these practices, it means that reflexive judgments about them across all age groups are biased negatively. It also suggests that the distribution of informed opinions has much greater parity among different age cohorts than it would first appear from the data.

This argument is further supported when we leave age out of the picture altogether and segment opinions by rudimentary exposure to configurable culture (see Figure 8.3). Among those who say they have heard of mash-ups, anime music videos, or machinima, the distribution of opinions is very similar to that for 18–25-year-old respondents. Yet among those who say they have never heard of any configurable cultural product, regardless of age, the distribution is more similar

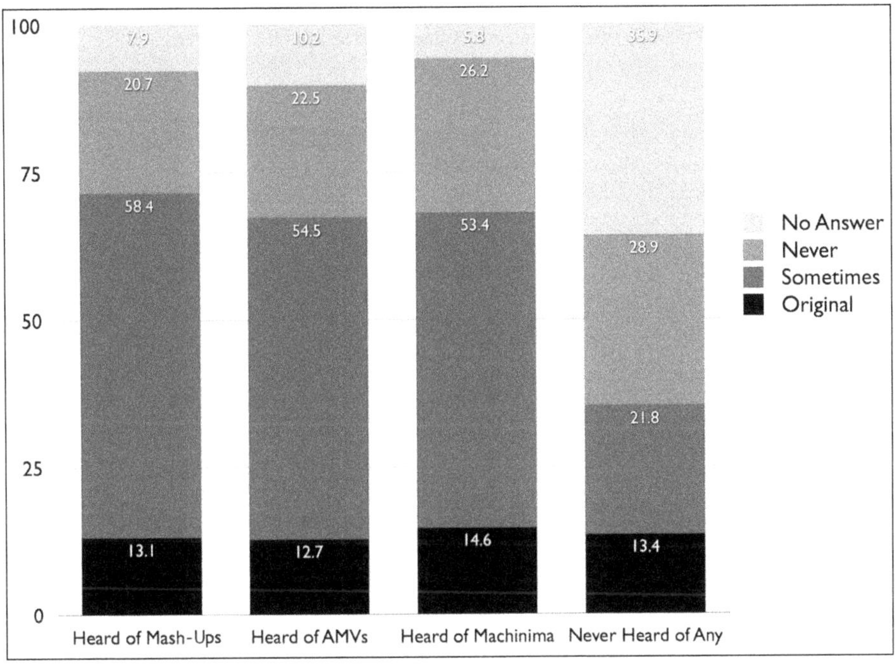

Fig. 8.3: Opinions about configurable culture by exposure, 2010.

to that of older respondents, with roughly a third (35.9%) reserving judgment and another 28.9% rejecting any chance of originality—and therefore cultural validity.

We also examined the relationship between income and configurable culture awareness, usage, and engagement, focusing on 2010 American survey respondents.[6] Income was not a consistent predictor of awareness; by and large, middle-income respondents showed slightly greater awareness of configurable cultural forms than did either the poorest or the wealthiest respondents. However, respondents above median income levels reported considerably higher degrees of usage than those below median income levels, and these figures tended to climb along with income. Configurable culture engagement levels also tended to be higher for those in higher income brackets. Figure 8.4 shows the percentage of respondents who reported engaging with at least one configurable cultural form within each of these media categories: news and politics, images, video games, film and television, and music.

In addition to examining the relationship between configurable cultural behaviors and demographics, we are also concerned with the capacity of these new forms and practices to contribute to shifts in the balance of cultural power. Specifically, theorists such as Jenkins and colleagues (2009) and Lessig (2008) have celebrated the democratizing potential of remixes and mash-ups, and warned

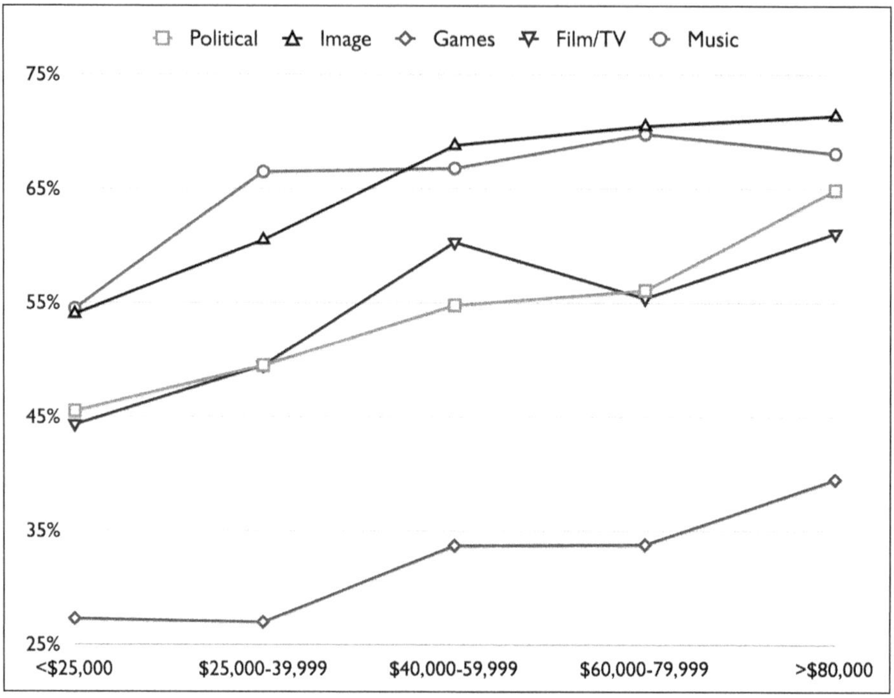

Fig. 8.4: American engagement with configurable cultural forms by income.

about the potentially chilling effects of copyright law, while others such as boyd and Hargittai (2008) and Brandimarte, Acquisti, and Loewenstein (2012) have debated whether engagement with configurable culture and social media poses risks to privacy and whether giving users tools to control the disposition of their personal data can mitigate those risks. We addressed both of these issues in our 2010 survey, asking respondents about their use of Creative Commons licenses, as well as their level of concern regarding online privacy and their experience modifying privacy settings at websites.

Although there is a growing awareness and general concern regarding copyright's role in regulating cultural behaviors around the world (Latonero & Sinnreich, 2013), the use of Creative Commons licenses by both producers and consumers is still relatively uncommon. According to our research, only 5.3% of U.S. adults have ever licensed their own work under a Creative Commons license, and 13.1% have searched for products that are open licensed or in the public domain. Outside of the United States, these figures are two to three times more prevalent; 17.3% of our non-U.S. respondents reported licensing their work under Creative Commons, and 31.7% of them have searched for, or used, openly licensed and/or public domain works.

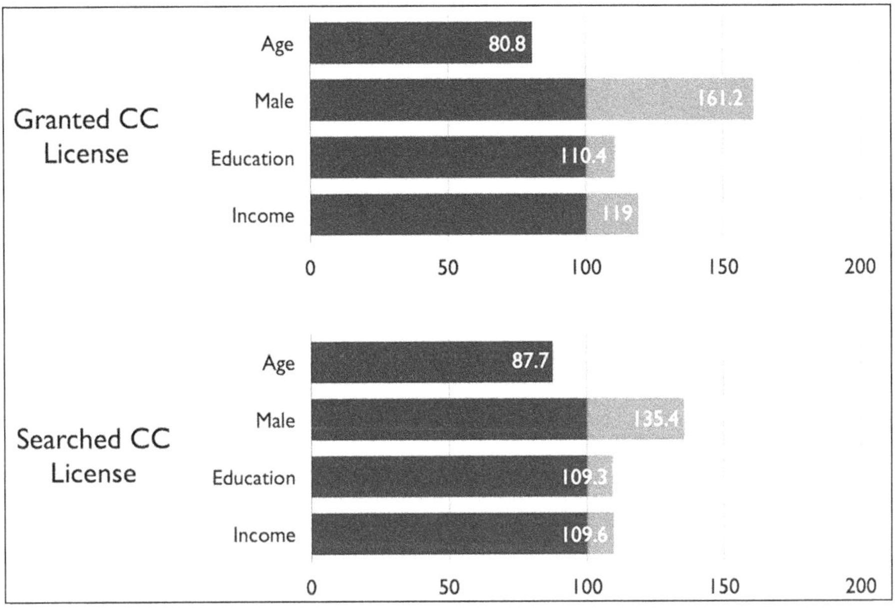

Fig. 8.5: Demographic profile of Creative Commons users, relative to survey baseline.

As with many other aspects of configurable culture, those respondents who embrace open licenses tend to be from demographic segments with greater access to both technology and the cultural capital to make use of it for creative purposes (see Figure 8.5). Specifically, respondents who applied open licenses to their own work and those who searched for others' openly licensed or public domain work tend to be wealthier, better educated, younger, and far more likely to be male than the overall population.[7]

On the whole, Internet users are very concerned about their privacy, with a mean score of 3.92 on a scale from 1 (not at all concerned) to 5 (extremely concerned). These scores vary widely by country, with respondents from the Philippines (4.6) and South Africa (4.5) expressing the greatest concern, and those from the United Kingdom and Turkey (each 3.3) expressing the least concern.[8]

As we have already discussed, age is a factor in awareness, engagement, and attitudes concerning configurable culture. However, age is not an appreciable factor when it comes to privacy concern; the mean level of concern was approximately 4 on a scale from 1 to 5 for each of the age groups we surveyed (Figure 8.6). On the other hand, age is a significant factor when it comes to *taking action* with regard to privacy; while 7 in 10 respondents aged 18–25 years reported that they have monitored or modified their privacy settings on a website, only about 4 in 10 aged 65 years and older reported having done

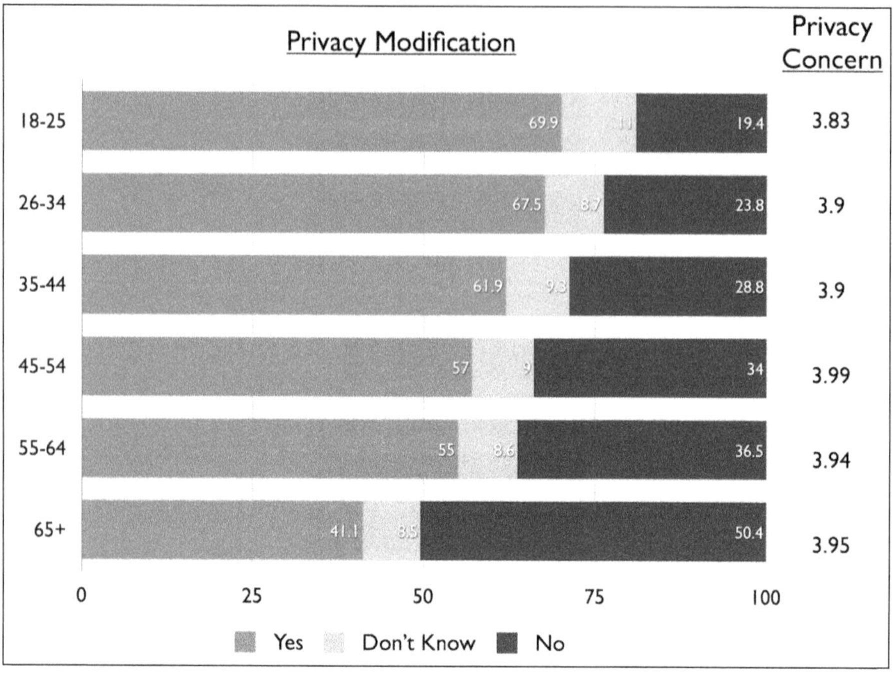

Fig. 8.6: Privacy concern and modification by age.

so. In other words, while privacy concern is universal among the online adult population, the older a person is, the less likely he or she will do something about it.

Like age, education level has a linear relationship with respondents' likelihood to monitor or modify their privacy settings on websites; specifically, the better educated respondents were, the more likely they were to modify their settings, and the less likely they were to say they did not know whether they had done so (see Figure 8.7). However, unlike age as a factor, education also correlated with the *level of overall privacy concern* among respondents. Those with doctoral-level degrees were far more concerned than most (mean value of 4.31 on a scale from 1 to 5), while those with a high school education or less were the least concerned (scores of 3.84 and 3.71, respectively). An interesting finding is that income was a far less successful predictor of privacy attitudes and behaviors than country, age, or education. Overall, levels of concern were nearly equivalent across income levels, and the likelihood of privacy modification hovered in the vicinity of 60% for each income group below $100,000 per year. Above this level, privacy modification spiked sharply, with 68.5% of those earning $100,000 to $150,000 and 79.3% of those earning more than $150,000 modifying their settings.

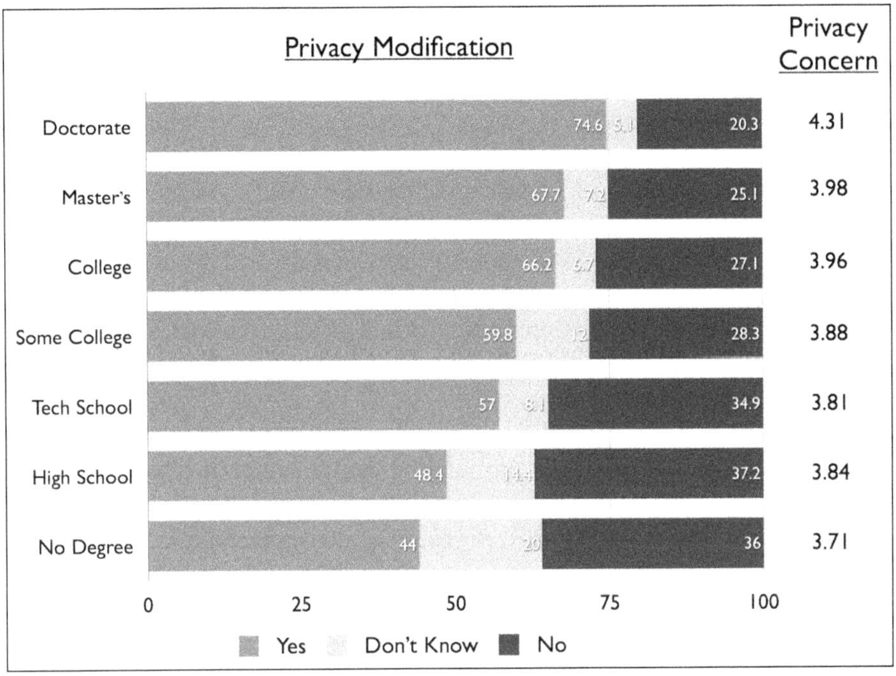

Fig. 8.7: Privacy concern and modification by education level.

CONCLUSION

The data from our surveys shed light on several widely held assumptions and beliefs regarding digital culture and society. First, engagement with configurable culture problematizes the traditional division between production and consumption but not, as some hold, simply by creating a third catchall category such as "produsage," "presumption," or "active" consumption. Rather, these practices inhabit a spectrum between marginal "production-adjacent" activities such as deejaying and mainstream "consumption-adjacent" ones such as creating playlists, with emerging practices such as music sharing and tagging inhabiting the ambiguous middle ground.

Second, though some argue optimistically that participatory culture, by virtue of its orthogonal relationship to traditional hierarchical structures of production and power, has an inherently democratizing effect on social organization, our data provide some justification for skepticism on that front. There is a clear relationship between income and engagement with configurable culture across a range of different subjects and platforms. In other words, rather than serving as an equalizer, these cultural forms may help to widen the cultural gap between the beneficiaries of our socioeconomic system and the ranks of the disenfranchised, thus reinforcing the class structures instantiated in traditional media organization.

Along similar lines, our data give us good reason to doubt whether open licenses such as those offered by Creative Commons and the Free Software Foundation are having a democratizing effect on cultural participation, as argued by scholars such as von Hippel (2005) and Galuszka (2012). As we demonstrate, those who use such licenses *for both production and consumption* tend to be younger, wealthier, better educated, and far more likely to be male than the general population. Thus, while they may contribute positively to structural changes in the media economy that provide greater opportunity to independent creators and innovative organizations, there is no evidence yet that these licenses actually ameliorate social inequities in a more general sense.

Our findings also suggest that some of the perceived wisdom about age as a factor in attitudes and behaviors surrounding digital culture is overly simplistic. For instance, though many have proposed that today's youth, raised as "digital natives," have a fundamentally different approach to configurable culture than do older generations weaned on mass media, our surveys suggest otherwise. True, our data show a considerable difference between younger and older respondents' willingness to accord configurable culture a degree of originality (which can be understood as an indicator of legitimacy). Yet the age gap is narrower when we account for respondents who do not have enough experience to render a strong opinion. The fact that the gap erodes when we look at exposure to configurable culture as the explanatory variable and age as a proxy for exposure suggests that there is nothing inherently native about younger people's relationship to digital media or, by the same logic, foreign about older people's digital media usage. This is good news because it suggests that increasing diffusion of digitally mediated cultural forms will continue to erode the age gap in the future.

Along similar lines, the proposition that younger people are less concerned with online privacy than older people is demonstrably disproven by our data. Though privacy concern varies widely with factors such as nationality and education, it remains remarkably consistent across all age groups surveyed. Our data show that younger adults care every bit as much as their elders do but that they are far more likely to have monitored or altered their privacy settings actively at websites, suggesting a higher level of expertise or perceived self-efficacy. This, in turn, may help to explain why, to casual observers, younger people seem almost recklessly willing to share information online. Much like the skilled skier whose penchant for black diamond slopes may seem reckless to a novice, younger users' decisions regarding privacy can only be understood and evaluated in relation to their levels of comfort and mastery over the challenge in question.

In summary, our survey data complicate and refute some of the more persistent ideas about digital culture and society that permeate both scholarly and popular debates. We acknowledge several limitations in our research; most important, we rely on a survey panel of online, English-speaking adults assembled via Web and e-mail, which undermines the generalizability of our findings. Additionally, our most recent data are from 2010; since then, mobile and social technologies have become both significantly more prevalent and complex, and the general public has become savvier about Internet surveillance by both commercial and governmental institutions, which is likely to influence sentiment about privacy. We aim to field a third survey in the near future to aid us in developing an even more nuanced, longitudinal understanding of these issues.

NOTES

1. This project was supported by a generous grant from the USC Annenberg Center on Communication Leadership & Policy.
2. Of our 3,055 respondents, 2,701 chose to report their nationality; in all, 92 different countries were represented, with 10 or more respondents from 26 different nations representing every populated continent.
3. Information about Intellisurvey can be found at http://www.intellisurvey.com.
4. Mean U.S. survey respondent age: 45.1 years; Mean U.S. adult age: 44.9 years.
5. We first introduced the concept of "adjacency" in Sinnreich, Latonero, and Gluck (2009).
6. We did not compare data from the 2010 and 2006 surveys because of changes in our methodology for capturing usage. We also opted to focus solely on American respondents because the variant national median income levels among international respondents would make a broader analysis far more complex.
7. On a country-by-country basis, these disparities are even greater. They are mitigated in these figures because non-Americans, who are most likely to use open licenses, also tend to earn less than Americans do.
8. It is interesting that these levels of concern do not appear to correlate consistently with actual privacy levels in these countries, as the relatively unconcerned United Kingdom has recently been called "the most surveillance-intense country in the democratic world" by Privacy International, while the same institution rates conditions in highly concerned South Africa as relatively benign.

BIBLIOGRAPHY

Aufderheide, P., & Jaszi, P. (2011). *Reclaiming fair use: How to put balance back in copyright.* Chicago, IL: University of Chicago Press.

Bosnjak, M., & Tuten, T. L. (2001). Classifying response behaviors in Web-based surveys. *Journal of Computer-Mediated Communication, 6*(3), article 6. doi:10.1111/j.1083-6101.2001.tb00124.x

boyd, d., & Hargittai, E. (2010). Facebook privacy settings: Who cares? *First Monday, 15*(8), 2.

Brandimarte, L., Acquisti, A., & Loewenstein, G. (2012). Misplaced confidences: Privacy and the control paradox. *Social Psychological & Personality Science.* Published online before print. Retrieved August 9, 2012. doi:10.1177/1948550612455931

Brenner, J., & Smith, A. (2013). 72% of online adults are social networking site users. *Pew Research Center's Internet & American Life Project.* Retrieved from http://pewInternet.org/Reports/2013/social-networking-sites.aspx

Bruns, A. (2008). *Blogs, Wikipedia, Second Life and beyond: From production to produsage.* New York, NY: Peter Lang.

Burwell, C. (2013). The pedagogical potential of video remix: Critical conversations about culture, creativity, and copyright. *Journal of Adolescent & Adult Literacy.* doi:10.1002/jaal.205

Denegri-Knott, J. (2006). Sinking the online "music pirates": Foucault, power and deviance on the Web. *Journal of Computer-Mediated Communication.* doi:10.1111/j.1083-6101.2004.tb00293.x

Deuze, M. (2007). *Media work.* Cambridge, MA: Polity.

Doran, C. J., & Littrell, R. F. (2012). Measuring mainstream U.S. cultural values. *Journal of Business Ethics,* 1–20. doi:10.1007/s10551-012-1515-z

Elkin-Koren, N. (1996), Public/private and copyright reform in cyberspace. *Journal of Computer-Mediated Communication, 2*(2), article 3. doi:10.1111/j.1083-6101.1996.tb00059.x

Ess, C. (2009). *Digital media ethics.* Oxford, England: Polity.

Galuszka, P. (2012). Netlabels and democratization of the recording industry. *First Monday, 17*(7). doi:10.5210/fm.v17i7.3770

Gunderson, P. A. (2004). Danger Mouse's grey album, mash-ups, and the age of composition. *Post-modern Culture, 15*(1). Retrieved from http://muse.jhu.edu/login?uri¼/journals/postmodern_culture/v015/15.1gunderson.html

Hargittai, E. (2010). Digital na(t)ives? Variation in Internet skills and uses among members of the "net generation." *Sociological Inquiry, 80*(1), 92–113.

Hargittai, E., & Hinnant, A. (2008). Digital inequality: Differences in young adults' use of the Internet. *Communication Research, 35*(5), 602–621.

Hargittai, E., & Hsieh, Y. P. (2010). Predictors and consequences of differentiated social network site uses. *Information, Communication & Society, 13*(4), 515–536.

Hargittai, E., & Shafer, S. (2006). Differences in actual and perceived online skills: The role of gender. *Social Science Quarterly, 87*(2), 432–448.

Hargittai, E., & Walejko, G. (2008). The participation divide: Content creation and sharing in the digital age. *Information, Communication & Society, 11*(2), 239–256.

Herman, B. D. (2012), Taking the copyfight online: Comparing the copyright debate in congressional hearings, in newspapers, and on the Web. *Journal of Computer-Mediated Communication, 17*(3), 354–368. doi:10.1111/j.1083-6101.2012.01575.x

Hill, K. (2013, April 24). Yet another study that says young people care less about privacy. *Forbes.* Retrieved from http://www.forbes.com/sites/kashmirhill/2013/04/24/yet-another-study-that-says-young-people-care-less-about-privacy/

Huq, R. (2003). From the margins to mainstream? Representations of British Asian youth musical cultural expression from bhangra to Asian underground music. *Young: The Nordic Journal of Youth Research, 11*(1), 29–48.

Jaszi, P., & Aufderheide, P. (2008). *Code of best practices in fair use for online video.* Washington, DC: American University Center for Social Media.

Jenkins, H. (2006). *Convergence culture: Where old and new media collide.* New York, NY: New York University Press.

Jenkins, H., Clinton, K., Purushotma, R., Robison, A. J., & Weigel, M. (2009). *Confronting the challenges of participatory culture: Media education for the 21st century.* Cambridge, MA: MIT Press.

Jocson, K. M. (2013). Remix revisited: Critical solidarity in youth media arts. *E-Learning and Digital Media, 10*(1), 68–82.

Karaganis, J. (2011). *The copy culture survey: Infringement and enforcement in the US*. Retrieved from http://piracy.americanassembly.org/wp-content/uploads/2011/11/AA-Research-Note-Infringement-and-Enforcement-November-2011.pdf

Keen, A. (2007). *The cult of the amateur: How today's Internet is killing our culture*. New York, NY: Crown.

Kim, M. (2007). The Creative Commons and copyright protection in the digital era: Uses of Creative Commons licenses. *Journal of Computer-Mediated Communication, 13*(1), 187–209. Retrieved from http://jcmc.indiana.edu/vol13/issue1/kim.html

Lanier, J. (2010). *You are not a gadget*. New York, NY: Vintage.

Latonero, M., & Sinnreich, A. (2013). The hidden demography of new media ethics. *Information, Communication & Society*, 1–22. doi:10.1080/1369118X.2013.808364

Lenhart, A., Madden, M., Smith, A., Purcell, K., Zickuhr, K., & Rainie, L. (2011). *Teens, kindness and cruelty on social network sites*. Washington, DC: Pew Research Center.

Lessig, L. (2004). *Free culture: How big media uses technology and the law to lock down creativity*. New York, NY: Penguin.

Lessig, L. (2008). *Remix: Making art and commerce thrive in the hybrid economy*. New York, NY: Penguin.

Levine, R. (2011). *Free ride: How digital parasites are destroying the culture business, and how the culture business can fight back*. New York, NY: Random House.

Lowood, H. E. (2006). High-performance play: The making of machinima. *Journal of Media Practice, 7*(11), 25–42.

McLeod, K. (2007). *Freedom of expression®: Resistance and repression in the age of intellectual property*. Minneapolis: University of Minnesota Press.

Mossberger, K., Tolbert, C. J., & Stansbury, M. (2003). *Virtual inequality: Beyond the digital divide*. Washington, DC: Georgetown University Press.

Ondrejka, C. (2004). Escaping the gilded cage: User created content and building the metaverse. *New York Law School Law Journal, 49*, 81–101.

Palfrey, J. G., & Gasser, U. (2008). *Born digital: Understanding the first generation of digital natives*. New York, NY: Basic Books.

Ross, A. (2006). Technology and below the line labor in the copyfight over intellectual property. *American Quarterly, 58*(3), 743–766.

Serazio, M. (2008). The apolitical irony of generation mash-up: A cultural case study in popular music. *Popular Music & Society, 31*(1), 79–94.

Shiga, J. (2007). Copy-and-persist: The logic of mash-up culture. *Critical Studies in Media Communication, 24*(2), 93–114.

Sinnreich, A. (2010). *Mashed up: Music, technology and the rise of configurable culture*. Amherst: University of Massachusetts Press.

Sinnreich, A. (2013). *The piracy crusade: How the music industry's war on sharing destroys markets and erodes civil liberties*. Amherst: University of Massachusetts Press.

Sinnreich, A., & Latonero, M. (forthcoming). Tracking configurable culture from the margins to the mainstream. *Journal of Computer-Mediated Communication*.

Sinnreich, A., Latonero, M., & Gluck, M. (2009). Ethics reconfigured: How today's media consumers evaluate the role of creative reappropriation. *Information, Communication & Society, 12*(8), 1242–1260.

Stallman, R. M., & Gay, J. (2009). *Free software, free society: Selected essays of Richard M. Stallman.* CreateSpace.

Taylor, T. L. (2006). *Play between worlds: Exploring online game culture.* Cambridge, MA: MIT Press.

Vaidhyanathan, S. (2001). *Copyrights and copywrongs: The rise of intellectual property and how it threatens creativity.* New York, NY: New York University Press.

Viégas, F. B. (2005). Bloggers' expectations of privacy and accountability: An initial survey. *Journal of Computer-Mediated Communication, 10*(3), article 12. Retrieved from http://jcmc.indiana.edu/vol10/issue3/viegas.html

Von Hippel, E. (2005). *Democratizing innovation.* Cambridge, MA: MIT Press.

Wagner, R. P. (2003). Information wants to be free: Intellectual property and the mythologies of control. *Columbia Law Journal, 103*, 995–1034.

Xie, B., Watkins, I., Golbeck, J., & Huang, M. (2012). Understanding and changing older adults' perceptions and learning of social media. *Educational Gerontology, 38*(4), 282–296.

CHAPTER NINE

iAuthor

The Fluid State of Creativity Rights and the Vanishing Author

KATHARINE SARIKAKIS AND JOAN RAMON RODRIGUEZ-AMAT

The "author" is a matter of copyright governance. An almost-mythical dimension in the public domain, she or he is constructed by state- and industry-led campaigns emphasizing the impact of copy theft on the livelihood of the "hero" of the cultural work. Copyright laws originate from the idealized author-creator (Silbey, 2008), an idea that varies across time and "constituencies" of thought. The question that motivates this chapter is: What is the place of the "author" in the current copyright regimes, particularly under the new conditions of production and consumption in the digital context? We discuss the conflictive transformation of authorship by juxtaposing available practices and understandings of authorship to its selective constructions found in copyright law across time and the terms and conditions of user-generated content in cross-media productions and so-called do-it-yourself (DIY) platforms. The aim is to identify the ways in which authorship is conceived in the governance of copyright. We argue that the figure of the author is shrinking in the governance of cultures of sharing, remixing, and nonprofessional production. We conclude with a critical reasoning of why these practical changes do not enter the debates and initiatives involving intellectual property policy regimes.

In recent years, the possibilities brought by technologies have multiplied the forms of authorship, which has become a focal point in public debate. Blogs (Edwards, 2011; Masnick, 2011a; Hart, 2011) report that Facebook hosts 140 billion photos, 4% of the 3.5 trillion photos ever taken. Siegler (2011) writes in Techcrunch that Instagram owned 150 million photos after just 9 months of being active and compares this iPhone application to Flickr, which took almost 24 months to reach 100 million pictures. Good (2011) writes in *1000 Memories:* "Already Facebook's photo collection has a staggering 140 billion photos, that's over 10,000 times larger than the Library of Congress."

One of the consequences of the Internet has been the capacity of users to tap into a wealth of content made available through cultures of sharing, combined with the expectation of "free" circulation of information on the Internet. Content, copyrighted or not, is the object of the Internet. The struggle over copyright is fought with numbers and legislative reforms. In a report commissioned by NBC Universal, it is estimated that a quarter of the traffic across all areas of global Internet (pornography not included) infringes on copyright laws (Envisional, 2011). The content industry is alarmed by the pace, numbers, and users' innovative approaches to circumvent laws, "norms," and technological and other impediments for the distribution of "copied"—but not copyrighted—work. Between 2004 and 2009, the Recording Industry Association of America (RIAA) estimates that approximately 30 billion songs were downloaded illegally on file-sharing networks (RIAA, 2011). The National Purchase Diary Group (NPD) reports that only 37% of music acquired by U.S. consumers in 2009 was purchased (Hill, 2011). The Institute for Policy Innovation (IPI) argues that the annual damages from global music piracy to the U.S. economy amount to $12.5 billion, 71,060 U.S. jobs lost, a loss of $2.7 billion in workers' earnings, and a decrease of $422 million in tax revenues ($291 million from personal income tax and $131 million from corporate income and production taxes) (Siwek, 2007).

The numbers in these reports may be contestable, but they demonstrate two things. First, the culture industry—and, in particular, the content industry—is anxious about its market position. However, this anxiety points to the fact that it is struggling to come up with and settle into new business models that can monetize users' differentiated from previous norms and expectations patterns. Second, regardless of the accuracy of financial estimations of loss, current uses of the Internet challenge both established modes of the culture industry and its legislative framework. They also challenge us to rethink hitherto accepted norms and assumptions of "the author" with whom the industry and regulator are concerned.

COPYRIGHT, THE "MECHANICAL" REPRODUCTION OF CONTENT, AND THE MULTIDIMENSIONAL AUTHOR

Intellectual property rights are assumed to protect investments related to the production of cultural goods by emphasising the relation of a maker and her or his product in asserting a right to ownership over it. The focus is on the principle of remuneration and compensation for the investment of resources—whether economic, intellectual, or other—and the benefit of distribution, exposition, licensing, or selling. An important dimension of intellectual property rights is copyright: The right to copy, publish, and develop a certain work presumes the existence of an owner of this right. The owner is assumed to be the author of the work. However, the notion of the author is not straightforward. Digital media, reproduction, sharing, and remixing of content have given rise to new practices and understandings of old concepts involving artistic expression. The author becomes so ubiquitous that she or he disappears; theoretically, at least, digital media allow for an infinite number of authors to blossom. It is questionable whether existing legal frameworks can cope with this challenge that the transformation of authorship brings. It is, therefore, useful to see to what extent the regulator has sought to reflect new realities in the term author, as debates concerning authorship constitute a key aspect in current copyright policies. The author appears to embody the inner reason for every form of regulation and protection of intellectual property. However, authorship "is a contingent amalgam of diverse attributes, statuses, and persons" (Saunders, 1992, p. 235). The concept did not emerge historically from a single point or as the product of a cumulative evolution; rather, the author is the result of various and diverse lines of thought and practical needs. Epistemologically, the author appeared as a product of a rupture in the forms of knowledge. Historian Elisabeth Eisenstein (1980) demonstrates that the conditions for knowledge changed with the print press, which marked a particular bend in the forms of reproducing and distributing knowledge. What until then worked as an anonymous continuity of layered comments and variations of hand-copied documents became visibly distinguishable.

Printed books and the mechanical reproduction of content created an additional level of interlocution that forces a "signature" in the space between text and reader. The reader, commentator, or critic is distinguished from the author, forcing a particular form of individuality in which every reader can have an original opinion, different from anybody else's. Equality in the difference of individuals is a product of the invention of print and marks the birth of the author. Scholars identify the dichotomization in the continuity of knowledge around the mid-seventeenth century (Derrida, 1967; Foucault, 1968; Eisenstein, 1980; Ong, 1982). The separation between idea and expression complements and reinforces the segregation between thinker and thought. In this case, what is "immaterial"—idea—is other than its "materialization"—expression. These notions create a constellation for a new form of knowledge that assumes that which is thought is different ontologically from that which is said. Those historical epistemic scenaria created the conditions for regulation and formalization of copyright laws very similar to the ones known today. The most illuminating example is England's creation of the Statute of Anne.[1] This is considered to be the first copyright law that came into force in 1710 to protect the country's flourishing publishing market from foreign illegal copies; but it served the purpose of equalizing the recently united kingdoms and markets of Scotland and England.

A second epistemic change is identified around the French Revolution. Around 1789, the national State of Law consolidated and, with it, the legal concept of the citizen. The switch from villain to citizen also granted a definite persona to the author (Newlyn, 2000). Whereas the Statute of Anne considered the author as a maker and an artisan, romanticism paid particular attention to the link between the work and spirit of the author. The romantic author would become fundamental in legislative developments. The owner of rights according to the Statue of Anne still did not possess the rights of a full individual. In 1774, a tribunal failed the artisan in favor of the publisher: "The judges did determine that an author had a perpetual copyright to a work he or she created—but that right disappeared the minute the book was published!" (Gantz & Rochester, 2005, p. 29). The intentions of the Statute of Anne protected the investment by English publishers; protecting the author had little to do with it (Rose, 1993).

With the start of the nineteenth century, the concept of the romantic author implied that any intellectual work was the spiritual and original expression of a person. The law incorporated the dimension of moral rights, but separately from rights that secure material remuneration. It marked the point of rupture between copyright that creates the artist along with his or her licensed rights and copyright as the apparition of so-called moral rights. Between the author as a singular individual and as a profit maker who recoups investment, cultural and intellectual debates have suggested other forms of authorship that do not find expression in copyright regimes. For instance, the literary and philosophical discussion of the late 1970s suggested dissolving the author in the social practice of the discourse. Authors like Roland Barthes (1977), Michel Foucault (1977), Julia Kristeva (1982), and Jacques Derrida (1998) wrote influential texts that "sentenced the author to death." Such approaches placed interpretation at the center of the processes of communication and, thus, the author was displaced to the margins. The author lost his or her interpretive authority. Socially, the author can be identified still in two domains: first, the context of the creative process; second, as a singular actor who enjoys social recognition. Ultimately, the social recognition of the author is associated with the aura of the romantic author. That aesthetic movement argued (Safranski, 2007; Newlyn, 2000) that the writer's feelings and expression are one and the same because the author exposes her whole life in writing.

The author for the romantics was not only a celebrity; as Lucy Newlyn (2000) shows, authors also were anxious for both their popularity and place in the network of printers, publishers, and critics. Both aspects fit well in a climate of an expanding book industry in sales and marketing. Writers usually thought of the public as an anonymous mass, while critics and publishers employed mutually beneficial marketing strategies that exploited authors' presumed literary superiority.

The author was also a product in a competition market. It is at this junction that the need to regulate ownership, originality, and authenticity becomes paramount. Authors had to distinguish themselves from scribers; originality was a commercial asset and so was the ownership of ideas (Newlyn, p. 13).

The political economy of authorship brings the author as an abstract idea and specific individual to the space between public and publisher, labor and creation. The economic rationale around the equation of investment-benefit-consumption typical of the cultural industries places the author closer to a proprietor than to a creative worker (Saunders, 1992; Rose, 1993). This would explain simultaneously the apparition of moral rights as forms of protecting the personal dimension of the author and their formulation as part of related rights in the international copyright conventions. The enormous resources invested in the process of production, publication, and distribution had to be compensated by defining intellectual works as commercial goods. Most of the technical discussion about ownership and authorship in copyright regimes stands in between this double logic of authorship as a personal expression of an individual and ownership as an economic effort by the publisher.

Often, both logics integrate in a legislative model that takes both sets of interests simultaneously; but sometimes there are contradictions between the author and the producer. In the Statute of Anne, the need to define the author in law initially was not as important as the need to define the proprietor (as investor) of the works. It was with the nineteenth century that related rights served to ameliorate the disagreement between author-celebrities and oligopolies of publishers. It is at this intersection of interests, where the philosophy of intellectual property as a form of licence, exchange of rights, transfer, and representation can be understood. Music, film, and computer programming have generated vast investment in important cultural industries on a global scale during the last century. Debates arose about copyright and the problem of moving from investment by a single publisher and the personal effort of a single author to organized industries involving thousands of employees in the creative process. As law is a path-dependent process, the logic of economic return remained in the copyright of works under collective authorship, forms of licensing of rights by employment, or the redefinition of author to include other activities involved in intellectual work, such as film production and directorship.

This definitional expansion continues in the twentieth century's international copyright laws. In 1994, the Agreement on Trade-Related Aspects of Intellectual Property Rights (TRIPS) was not only an update of the Berne Convention for the Protection of Literary and Artistic Works, it was also an expansion of objects of copyright in the context of digitalization. It created a new point of reference for the definition of the author, based on the transformations in the conditions of media production, profit, and investment on a global scale. It is often argued that technology closes the gap between producer-creator and consumer-user, as it allows the blooming of a thousand authors. Already in the 1970s, the term "prosumer" came to characterize the proactive public as consumers contributing to the development of a product as semi-professional consumers who use products as if they were specialists, as well as creators and sellers (publishers) of their own products. These meanings of prosumer indicate that previously clear lines among consumers, producers, users, and fans are blurred: the receiver is also the sender. This scenario permeates the industry of production and deforms the structure of markets of goods as they historically are conceived. Consumers' active participation in the production process gives rise to new forms of product development. But also, the very idea of author changes, as "authorship" expands via computer programming, for example, to the making of multiple narratives as options to be chosen and reworked by publics in the context of online narratives. Electronic literature, for example, has its own dedicated organization (ELO) and is collected and archived by the Massachusetts Institute of Technology in Boston, not as a library of books but in the form of computer servers (Martín, 2011). Authorship in these conditions multiplies and moves away from an easily identifiable writer or even publisher.

Merchandise also contributes to this diffusion of authorship, through the phenomenon of "transmedia storytelling," which has become one of the most profitable strategies of production of all times, based on the principle that "each franchise entry needs to be self-contained enough to enable autonomous consumption" (Jenkins, 2003). At the same time, production through the availability and easiness of technology transforms producers' authority, which raises important questions as to whether the author or creator is identified (Rodriguez-Amat & Sarikakis, 2012). There is an interesting contradiction here. On the one hand, the structural transformation of the industry[2] means that the author often disappears, subsumed in a larger network of developers in a transnational enterprise, where the input of consumers-users alters a product significantly. On the other hand, in order to maintain control over the process of transformation and appropriation of the product by users, the industry reverts to the romantic notion of a creator, whose livelihood is damaged through free circulation of culture. If the increase in number of writers, copyists, translators, and readers somehow forced the emergence of copyright in the eighteenth century, the conditions generated by digitalization are forcing further definitional and conceptual changes.

THE AUTHOR IN LAW

The legal landscape of intellectual property has changed significantly in the past two decades, not only due to the expansion of the Internet but also due to the transformation of the structure of the industry and its products. The author is constructed diversely along the various copyright regimes. For instance, the law has forced the denaturalization of the author, who is rooted out from assumptions related to natural law. Such an operation distinguishes, again, two forms of authorship that are often echoed in jurisprudence (Damstedt, 2003). On the one hand, if the author is a natural element of every text, then she or he cannot be changed, sold, transferred, or modified. On the other hand, the definition of authorship as incorporated in juridical language must leave the limits and conditions of authorship explicit and eventually open to discussion.

Current concerns around copyright related to the regulation of cultural manifestation make, arguably, the author-owner omnipresent, thanks to technology. The author is omnipresent but at the same time invisible. Copyright ideas are less preoccupied with the maker of a work and more with the possibility of control over—and profitability of—the work and, increasingly, of the user. In this direction, Lessig in his *Love of Culture* (2010) argues that Google Books, an 18-million-book library project, is a dangerous vehicle to control content, where quotes, pages, and sentences are traceable, accounted, and subject to licensing. He says, "We are about to make every access to our culture a legally regulated event." Or again: "We are about to make a catastrophic cultural mistake" (Lessig, 2010). Indeed, international policy provisions are poor in constructively and creatively imagining and providing for the creator.

Ultimately, without precise, flexible, or comprehensive definitions about the author, the focus of the law falls on ownership of the rights to exploitation of the work. The 1996 Copyright Treaty of the World Trade Organization (World Intellectual Property Organization Copyright Treaty) has a preamble by which it recognizes the need to maintain a balance between the rights of authors and the larger public interest. Considerations about the author in the Copyright Treaty of the WTO are clear in Article 6 of the Right of Distribution, stating, "Authors … shall enjoy the exclusive right of authorizing the making available to the public of the original and copies of their works through sale or other transfer of ownership." Following this law—assuming both author and publisher are equals in negotiating power—opens the floor for individualized negotiations between the two parties—including the total transfer of rights. The updates of the Berne convention from 1971 (and its 1979 amendment) define the author in terms of proprietary rights. The moral rights dimension of authorship is exhausted with the right of the author to claim authorship of the work.

The European Union's approach does not offer a definition of the author who is subsumed by rights holders of distribution and publication, as the directive imposes responsibilities for the identification of authors and proof of permission to publish (European Parliament and European Council, 2001, para. 55). Rather, the 2004 Directive (European Parliament and European Council, 2004) conflates authorship as "making" with management:

> Since copyright exists from the creation of a work ... the author of a literary or artistic work is regarded as such if his/her name appears on the work. A similar presumption should be applied to the owners of related rights since it is often the holder of a related right, such as a phonogram producer, who will seek to defend rights and engage in fighting acts of piracy. (European Parliament and European Council, 2004, para. 19)

Supranational and international policies provide legislative principles, but it is at the level of the national legislature where a clear definition of authorship may be developed. UK Copyright Law offers some precision in the First Part of the Copyright, Designs and Patents Act 1988 (Amendment) Regulations 2010. In the first Chapter of Subsistence, ownership and Duration of copyright, Article 9 is related to authorship of work. According to the Act "'author,' in relation to a work, means the person who creates it." It makes specific definitions depending on the medium (e.g., broadcast, film, sound). In the case of computer-generated content "the author shall be taken to be the person by whom the arrangements necessary for the creation of the work are undertaken" (§3). This particular definition has to do with the creator of the work and the particularities of the language in which the work takes form. But in terms of rights, the author's moral rights "are not assignable" (article 94, chap. 5). They are part of the heritage extended by the Berne Convention.

France refers to the nature of the right of the author (*Nature du droit d'auteur*) in chapter 1 (article 111–1):

> *Art. L. 111–1. L'auteur d'une oeuvre de l'esprit jouit sur cette oeuvre, du seul fait de sa création, d'un droit de propriété incorporelle exclusif et opposable à tous.*
>
> *Ce droit comporte des attributs d'ordre intellectuel et moral ainsi que des attributs d'ordre patrimonial...*
>
> *L'existence ou la conclusion d'un contrat de louage d'ouvrage ou de service par l'auteur d'une oeuvre de l'esprit n'emporte aucune dérogation à la jouissance du droit reconnu par l'alinéa 1er.*
>
> (The author of a (intellectual) work enjoys over this work, by the only fact of its creation, a right of exclusive incorporeal property. This right implies attributes of intellectual and moral order as well as attributes of property determined by the first and third books of the present code. The existence or the ending of a contract of work rental or service by the author of an intellectual work does not mean any derogation to the enjoyment of the right recognized in the first paragraph.)

The emphasis on and durability of the concept of intellectual work (*oeuvre de l'esprit*) of this formulation is the sign of the value of moral rights in the French copyright context. Nevertheless, the importance of the relationship between author and work does not result in an uncontested or comprehensive description of the author. According to chapter 3 of the entitled for the right of authorship, article 113–1 states that the quality of the author belongs, except in the case of proof of the opposite, to the one or those under the name of which the work is diffused.

In turn, Spanish copyright laws work similarly but underline the human nature of the author in two dimensions: as natural person and as juridical person. Whereas the first means any human of having rights, the second means any entity entitled to own rights. The fine difference between natural person and juridical person helps build an interesting definitional space between the author and the owner of rights. In the *Spanish Law of Intellectual Property (RDL 1/1996) Title II, Chapter I, Article 5, se considera autor a la persona natural que crea alguna obra literaria, artística o científica* (Author will be considered the natural person who creates a literary, artistic, or scientific work) but also *asimismo se benefician de esta protección personas jurídicas en los casos expresamente previstos en ella* (other juridical persons will be allowed to benefit from it in the cases expressly foreseen in it). It is particularly interesting to consider this gap, because it shows the difference between the unavoidable humanity of the creator (owner of moral rights) and the rights of authorship that can be modified and owned by entities not necessarily human but juridically identified: institutions, enterprises, brands, and associations. The assimilation of rights is resolved in "presumption of authorship, anonym works or pseudonyms" (article 6 of the RDL 1/1996) when it is established that "when the work is anonymously diffused or under pseudonym or signature, the exercise of the rights of intellectual property will correspond to the natural or juridical person that brings it to light with the consent of the author, while the latter do not reveal their identity."

It is argued that the German tradition engages further with the rights of intellectual property, particularly concerning moral rights (Saunders, 1992). The central figure of the author in German law is "idiosyncratic." Whereas the word *Autor* exists in the German language, the law refers to works as *persönliche geistige Schöpfungen* (personal intellectual creations) (*Urheberrechtsgesetz* BGBl I S. 173, section 2). *Werke … sind nur persönliche geistige Schöpfungen* (Works … are only personal intellectual creations). The author is the *Urheber*, the originator, the creator; thus paragraph 7 of section 3 reads: *Urheber ist der Schöpfer des Werkes* (The originator is the creator of the work) and, extensively, the intention of copyright law in section 4, article 11 reads that the rights of authorship (*Urheberrecht*) protect the originator in their intellectual (*geistigen*) and personal relation to the work and to its uses.

The Austrian legal frame of copyright defines work as property of intellectual creation in the area of literature, musical art, pictorial art, and film art: *Werke im Sinne dieses Gesetzes sind eigentümliche geistige Schöpfungen auf den Gebieten der Literatur, der Tonkunst, der bildenden Künste und der Filmkunst.* The author is the one who has created/originated the work (*[1] Urheber eines Werkes ist, wer es geschaffen hat (§10, Abschintt II)*). In the article §8, *Miturheber*, the Austrian law considers the collective author or the co-creator and defines it as follows: If a work has been made by various, without each part being properly distinguished, they are co-creators of the work (*Haben mehrere ein Werk gemeinsam geschaffen, ohne daß sich ihre Anteile gesondert verwerten lassen, so sind sie Miturheber des Werkes*). This is a consideration that can be also found in the other copyright regimes considered.

Whereas these differences in the formulation of the legal definition of authorship appear to invite a discussion around cultural and linguistic articulations of the author, in the European tradition the models reviewed in these pages consider moral rights without making an attempt to provide a suggestion about the various possibilities of authorship. With the exception of British law, the originator and creator of a piece of work is assumed to be a person with a limited role in the copyright and right ownership. When thinking of new methods of production and distribution, re-usage, and revision of cultural goods, the Creative Commons formula worked as an alternative; but critics state that CC is based on traditional copyright itself (Toth, 2005; Dvorak, 2005). However, still, a whole range of authors and authorship processes are left out of scope, while the supremacy of publishers is maintained.

THE VANISHING AUTHOR

The author seems to be vanishing in the face of major cultural transformations. Conditions of production and consumption push the central role that the author briefly enjoyed to the margins of processes like mixing, sharing, merging, and eventually consuming and choosing. The number of photographs uploaded onto platforms such as Facebook or Instagram every hour and the number of hours of video uploaded daily on YouTube or Vimeo are fair signs of an exploding volume of cultural production. With it, an expanded frame of authorship is contributing to "the amateur culture" (Hart, 2011; BBC, 2005) irrespective of what its artistic value is (should be). The notion of amateurism obscures values, such as quality (excess against scarcity) of production of cultural goods and authority of the author as (recognized) creator. Both aspects are dimensions reminiscent of the romantic discourse (Newlyn, 2000) and coincide in intentions and forms with the campaigns pushed worldwide against consumption of copyrighted materials. The discourse separating amateur from professional authors undervalues and leaves the work of the amateur user unattended. Meanwhile, the multinational Virgin Mobile Australia uses a picture of a 16-year-old girl from Flickr in its advertising campaign (Associated Press, 2007); elsewhere, a photographer discovers his image published and multiplied worldwide as an icon for protest (Masnick, 2011b). Whereas the family of the girl sued Virgin, the young photographer embraced the publicity. Levi's promoted the hashtag #iamlevis to encourage users of Instagram to publish photographs of who might be the next public image of the denim brand (Soller, 2012). In those cases amateurs license their rights to the platforms where they upload their images and are left without legal protection as authors; even their moral rights are unprotected. These cases are presented often as isolated against the background of a growing culture of free access and ideas of "shareability" (Armano, 2011). They are becoming directives for marketing researchers, advisers, and companies; the app system by Apple and Android models is based on the authorship of large-scale amateurs. Collective participative forms of creating contribute, ultimately, to the vanishing of the author as conceived in dominant copyright legal understandings.

The 2011 Canadian copyright law (Bill C–11) attempts to provide for an expanded definition of authorship, while at the same time providing or even, potentially, claiming back some space for culture making by nonprofessional and/or noncommercial actors. This helps expand the definitional horizon further, by recognizing the spirit of the creator in others, who will make such use of copyrighted works. The Copyright Modernization Act of September 29, 2011 articulates signs in favor of moral rights and the extension of the conditions for fair use, hence the possibility of user/author for cases such as "education, parody or satire" (i.e., clauses 29.4 or 29.5) as forms of non-infringement; or even "29.21 (1) for the creation of a new work or other subject-matter in which copyright subsists under certain conditions." This formulation recognizes the creativity, originality, and, ultimately, authorship of mash-ups and remixes, which remain illegal under the current legal regime. But simultaneously, the Act is inscribed in the norms dictated by the World Intellectual Property Organization Copyright Treaty and the World Intellectual Property Organization Performances and Phonograms Treaty. This means the law is still criminalizing popular practices like burning CDs (even if it is for personal use) or unlocking technological protection measures put by producers to block the acquired devices and avoid piracy. The blog community has reacted to the excess of connivance of the Act with the big worldwide players of the culture industry (e.g., Geist, 2011).

Authorship was described as "highly visible in contemporary copyright law, [and] usually appears as a focus of consensus rather than debate" (Jaszi, 1991). The author is the main character knocked out of place. Bill C–11 decriminalizes certain uses of the digital media and certain intentions that were punishable until now. But this does not mean that the mixer, the educator, or the parodist obtain the degree of author, who seems to wither away in the midst of a crowd of improvised publishers, commentators, deejays, amateur photographers, and citizen journalists. One of the most profitable strategies of production is transmedia storytelling (Rodriguez-Amat & Sarikakis, 2012). The films and series increase and commercially disperse in a multiplication of formats first (DVD, Blu-Ray, Pay-tv, etc.); but also multiply the extension of their narratives in forms of gadgets, objects, action figures, comics, sequels, prequels, mobisodes, short movies, video games, and others. From the point of view of the protection of authorship rights, the conglomeration of stories and media make it particularly difficult to identify (and protect) an owner in the narrative world. The corporate solution has been to move out from the copyright system of authorship and to consider the group of stories, the merchandising, and the future developments (yet to be told or thought) as a commercial brand. Here, trademark legislation regulates the creation of platforms of participation where users and fans license their rights to the brand.

Structural changes mean that online distributors deal directly with authors in more confronting ways than the traditional mediators. The relation between the author and the consumer—publishers, distributors, and record producers—changes; writers, bands, and artists, bridge the middle man. Amazon deals directly with authors for higher commission (Streitfeld, 2011), Spotify negotiates with bands directly, and as cellist Zoe Keating says, "pays different moneys to different labels" (Houghton, 2011). Disputes with Spotify have spread along the Internet (Lindvall, 2011) and bands like Coldplay or Tom Waits or Adele do not allow the firma of "stream music" to publish their latest records (Robb, 2011). Thus, the logic of investment and protection that once originated in copyright law is lost somewhere.

As this chapter has demonstrated, the author comes and goes in the copyright regime. The author appeared as a particular condition related to the commercializing intentions of the publisher and the values of the individual as a creator. Progressively, the multiplication of practices and the extension of devices obliged the copyright system to adapt and consider the author in forms like collective works, licensing of employment, and so on. Current forms of cultural production seem to announce the next effacement of the author. Ultimately, the user becomes more of a consumer of the very products on which she or he elaborates—for free. Profit remains in the hands of the platform or the entity that facilitates the conditions for such a practice. It is not, thus, that the author disappears leaving no trace behind; rather, the author, as a full point in a process of labor, vanishes. The author is the user, the audience is the media, and it enjoys a complete other form, apparently more free, but effectively unprotected.

To be continued …

NOTES

1. The Parliament of Great Britain enacted the Copyright Act of 1709 8 Anne c. 19, An Act for the Encouragement of Learning, by Vesting the Copies of Printed Books in the Authors or Purchasers of such Copies, during the Times therein mentioned in April 1710 and it was repealed in July 1842.
2. We are aware that culture industries exhibit many differences in their organizational practices, but they also exhibit common traits. In the context of digital media and convergences, these traits gain a prime role in the market position of their products.

BIBLIOGRAPHY

Armano, D. (2011, October 6). Share-ability by design. *L+E. Logic and Emotion.* Retrieved from http://darmano.typepad.com/logic_emotion/2011/10/sharing.html

Associated Press. (2007, September 20). Virgin Mobile sued over Flickr image used in ad. *World Business on NBC News.* Retrieved from http://www.msnbc.msn.com/id/20896643/ns/business-world_business/t/virgin-mobile-sued-over-flickr-image-used-ad/

Barthes, R. (1977). The death of the author. Trans. R. Howard. *Image, music, text.* Athenaeum. Library of Philosophy. Retrieved from http://evans-experientialism.freewebspace.com/barthes06.htm

BBC. (2005, July 18). "Amateur culture" set to explode. *BBC News.* Retrieved from http://news.bbc.co.uk/2/hi/entertainment/4685471.stm

Berne Convention for the Protection of Literary and Artistic Works (1886) and further amendments. *WIPO Database of Intellectual Property. Legislative texts.* Retrieved from http://www.wipo.int/treaties/en/ip/berne/pdf/trtdocs_wo001.pdf

Bill C–11. Act to amend the Copyright Act. (2011). Retrieved from http://www.parl.gc.ca/About/Parliament/LegislativeSummaries/bills_ls.asp?Language=E&ls=C11&Mode=1&Parl=37&Ses=2&source=library_prb

Bundesgesetz über das Urheberrecht an Werken der Literatur und der Kunst und über verwandte Schutzrechte (Urheberrechtsgesetz). *StF: BGBl.* Nr. 111/1936 (StR: 39/Gu. BT: 64/Ge S. 19.) *Bundeskanzleramt Rechtsinformation System.* Retrieved from http://www.ris.bka.gv.at/Geltende-Fassung.wxe?Abfrage=Bundesnormen&Gesetzesnummer=10001848

Code de la Proprieté Intellectuelle. Version consolidée au 11 Septembre. (2013/2011). Retrieved from Legifrance.gouv.fr; the Public Service for the Diffusion of Right, http://www.legifrance.gouv.fr/affichCode.do?cidTexte=LEGITEXT000006069414&dateTexte=20111026

Copyright, Designs and Patents Act 1988 (Amendment) Regulations. (2010). No. 2694. Retrieved from http://www.legislation.gov.uk/uksi/2010/2694/made

Damstedt, B. (2003). Limiting Locke: A natural law justification for the fair use doctrine, Footnote 112. *Yale Law Journal 1179.* Retrieved from http://www.yalelawjournal.org/the-yale-law-journal/content-pages/limiting-locke:-a-natural-law-justification-for-the-fair-use-doctrine/

Derrida, J. (1967). *L'écriture et la différence.* Paris: Éditions du Seuil. Retrieved from http://www.jacquesderrida.com.ar/frances/ecriture_difference.pdf

Derrida, J. (1998). *Of grammatology.* Baltimore, MD: Johns Hopkins University Press.

Dvorak, J. C. (2005, July 18). Creative Commons humbug. PCMag.com. Retrieved from http://www.pcmag.com/article2/0,2817,1838244,00.asp

Edwards, C. (2011). Facebook's 140 billion photos represent 4% of photos ever taken by humans. *ChasNote Metrics, successes & flaming disasters in digital marketing.* Retrieved from http://chas-note.com/2011/09/19/facebooks-140-billion-photos-represent-4-percent-of-photos-ever-taken-by-human/

Eisenstein, E. (1980). *The printing press as an agent of change: Communications and cultural transformations in early-modern Europe, Vol. 1.* Cambridge, England: Cambridge University Press.

Envisional. (2011, January). *Technical report: An estimate of infringing use of the Internet January 2011.* Cambridge, England: Envisional. Retrieved from http://documents.envisional.com/docs/Envisional-Internet_Usage-Jan2011.pdf

European Parliament and European Council. (2001). *Directive 2001/29/EC on the harmonization of certain aspects of copyright and related rights in the information society.* Retrieved from http://eur-lex.europa.eu/LexUriServ/LexUriServ.do?uri=CELEX:32001L0029:EN:HTML

European Parliament and European Council. (2004). *IPRED or Directive 2004/48/EC on the enforcement of intellectual property rights.* Retrieved from http://eur-lex.europa.eu/LexUriServ/LexUriServ.do?uri=CELEX:32004L0048R(01):EN:NOT

Foucault, M. (1968). *The order of things: An archaeology of the human sciences.* London, England: Vintage.

Foucault, M. (1977). What is an author? In *Language, Counter-Memory, Practice* (pp. 124–127). New York, NY: Cornell University Press. Retrieved from http://evans-experientialism.freewebspace.com/foucault3.htm

Gantz, J., & Rochester, J. (2005). *Pirates of the digital millennium: How the intellectual property wars damage our personal freedoms, our jobs, and the world economy.* London, England: Financial Times.

Geist, M. (2011). Geist: Why Canada's new copyright bill remains flawed. Star.com. Retrieved from http://www.thestar.com/business/article/1063099-geist-why-canada-s-new-copyright-bill-remains-flawed

Gesetz über Urheberrecht und verwandte Schutzrechte (Urheberrechtsgesetz) vom 9. September 1965 (BGBl. I S. 1273; 2013). Retrieved from http://www.gesetze-im-internet.de/urhg

Good, J. (2011, September 15). How many photos have ever been taken? 1000memories blog. Retrieved from http://1000memories.com/blog/94-number-of-photos-ever-taken-digital-and-analog-in-shoebox

Hart, T. (2011, September 26). Does amateur creativity make copyright obsolete? *Copyhype. Understanding copyright wars.* Retrieved from http://www.copyhype.com/2011/09/does-amateur-creativity-make-copyright-obsolete/

Hill, E. (2011, October 11). Caught in the act. *The Pendulum.* Retrieved from http://www.elonpendulum.com/2011/10/caught-in-the-act/

Houghton, B. (2011, September 26). Zoe Keating on Spotify, fairness to indie artists & music's niche economy. Hypebot.com. Retrieved from http://www.hypebot.com/hypebot/2011/09/zoe-keating-on-spotify-fairness-to-indie-artists-musics-niche-economy.html

Jaszi, P. (1991). Toward a theory of copyright: The metamorphoses of "authorship." *Duke Law Journal* (2), 455–502. Retrieved from http://www.jstor.org/stable/1372734

Jenkins, H. (2003). Transmedia storytelling: Moving characters from books to films to video games can make them stronger and more compelling. *Technology Review, 10.* Retrieved from http://www.technologyreview.com/biotech/13052/

Kristeva, J. (1982) *Powers of horror. An essay on abjection.* New York, NY: Columbia University Press.

Lessig, L. (2010). For the love of culture. Google, copyright, and our future. *New Republic.* Retrieved from http://www.tnr.com/article/the-love-culture

Lindvall, H. (2011, February 1). Spotify should give indies a fair deal on royalties. *Guardian.* Retrieved from http://www.guardian.co.uk/media/pda/2011/feb/01/spotify-royalties-independents

Martín, J. (2011, March 9). Con leer no basta. *El Pais.* Retrieved from http://www.elpais.com/articulo/portada/leer/basta/elpepuculbab/20110903elpbabpor_4/Tes

Masnick, M. (2011a, September 23). Facebook hosts 4% of all photos ever taken in history. Techdirt.com. Retrieved from http://www.techdirt.com/articles/20110923/14535516079/facebook-hosts-4-all-photos-ever-taken-history.shtml

Masnick, M. (2011b, March 9). The "stolen" scream: Photographer discovers his image is everywhere … and embraces it. Techdirt.com. Retrieved from http://www.techdirt.com/blog/casestudies/articles/20110309/05100213418/stolen-scream-photographer-discovers-his-image-is-everywhere-embraces-it.shtml

Newlyn, L. (2000). *Reading, writing and romanticism. The anxiety of reception.* Oxford, England: Oxford University Press.

Ong, W. (1982), *Orality and literacy: The technologizing of the word.* London, England; New York, NY: Methuen.

Real Decreto Legislativo 1/1996. (1996, April 12). Ley de Propiedad Intelectual. Official Spanish Bulletin (B.O.E.) núm. 97, de 22-04-1996. Retrieved from http://civil.udg.es/normacivil/estatal/reals/lpi.html

RIAA (Recording Industry Association of America). (2011). *For students doing reports.* Retrieved from http://www.riaa.com/faq.php

Robb, J. (2011, October 30). Coldplay, Tom Waits and Adele pull their music from Spotify. *Louder than war.* Retrieved from http://louderthanwar.com/featured/coldplay-tom-waits-and-adele-pull-their-music-of-spotify

Rodriguez-Amat, J. R., & Sarikakis, K. (2012). The fandom menace or the phantom author? On sharecropping, crossmedia and copyright. In I. Ibrus & C. Scolari (Eds.), *Crossmedia innovations.* London, England: Peter Lang.

Rose, M. (1993). *Authors and owners: The invention of copyright.* Cambridge, England: Harvard University Press.

Safranski, R. (2007). *Romantik. Eine deutsche Affäre.* München, Germany: Carl Hanser Verlag.

Saunders, D. (1992). *Authorship and copyright.* London, England: Routledge.

Siegler, M. G. (2011). The latest crazy Instagram stats: 150 million photos, 15 per second, 80% filtered. TechCrunch.com. Retrieved from http://techcrunch.com/2011/08/03/instagram-150-million

Silbey, J. (2008). Mythical beginnings of intellectual property. *George Mason Law Review, 15*(2), 319–379.

Siwek, S. (2007, August 21). *The true cost of sound recording piracy to the U.S. economy.* Retrieved from http://ipi.org/IPI%5CIPIPublications.nsf/PublicationLookupFullText/5C2EE3D-2107A4C228625733E0053A1F4

Soller, K. (2012, June). Levi's to cast an ad campaign using Instagram. Esquire: The style blog. Retrieved from http://www.esquire.com/blogs/mens-fashion/levis-instagram-campaign-010612

Streitfeld, D. (2011, October 16). Amazon signs up authors, writing publishers out of deal. *New York Times.* Retrieved from http://www.nytimes.com/2011/10/17/technology/amazon-rewrites-the-rules-of-book-publishing.html?_r=3&hp

Toth, P. B. (2005) Creative humbug. Indicare. Retrieved from http://www.indicare.org/tiki-read_article.php?articleId=118

World Intellectual Property Organization. (1996). WIPO Copyright Treaty (WCT) (adopted in Geneva on December 20, 1996). Retrieved from http://www.wipo.int/treaties/en/ip/wct/pdf/trtdocs_wo033.pdf

World Trade Organization. (1994). *Trade agreements. Trade-Related Aspects of Intellectual Property Rights (TRIPS).* Retrieved from http://www.wto.org/english/docs_e/legal_e/27-trips.pdf

CHAPTER TEN

The New Reputation Custodians

Examining the Industrialization of Visibility in the Reputation Society

NORA A. DRAPER

In a 2012 *New York Times Magazine* article, Lizette Alvarez documents a change in a time-honored college ritual: spring breakers are moderating their behavior in view of the long-term consequences of their actions. The source of this trepidation? The smartphones in the pockets of their peers—each one equipped with a camera, ready to capture antics for personal commemoration and public circulation online. While anecdotal, this story illustrates the now-mundane reality that ubiquitous recording devices and accessible publishing platforms allow the performances of ordinary people to be easily decontextualized and rebroadcast for vast and unintended audiences. Popular media outlets rehearse anecdotes and issue warnings about the negative implications of these viral performances. Academics warn that the information we intentionally and unintentionally share online is used to create persistent reputations from which we cannot escape (e.g., Turow, 2011). If the spring breakers who spoke to Alvarez are any indication, people—even youth, popularly portrayed as eschewing privacy in favor of a cultural of extreme visibility—have heeded the advice.

The *Times* article also alludes to a parallel logic. The college students Alvarez interviewed reveal their muted behavior is part of broader strategic project. Armed with an understanding that potential employers use online search as a way to vet candidates, they imagine their digital presence—a collection of websites, blogs, and social network profiles—as a cursory résumé. Despite the risks, one's digital presence is also considered a value store to be cultivated, managed, protected, and, eventually, mined. The online reputation management (ORM) industry, aimed at helping individuals to create, protect, and, if necessary, fix their digital presence, has grown quickly from a digital cottage industry to a well-funded enterprise. ORM firms, which emerged to fill the gap left by laws that have been slow to evolve to protect individual reputation in the digital era, encourage individuals to promote as well as protect their online identity. Through an analysis of the public discourse of this emerging industry, including publicity statements, company websites, and how-to manuals, this chapter explores how the industrialized practice of online identity management balances anxieties about the fragility of reputations in the digital era with strategies to create value through the creation of a profitable image.

DIGITAL VISIBILITY: REPUTATION, PRIVACY, AND IDENTITY ONLINE

Despite being used interchangeably, reputation and identity are distinct concepts. Reputation, which is commonly defined as the "shared, or collective, perception about a person" (Nock, 1993, p. 2), is a value constructed by others and used to assess the likely future actions of an individual. People may influence their reputation through strategic self-presentation, but the concept refers to a construct created by others as a proxy for trust. Although an individual's reputation is created by others, it has been treated in the law as the property of the individual to whom it refers. In this view, reputation has value that can be cultivated and mined; therefore, damage to reputation is often articulated in terms of loss. John Clippinger (2011) describes reputation as a construct with redemptive or stored value, derived through the trust-based networks in which it is situated. As early as 1890, E. L. Godkin described the socializing function of reputation noting: "The love of reputation is the most powerful motive to good conduct—perhaps the very strongest guarantee the community has for the good conduct—of the citizen" (p. 59). In intimate societies where individuals rely on sustained interaction, reputation serves as a way to build community trust. In diffuse societies where individuals cannot rely on the familiarity that comes with repeated interaction, portable reputation metrics—including credit scores and identification schemes—act as third-party guarantors (Nock, 1993).

Unlike reputation, which is constructed by others on behalf of an individual, identity is generally understood as an interior construct. While premodern thinkers often treated identity as innate and consistent (see Taylor, 1989), modernist academics have argued identities are strategic and evolving constructions that differ depending on circumstance. Erving Goffman (1959), for example, describes self-presentation as a performance that is continuously and situationally defined. The performances that make up one's identity, he notes, are scripted to adhere to the expectations of the audience. As a result, the individual will play several roles over the course of his or her life. Anthony Giddens (1991) positions the late-modern self as a reflexive project where individuals experiment with various identities. For Giddens, there is an inherent risk in the modernist identity project; as individuals experiment with different identities they choose between the "indefinite range of potential courses of action," in effect deciding between "possible worlds" with all the positive and negative implications of those decisions (pp. 28–29). Reputation and identity are, of course, closely related insofar as public performances may inform one's reputation.

It is also useful to note the relationship between privacy and reputation. In their treatise on privacy, Samuel Warren and Louis Brandeis (1890) draw on appeals for the legal protection of reputation to make their own claim for the value of privacy. Defining privacy as the "right to be let alone," Warren and Brandeis argue for a legal right to privacy in addition to the laws governing damage to reputation. The lawyers argue that the right to privacy is related to the principle of inviolate personality, which protects the unwanted communication of an individual's thoughts, emotions, and sensations, "whether expressed in writing, or in conduct, in conversation, in attitudes, or in facial expressions" (p. 206). In short, for Warren and Brandeis, privacy guarantees "the right to one's personality" (p. 207). This influential definition positions privacy as a way of carving out space for personality, as distinct from reputation.

The introduction of new media technologies challenges existing norms of privacy by altering circumstances of interaction and creating new opportunities for capturing, sharing, and archiving information. In his defense of reputation, Godkin (1890) is concerned with the role of newspapers in the spread of gossip beyond community boarders and the persistence of written content that made it difficult to amend. Warren and Brandeis (1890) write about the perversion of privacy by journalists using photography to interfere in the private lives of individuals. Similarly, the emergence of digital media platforms has forced a reexamination of social norms around privacy. danah boyd (2007) argues digital information is persistent, searchable, and replicable; features that make it difficult to ensure complete removal of information once it has been shared. If the content has been downloaded, copied, or cached even once, tracking down the reproductions is nearly impossible (Lipton, 2010). These characteristics, coupled with the near-ubiquity of recording technologies, make it more difficult for people to fade into "practical obscurity" (Strahilevitz, 2008), hoping their public indiscretions will be ignored or forgotten. boyd also argues that we have limited awareness of our audiences when using digital platforms to post or share information, making it difficult to know how to pitch one's self-presentation.

As a result of digital platforms that encourage the use of authentic or real-world identities (Marwick, 2005), much of the identity work that took place in offline spaces now takes place within semi-public online spaces. As a result, online self-presentation often follows a set of strategic practices that balance the opportunities and risks associated with the persistent visibility of online identity. Theresa Senft (2008) uses the term "micro-celebrity" to describe the use of the Web by ordinary people to create and promote a persona that will increase audience reach and popularity. Noting the conflation between self-presentation by public figures and ordinary people, Lynn Schofield Clark (2013) notes that in negotiating appropriate digital disclosure about their own lives, young people turn to celebrities as models. The level of calculation associated with various forms of identity performance suggests individuals are not simply engaging in self-presentation online but also in self-promotion. The range of strategies to develop a compelling online image has been referred to as personal branding (Marwick & boyd, 2010) or self-branding (Banet-Weiser, 2012). Alison Hearn (2008) suggests the explosion of self-branding practices in the twenty-first century originated in the 1990s out of a post-Fordist economy characterized by mobility, subcontracting, and decentralized production. These practices, she argues, turned the self-reflexive project of identity formation described by Giddens into an economic process where value is extracted through the labor of self-presentation. Similarly, Sarah Banet-Weiser (2012) argues society's current fetishization of visibility encourages individuals to "cultivate a self-brand" (p. 56).

IN THE EYES OF THE LAW: LEGAL APPROACHES TO DIGITAL REPUTATION

Much has been made of the limits of the law to protect personal privacy and respond to threats to reputation in the digital era. In response, the European Union has proposed Right to Be Forgotten legislation, which would give individuals the right to request removal of information found online regardless of how it got there (European Commission, 2012).[1] The legislation has not been well received by commercial platforms, which do not want responsibility for adjudicating content and prefer to act as neutral publishers. Criticism has also come from some legal scholars who fear the proposed legislation teeters too close to the slippery slope of online censorship (e.g., Rosen, 2012). Right to Be Forgotten legislation raises a number of key issues regarding how information is stored, shared, and used once it is published, as well as who has ownership over digital content.

Unlike countries in Europe, the United States does not have comprehensive privacy legislation. In the United States, reputation is primarily addressed using defamation law, which creates liability when published information harms an individual by lowering his standing in the eyes of his peers (Warren & Brandeis, 1890). Defamation cases face a number of challenges, most prominently, the strength of free speech rights guaranteed by the U.S. Constitution's First Amendment. These challenges make it risky to use legal avenues for content removal. Even if a case is successful, the process is likely to be costly, both in terms of time and financial resources. In the time it takes for a case to work its way through court, the offending content will likely remain online (Fertik & Thompson, 2008; Wilson, 2011), potentially bringing increased visibility to a case (Solove, 2007).

The specific characteristics of digital media platforms that allow for coproduction among various users further contribute to the difficulties of regulating online speech. When news was primarily disseminated through established media outlets, those companies were understood to have a responsibility for their published content. Determining responsibility for digital content when one individual or company is rarely responsible for creation, publications, and display is more complicated. Moreover, U.S. legislators passed Section 230 of the Communications Decency Act of 1996, which prevents third-party providers from being sued for infringing content. As a result, aggrieved parties are left with the less lucrative option of pursuing the individual responsible for posting the content (Solove & Schwartz, 2009). Burdens of proof also become increasingly punitive in the digital era when identities can be obscured (Lipton, 2010; Marwick, Diaz, & Palfrey, 2010).

Cass Sunstein (2009) has proposed a number of options for reconciling existing laws with the need for enhanced reputation protections. The first is a right to demand retraction in cases where a statement is deemed to be both false and damaging. A website that refuses to do so after being notified of the infringing content could be liable for damages. A second recommendation allows the individual to request removal of defamatory content from websites through a takedown provision modeled on the "notice and takedown rights" for copyrighted content contained in the Digital Millennium Copyright Act of 1998. This solution has similarities to the European Union's Right to Be Forgotten legislation, insofar as it transfers the onus of deciding whether content should be exempt to publishers. Sunstein's third suggestion is a system of damage caps and schedules where the reputation of speakers would suffer if they were found to be spreading falsehoods. This is similar to some of the reputation systems currently operating in online markets (e.g., eBay), online review sites (e.g., Yelp, Amazon), and online communities (e.g., Reddit).

Some commentators suggest the law is not the ideal venue through which to ensure greater privacy protections and reputation control online. The law, they argue, moves too slowly and is more likely to stifle innovation than to provide comprehensive solutions. Observers have offered alternatives to regulation including educational initiatives, changes to social norms (Marwick et al., 2010; Sunstein, 2009), reputation insurance programs (Morozov, 2012), the opportunity to file for reputational bankruptcy (Zittrain, 2008), and the use of private companies to help sanitize online representations (Marwick et al., 2010; Solove, 2007; Zittrain, 2008). The growth of commercial outlets that—for a fee—help individuals manage their digital presence illustrates how personal branding is positioned in response to the risks and opportunities associated with digital identity. The logics of this industry, which reveal the application of economic and advertising discourses to theories of the self, are discussed below.

ONLINE REPUTATION MANAGEMENT: THE INDUSTRIALIZATION OF VISIBILITY

The field of online reputation management (ORM) has its roots in public relations (PR) and is concerned primarily with the development, curation, and protection of its clients' digital images. The handbook Online Reputation Management for Dummies offers the following definition:

> **What is online reputation management?**
>
> Online reputation management is the process of ensuring that the right information appears when people look you (or the name of your brand) up in search engines like Google, Bing, or Yahoo!, or on social networks like Facebook, Twitter, or LinkedIn. The idea is to minimize negative content and to promote flattering content (Stradtman, 2012, p. 10).

A 2008 *Business Week* article outlined the growth of ORM "in response to the explosion of social media that amplified the voices of individual Internet users" (Tozzi, 2008). In the same year, analysts predicted that ORM would likely grow into a $250 million industry by 2011 (Beal, 2008). Five years later, *Business Week* noted ORM could be a $5 billion industry by 2015 (McNichol, 2012). While the industry's focus tilts toward the needs of businesses and celebrities—those who have traditionally sought the services of PR firms—a small but growing segment focuses on the need for "ordinary" individuals to build, manage, and defend their online reputations.

Industry Logic

ORM is shaped by the assertion that what people "find online will shape how they think about you, for better or worse" (Fertik & Thompson, 2010, p. 2). The industry defines reputation as the information found in an online search for a person, whether or not it is actually about them (Francesconi, 2010). Industry discourse makes no distinction between online and offline reputation; in the digital era, it argues, a person's online reputation is his or her reputation. And while the amount of information online is vast, the part that makes up an individual's reputation is quite small. Only information that is returned on the first page or two of search results is considered part of one's reputation. The ORM industry is composed of three central logics. The first states that your reputation is your brand. The second is that brands are vulnerable. The third argues the best way to protect a brand is to control the surrounding narrative.

ORM draws on branding rhetoric in its explanation of the value of an individual's digital image. One ORM how-to guide for individuals states: "Your online image is your personal brand on the Internet" (Francesconi, 2010, p. 225). Much as online review websites like Yelp and TripAdvisor have become the primary points of engagement for consumers evaluating businesses, ORM positions one's online image as a résumé. The ORM firm Brand.com (formerly Reputation Changer) warns that "86% of recruiters said that a good online reputation would increase the chances that they'd hire a candidate." Warnings about potential employees being passed up because of something revealed in an online search are so prevalent that colleges and universities provide seminars on Putting Your Best "Facebook" Forward, which offers strategies for sanitizing online representations. In 2009, Brand-Yourself, an ORM company targeted at individuals, partnered with Syracuse University to give graduating students a free six-month subscription to the company's reputation management service.

ORM focuses on both the creation of an effective personal brand and on the protection of that image. There is a pervasive sense across industry texts that one's reputation is consistently under threat. One how-to guide states, "We all have reputations and our own personal brands that can get damaged, perhaps irreparably, from our online conduct or from our conduct that is captured and distributed online" (Wilson, 2011, p. 11). Characterizing the sources of these threats as internal or external, malicious or unintended, industry rhetoric cautions that individuals must monitor their digital presence to be aware of any potential damage to their digital image.

ORM embraces the notion that there is no such thing as privacy online (Beal & Strauss, 2008). Further, industry guides suggest naïve expectations regarding online privacy put people, and their reputations, at risk. ORM encourages individuals to control the narrative around their own brand by creating a consistent or boiler-plate profile that is repeated across various online platforms (Tabin & Agranoff, 2010). The logic behind this approach is that if an individual fails to take control of his or her online identity, someone else will do it for them (Fertik & Thompson, 2010; Francesconi, 2010; Tabin & Agranoff, 2010). Particular tools are discussed below, but the primary strategy is referred to as "radical transparency" (Whitfield, 2012). This approach borrows directly from public relations, where it is used to help companies deal with crises by getting out in front of negative stories. The logic behind radical transparency is that by "being open and honest online, admitting mistakes, engaging stakeholders in discussions about your brands, and even revealing your internal processes" (Beal & Strauss, 2008, p. xxiv), companies mitigate damage to their reputations. The way the approach is applied in ORM may be more appropriately titled "strategic transparency." Much like commercial brands, individuals are encouraged to share only the information that will create a brand that is inoffensive, consistent, and legible.

Industry Tools

Although companies do not publicize specific strategies, there are a few commonly used ORM techniques. While companies may attempt to have information removed from websites by contacting publishers and host sites, issuing take-down requests, or bringing legal action, seeking information removal can be futile. Therefore, the industry relies primarily on burying, rather than removing, content. To bury unwanted content, ORM companies use a method called search engine optimization (SEO), which involves creating positive or neutral content that appears attractive to search algorithms, thereby boosting favorable content while simultaneously burying negative content. SEO is built on the logic that people rarely scroll beyond the first or second page of search results; therefore, if negative content can be relegated to the later pages, it is far less likely to be discovered. To ensure a positive image, ORM firms rely on the stable features of search algorithms to create content that likely will dominate search results.

Reputation management relies on early detection to bury negative content. As a result, ORM recommends monitoring the Internet for the appearance of content related to one's name. Additionally, many packages from ORM firms offer pervasive monitoring to head off negative content. These strategies involve self-surveillance and surveillance of others—particularly those in one's social network—who might cause inadvertent damage. Strategies include setting up alerts, such as Google Alerts, Yahoo! Alerts, and Windows Live Alerts, which provide instant notification whenever a certain word or phrase is indexed by a particular search engine (Tabin & Agranoff, 2010). ORM experts encourage people to set up alerts for their own names so that they are notified whenever their names appear in newly indexed content and to continuously monitor the representations of those in one's social network whose profiles may reflect poorly on their own image.

IS ORM A VIABLE SOLUTION?

In his seminal work on the state of reputation in the digital era, legal expert Daniel Solove (2007) notes the potential role of commercial ORM to act as part of broader legal reforms designed to give people greater recourse when their online reputations have been tarnished: "Another promising development is the rise of services like ReputationDefender [now Reputation.com], a company that helps people find and remove harmful information about themselves online. … Such services can help make informal ways of resolving the problem more efficient" (p. 192). The market model, however, faces a number of practical limitations. Additionally, the industry's support for the notion that no online space is private means that there is no venue for online behavior that a person might not want as part of his or her digital reputation. In the following section, I explore the benefits and drawbacks of ORM before turning to some implications of this practice.

ORM Is Invisible but Slow, Uncertain, and Costly

As previously noted, one drawback of using the legal system to deal with online content is the increased visibility it brings. ORM techniques have the benefit of making the disappearance of the offending content largely invisible to everyone except for those paying particularly close attention to the search results for a particular term. While this is an important advantage, ORM suffers from the same issues of speed and cost that plague legal approaches. Even when using SEO strategies, influencing search results is a difficult and slow process. Search engines like Google, Bing, and Yahoo! use crawlers to scan the Web, record links and content, and index pages to ensure quick retrieval for future searches. Crawlers may not visit each page every day, so changes to webpages may take time to be indexed by search engines. One guide suggests the results of a successful campaign may take 8 to 12 weeks (Tabin & Agranoff, 2010) and most ORM firms do not guarantee results. Moreover, the cost of ORM services can be prohibitive. Reputation.com offers some free services, but packages can costs individuals around $2,000 per year (Bronstad, 2012). That price is likely to increase for those with more severe damage to their online images. Even with companies dedicated to creating tools for individuals and a host of do-it-yourself guides, the task still requires time and technical skill. These factors are likely to create a divide between individuals with and without the resources to manage their online image.

ORM Does Not Need the Cooperation of Host Website or Original Poster

Although experts may attempt to have content removed from a site by negotiating with the host or original poster, they tend not to focus on the removal of content, opting instead to bury negative content beneath more flattering search results. This gives ORM the advantage of avoiding negotiations with websites and platforms that prefer not to adjudicate content. This practical advantage of ORM raises a more philosophical concern.

ORM Techniques Avoid Due Process

Part of the reason barriers to proving defamation are high is because of the value placed on free access to information. Judge Richard Posner (1978/1979), a critic of expansive privacy laws, argues that significant harm is done when individuals conceal discrediting information. The concern raised here is not so much that people might be able to conceal information about their previous dealings—this has always been the case—but that ORM practices institutionalize the availability of resources for sanitizing reputations to certain people.

ORM Industry Lacks Regulation or Ethical Oversight

While ORM firms share an underlying logic, a general definition of reputation, and a set of standard practices, the industry lacks ethical norms or regulatory oversight. While many ORM firms have positive reputations and perform services consistent with existing laws, others are engaged in practices that reflect poorly on the industry. Some firms have been accused of engaging in "black hat" SEO tactics, which include attempts to trick a search engine into believing a webpage's content is of value (Reputation Changer, 2012). Further, some companies have been accused of sabotaging clients' online reputations using information provided by the client to ensure continued business (Net Security, 2012). A website called Incautious Porn (incautious.org) draws attention to this practice and warns individuals that if they have visited a pornographic website, their name and telephone number may have been recorded. What's more, Incautious Porn claims to be creating paintings that contain this information and selling them for 50 euros. The site will allow people to search the database for their own name and phone number for 10 euros and, if found, remove the information for 1,000 euros to ensure it will not be included in any of the company's "art projects." Unlike the PR industry, with its governing body and ethical principles (e.g., the Public Relations Society of America's Codes of Ethics), the ORM industry lacks profession-wide standards.

ORM Relies on and Supports Powerful Media Agents

ORM challenges the supposed neutrality of search engines by manipulating results through an understanding of algorithmic patterns. One Google representative notes: "While there is nothing in our guidelines that explicitly forbids reputation management, if we uncover link schemes or other violations, we reserve the right to take action in response" (as cited in Chiaramonte, 2012). However, the industry's reliance on SEO reinforces the power of a small number of search engines as the primary Internet portals. Since even ORM experts are not privy to the algorithms used by search engines to rank content, they have to rely primarily on a number of stable components of the formulas. This generally means hosting content on popular and established websites, including social network sites and the webpages of established companies. The reliance on these websites supports an existing disparity where the bulk of online traffic is concentrated among a small number of websites. Rather than trying to subvert the current logics of the online ecosystems, which allow a limited number of players to control an increasingly dominant view of "reality" (Vaidhyanathan, 2011), standard approaches in the ORM industry operate within these principles and lend additional support to the inequitable distribution found online.

ORM Supports a Culture of Visibility

ORM solutions promote visibility as both a risk factor and a solution to the presence of negative online content. The industry suggests that people make assumptions based on the absence of content and that the lack of a profile can send troubling signals to others. For example, the absence of information about one's activities in his professional field may suggest to others that he is not a leader or expert in that area (Francesconi, 2010, p. 36). Making the argument for more, rather than less, information, ORM follows the mantra that "dilution is the solution to pollution" (Tabin & Agranoff, 2010, p. 48). Positioning visibility as a necessity limits the options for those uninterested in having an online presence. Individuals are encouraged to create innocuous profiles that will appeal to all members of their invisible online audience. As a result, those aspects of one's identity that are not reflective of the mainstream are likely to be excluded from his or her digital profile. This raises the question of what will happen to dangerous ideas—the unpopular notions that push mainstream thought in uncomfortable but essential ways. As Rosen (2004) asks, with everyone living "'under the microscope" where will we find opportunities for the risk taking that leads to innovation and social change?

GOVERNING A REPUTATION SOCIETY: A MIXED APPROACH

Digital reputations are growing in scope and influence. While it is difficult to assess how important an individual's search results are to his or her success in the social or economic world, there are communities on the Internet where the weight of one's reputation is evident. Across the Internet, communities are using reputation systems to evaluate products, services, and individuals (Masum, Tovey, & Zhang, 2011). Much like the introduction of portable reputation mechanisms to industrialized society, reputation systems are designed to generate trust and accountability in otherwise anonymous spaces. These mechanisms can be extremely powerful agents for regulating communities and creating new markets. The success of cooperative commercial ventures like Airbnb, Wheelz, and eBay demonstrate the capability of these services to create communities and support sustainable commerce. The power of these systems to ensure pro-social community norms is countered by the power of reputation to act as a stigmatizing force for those unlucky enough to have lost their privileged status.

There are those who believe that the growth of online reputation systems will lead to a new economic system in which individuals will be evaluated using metrics based on past interactions, behaviors, and, presumably, other data points deemed relevant. One advocate for the power of this new social order writes: "Welcome to the reputation economy, where your online history becomes more powerful than your credit history" (Botsman, 2012). Regardless of whether or not the reputation society evolves the way some analysts suggest, digital reputation metrics are likely to play an increasingly important role in how individuals are viewed and how decisions are made. Klout and Kred—two companies that aim to measure and reward individuals' online influence—are examples of this movement. Given the absence of regulatory or review mechanisms in most of these reputation systems, as well as the inability of existing legal structures to deal with the challenges they pose, the ORM industry fills a gap by creating extra-legal avenues for dealing with damaged reputations. However, in consideration of the drawbacks outlined above, ORM should not be understood as a long-term solution to dealing with challenges to privacy and reputation in the digital era. To the extent that the industry promotes reputation as a suitable metric for assessing individual worth and makes available the tools for controlling one's image within this system, it will exacerbate existing inequalities around access and visibility.

Alternative approaches that focus on education, social norms, and self-regulation represent preferable long-term solutions. Educational programs can borrow from industry practices, for example, the creation of alerts to notify individuals when their name appears in a search database and the adjustment of privacy policies on social network and community websites. These efforts should, however, avoid the industry language that invokes a constant state of threat and the need for network surveillance, both of which may have the unintended consequence of sanitizing the Web through the chilling of controversial or unpopular speech. The work of both Banet-Weiser (2012) and Hearn (2008) remind us that self-branding practices limit discourses of the self and reproduce normative identities by encouraging individuals to adhere to familiar and uncontroversial narratives.

Anecdotes, like the one cited at the outset of this chapter, suggest norms are beginning to change. Every effort should be made, however, to ensure that fear of digital disclosure does not stifle creativity, identity play, or dissent. Media literacy programs should focus on encouraging more generous approaches to online reputations that consider the contextual and partial nature of information found online. Rather than stressing the logic that the information found about an individual online is his or her reputation, we should encourage contemplation of the complexities of human behavior. Social norms should aim to respect the intended boundaries between various audiences and reassert a difference between reputation and identity.

The consistency and palatability demanded by branding practices is antithetical to identity experimentation and development. The importance of privacy—or at least of "forgetting"—is the ability to try on identities without having them stick as part of one's permanent reputation or brand. Insofar as ORM insists that digital technology has eradicated privacy, it removes the essential distinction between identity, which must include space for experimentation, with an approach to reputation that highlights the need for an individual to create a unified, permanent, and profitable image. There is a need to reshape this rhetoric to ensure continued spaces for identity play that does not harm the individual's standing in the reputation society—whatever that society may look like.

NOTES

1. Argentina has been negotiating a similar legislative approach.

BIBLIOGRAPHY

Alvarez, L. (2012, March 16). Spring break gets tamer as world watches online. *New York Times.* Retrieved from http://www.nytimes.com/2012/03/16/us/spring-break-gets-tamer-as-world-watches-online.html?_r=0

Banet-Weiser, S. (2012). *Authentic™: The politics of ambivalence in a brand culture.* New York, NY: New York University Press.

Beal, A. (2008, May 28). First estimate for growth of search engine reputation management industry. *Marketing Pilgrim.* Retrieved from http://www.marketingpilgrim.com/2008/05/first-estimate-for-growth-of-search-engine-reputation-management-industry.html

Beal, A., & Strauss, J. (2008). *Radically transparent: Monitoring and managing reputations online.* Indianapolis, IN: Wiley.

Botsman, R. (2012, August 20). *Welcome to the new reputation economy.* Wired.co.uk. Retrieved from http://www.wired.co.uk/magazine/archive/2012/09/features/welcome-to-the-new-reputation-economy.

boyd, d. (2007). Why youth (heart) social network sites: The role of networked publics in teenage social life. In D. Buckingham (Ed.), *Digital learning: Youth, identity, and digital* (pp. 119–142). Cambridge, MA: MIT Press.

Bronstad, A. (2012, January 9). Building an online reputation can be tricky: Lawyers find that maintaining an online reputation isn't easy. *National Law Review.* Retrieved from http://www.law.com/jsp/nlj/PubArticleNLJ.jsp?id=1202537637854&slreturn=1

Chiaramonte, P. (2012, January 20). Exclusive: Online reputation manager hacked websites to "inject" illegal code. *Fox News*. Retrieved from http://www.foxnews.com/scitech/2012/01/20/google-cide-online-reputation-managers-can-wipe-from-web/

Clark, L. S. (2013). *The parent app: Understanding families in the digital age*. Oxford, England: Oxford University Press.

Clippinger, J. H. (2011). An inquiry into effective reputation and rating systems. In H. Masum & M. Tovey (Eds.), *The reputation society. How online options are reshaping the offline world* (pp. 25–35). Cambridge, MA: MIT Press.

European Commission. (2012). *General Data Protection Regulation*. Retrieved from http://ec.europa.eu/justice/data-protection/document/review2012/com_2012_11_en.pdf

Fertik, M., & Thompson, D. (2010). *Wild West 2.0: How to protect and restore your online reputation on the untamed social frontier*. New York, NY: American Management Association.

Francesconi, A. (2010). *Who are you online: Why it matters and what you can do about it!* Layton, UT: WhooRu.

Giddens, A. (1991). *Modernity and self-identity: Self and society in the late modern* age. Stanford, CA: Stanford University Press.

Godkin, E. L. (1890). The rights of the citizen to his own reputation. *Scribner's Magazine, 8*(1), 58–67.

Goffman, E. (1959). *Presentation of self in everyday life*. New York, NY: Anchor.

Hearn, A. (2008). "Meat, mask, burden": Probing the contours of the branded "self." *Journal of Consumer Culture, 8*(2), 197–217.

Lipton, J. D. (2010). *Repairing online reputation: A new multi-modal regulatory approach*. Retrieved from http://works.bepress.com/jacqueline_lipton/10

Marwick, A. E. (2005). *Selling your self: Online identity in the age of a commodified Internet*. Unpublished master's thesis, University of Washington, Seattle, WA.

Marwick, A. E., & boyd, d. (2010). I tweet honestly, I tweet passionately: Twitter users, context collapse, and the imagined audience. *New Media & Society, 13*(1), 114–133.

Marwick, A. E., Diaz, D. M., & Palfrey, J. (2010). Youth, privacy and reputation. The Berkman Center for Internet & Society at Harvard University. Retrieved from http://cyber.law.harvard.edu

Massa, P. (2011). Trust it forward: Tyranny of the majority of echo chambers? In H. Masum & M. Tovey (Eds.), *The reputation society: How online options are reshaping the offline world* (pp. 152–161). Cambridge, MA: MIT Press.

Masum, H., Tovey, M., & Zhang, Y. (2011). Introduction: Building the reputation society. In H. Masum & M. Tovey (Eds.), *The reputation society. How online options are reshaping the offline world* (pp. xv–xxi). Cambridge, MA: MIT Press.

McNichol, T. (2012, February 2). Fixing the reputations of reputation managers. *Bloomberg BusinessWeek*. Retrieved from http://www.businessweek.com/magazine/fixing-the-reputations-of-reputation-managers-02022012.html

Morozov, E. (2012, February 20). We need mandatory insurance to protect online reputations. Slate.com. Retrieved from http://www.slate.com/articles/technology/future_tense/2012/02/_right_to_be_forgotten_how_facebook_google_and_other_companies_can_protect_internet_user_privacy_.html

Net Security. (2012, January 23). Online reputation manager suspected of illegal code injection. Retrieved from http://www.net-security.org/secworld.php?id=12267

Nock, S. L. (1993). *The costs of privacy: Surveillance and reputation in America*. New York, NY: Aldine de Gruyter.

Posner, R. A. (1978/1979). Privacy, secrecy, and reputation. *Buffalo Law Review, 28*(1), 1–55.

Reputation Changer. (2012, January 30). Consumer alert: ReputationChanger.com warns consumers of reputation management companies who engage in black hat SEO. *Reuters.* Retrieved from http://www.reuters.com/article/2012/01/30/idUS92264+30-Jan-2012+PRN20120130

Rosen, J. (2004). *The naked crowd: Reclaiming security and freedom in an anxious age.* New York, NY: Random House.

Rosen, J. (2012). The Right to Be Forgotten. *Stanford Law Review Online, 64*, 88–92.

Senft, T. M. (2008). *Camgirls: Celebrity and community in the age of social networks.* New York, NY: Peter Lang.

Solove, D. J. (2007). *The future of reputation: Gossip, rumor, and privacy on the Internet.* New Haven, CT: Yale University Press.

Solove, D. J., & Schwartz, P. M. (2009). *Information privacy law* (3rd ed.). New York, NY: Aspen.

Strahilevitz, L. J. (2008). Reputation nation: Law in an era of ubiquitous personal information. *Northwestern University Law Review, 102*(4), 1667–1738.

Sunstein, C. (2009). *On rumors.* New York, NY: Farrar, Straus & Giroux.

Tabin, H., & Agranoff, C. (2010). *Do it yourself online reputation management: A step-by-step guide to building or repairing your online reputation.* Grand Junction, CO: Pendant.

Taylor, C. (1989). *Source of the self: The making of the modern identity.* Cambridge, MA: Harvard University Press.

Tozzi, J. (2008, April 30). Do reputation management services work? *BusinessWeek.* Retrieved from http://www.businessweek.com/smallbiz/content/apr2008/sb20080430_356835.htm

Turow, J. (2011). *The daily you: How the new advertising industry is defining your identity and your worth.* New Haven, CT: Yale University Press.

Vaidhyanathan, S. (2011). *The Googlization of everything (and why we should worry).* Berkeley: University of California Press.

Warren, S. D., & Brandeis, L. D. (1890). The right to privacy. *Harvard Law Review, 4*(5), 193–220.

Whitfield, J. (2012). *People will talk: The surprising science of reputation.* Hoboken, NJ: John Wiley.

Wilson, T. (2011). *Manage your online reputation: Don't let angry clients, jealous lovers, or ruthless competitors ruin your image.* North Vancouver, BC: Self Council.

Zittrain, J. (2008). *The future of the Internet and how to stop it.* New Haven, CT: Yale University Press.

PART FOUR

Challenging THE Record: Documents, Evidence, Materiality

CHAPTER ELEVEN

Possibilities for Queering Surveillance Infrastructure

The Case of the Quantified Self

DAVID J. PHILLIPS,[1] BRIAN J. HARDING, AND DANIELLE LEIGHTON

Much critical research focuses on the use of surveillance technique as a means of normalizing, managing, and policing populations (Gandy, 1993; Haggerty & Ericson, 2006; Norris & Armstrong, 1999). Others attempt to understand how surveillance can be engaged in the constitution of non-normative identities and perverse social configurations (McGrath, 2004; Koskela, 2009). This research joins that latter group. It brings together surveillance theory, queer theory, and infrastructure studies in an attempt to understand how systems and practices of surveillance can be made accessible to individuals and groups to interrogate normalizing practices, and to further their own explorations and constructions of self in relation to others. It tries to imagine what a queer infrastructure of surveillance might look like.

Surveillance here is understood in a specific sense as a four-stage process of knowledge production. In the first stage, members of a population are individualized and made uniquely identifiable. In the second stage, the actions or attributes of these uniquely identified individuals are monitored and recorded. In the third stage, the recorded data are conglomerated across the population and subjected to analysis to discover categories, patterns, and norms. In the final stage, this new population-level knowledge is applied back to the population, to individuals within it, and to the surveillance process itself (Foucault, 1977; Agre, 1994). This kind of surveillance is, at its heart, actuarial and statistical; it isolates individual behavior to understand populations, then uses that knowledge as the lens through which to understand individuals. It is an exercise in normalcy, deviance, typification, valuation, and risk management.

Queer theory is concerned with the politics and pragmatics of inhabiting contested and constructed identity positions. From a queer theoretical perspective, identities are performed and performative; they are not given or preordained but are continually brought into being—calling upon, straining, or reinforcing the structures that are both medium and outcome of the performance (Goffman, 1959; Giddens, 1984; Butler, 1998). Identities are useful. People strive to enact certain ideal identities in certain settings in order to be recognized and treated as a certain sort of person, with a certain social position. Moreover, these identity performances inform our subjective embodied sense of self. They recursively reconstitute the ideals, desires, and fears that impel them. Thus, identity mediates between the individual and the social; it is a product of exterior relations and interior subjectivity (Lemke, 2008). One project of queer theory is to explore structural possibilities for the production of the non-normative and the transgressive—to resist, co-opt, or destabilize hegemonic identity and knowledge structures.

Infrastructure studies engage the forging and maintenance of relatively stable, heterogeneous networks of ideology, law, money, and machines that mediate and support relatively stable practices. Infrastructure studies address not merely I-bars and girders, wires and pipes—it also considers as a primary analytic focus the human activities that are supported by and, in turn, support those material artifacts. It is concerned with the work that goes into making that constellation of society, machine, and power enduring (Star & Bowker, 2002).

This chapter uses these lenses—surveillance, queer identity, and infrastructure—to understand the quantified self (QS) movement as a moment in the evolution of surveillance practice. Quantified self is a loose affiliation of practitioners who monitor their own activities, in order to make sense of themselves and their relation to the world. Interaction among QS practitioners occurs through blogs and occasional regional meet-ups where QSers report their experiences with self-tracking. May 2011 saw the first national conference of QSers in Mountain View, California—the heart of Silicon Valley. The research team attended that conference and interviewed participants after its conclusion. Unattributed quotes in this article are from those interviews. We wondered what people were doing, what sense they were making of themselves, how that sense of self was useful to them or others, what resources they called upon in their practice, and how those resources were made available to them. What follows is first a description of our findings, then a critical analysis discussing the ways in which trends toward certain institutional and cultural configurations of self-tracking integrate surveillance practice—and the production of identities—toward, within, or against particular systems of power.

PRACTICES AND TOOLS

Our first area of observation was practice. We wanted to know just what QSers were doing, and what tools they were using as QSers. Informed by our own understanding of surveillance, we categorized this practice into three areas: data creation, data storage and access, and analysis and sense making.

Data Creation

We noticed three modes of data creation. The first employed automated sensing, the second self-reflection, and the third involved the gathering of existing data that had been generated for other reasons.

Automated Sensing: Rich Data with Minimal User Intervention

Perhaps the most common method of automated sensing involved the use of small, low-power sensors capable of wireless data transfer. Some of these devices measure biometrics. For example, the Zeo device (myzeo.com) is a headband incorporating electroencephalography (EEG) sensors. But not all the sensors are biometric. For example, the Fitbit (fitbit.com) is a miniature, wearable accelerometer. In some sense the successor to the pedometer, the Fitbit detects and records the wearer's motions and produces a constant stream of kinetic data generated with minimal effort on the part of the user. This data is used to make inferences from the movement of the wearer's body as to other attributes of the wearer—the quality of his or her sleep, perhaps, or the amount of physical activity undertaken.

Self-Reflection

While some data is produced automatically, other data-creation practices require active intervention or self-reflection. QSers may keep written journals or other records, regularly recording some aspect of their life. Projects may involve complex data-generation practices. For example, the evaluation of a self-administered non-standard treatment for Crohn's disease involved monitoring and recording bowel movements, digestive pain, weight fluctuation, hemoglobin levels, and muscle mass. None of these measurements were automated and some, such as pain level, required subjective measures.

Found Data

QS practice also makes use of found data—the copious effluent of daily life. E-mail archives are a rich source of such data, allowing one QSer to chart graphs for the 10 individuals with whom she or he conversed the most each month.

"Life-logging" involves the cross-referencing and integration of all sorts of found data. Two QSers used life-logging through the terminal illness of their infant daughter, encouraging her caregivers to record all of the data that the treatments generated and to compile it in a single, comprehensive source. Data collected included all inputs, outputs, and care activities—information that is continuously generated during medical treatment but most often left to disappear.

In summary, surveillance requires active data gathering. This entails decisions based on the cost of the data gathering and the presumed usefulness of the data. QS practice generally relies on low-cost data. These costs are kept low by two mechanisms. The first is the integration of the data-gathering process into commercial services using standard, mass-produced sensing devices, such as FitBit and Zeo. Data gleaned from the informational flotsam of everyday life is also low in cost.

But low cost is not the only criteria in deciding on data-collection practice. Some data, particularly data that will be used to understand severe health issues or other idiosyncratic concerns, require significant effort to produce.

This structure of the cost of data creation has implications for regular practices of knowledge creation that will be discussed later.

Data Storage and Access

Of course, data, once created, must be stored and made accessible. The availability of these tools—who has access to what data and under what conditions—is another aspect of the infrastructure of knowledge making.

In the context of QS, the storage and retrieval of data follows two significant models: local, on-site storage and remote, off-site, cloud-based storage. The majority of technology-focused business models in the consumer self-tracking device market store data in the cloud. For example, both Zeo and Fitbit, by default, stream data generated by their devices first to local base stations and then to remote servers operated by the companies. Once on the server, the individual's data are available to that individual, but generally only through proprietary analytic interfaces that provide little opportunity for customized or individualized analysis. While, in both cases, the base station (or the tracking device itself) is able to perform and display simple analytics—the ZEO base station can calculate and display the "ZQ" sleep score, and the Fitbit monitor features a flower icon that grows and shrinks in relation to the user's activity levels—for more complex analysis, including longitudinal analysis or comparisons to other users, data usually must be transferred to the companies' servers. There is some play in these models, though. Zeo allows the QSer to stream it from the device to the QSer's computer or to download it from the server in a spreadsheet format (developers.myzeo.com). Subscribers to Fitbit's premium service can access and download "daily summary data," but this is not the raw data that is generated by the Fitbit device (blog.fitbit.com/?p=360).

The QSer's data may be available to other parties. Often this takes the form of sharing data with a small group of self-selected friends. Data also may be conglomerated into population-wide statistics. Fitbit subscribers can compare their own data to their peers' through anonymized demographic data; for example, comparing one's weight to the mean weight of 40-year-old women (www.myzeo.com/sleep/dozer).

Within QS, collaboration is a core value and striven-for ideal. CureTogether, a health-related website with founders who are involved heavily in the QS movement, represents one such form of social data (www.curetogether.com). CureTogether helps individuals share their knowledge about and experience with their health conditions. For each symptom or condition, users can also contribute information regarding their experiences with certain treatments and whether they were effective or not. Simple statistics on the perceived success of each treatment are displayed in bar charts. Thus, CureTogether provides to each of its users an aggregate view of all of its users' data.

Just as innovations in sensor technology make data generation effortless, the "cloud" model of data storage produces an ambient collection of data with minimal input on the part of the user. The model also imposes constraints. Once the data is contributed by QSers and housed on an external server, the data holders control access according to third-party policies and tools. Local storage of data circumvents the reliance self-interested third parties, and significant work is being done among QSers to promote that. The ICD project, in which data is culled from an implantable cardioverter-defibrillator (ICD), is very much an effort to sidestep these institutional interests in data management. Typically, an ICD will record an individual's cardiac activity and send that data, via a low-power radio transmitter, a modem, and a phone line, to the device manufacturer. If cardiac anomalies are present, the manufacturer forwards a descriptive code to the individual's insurance provider, which alerts the individual's doctor, who contacts the individual. The ICD, as a data-generating device, is, thus, one element of an infrastructure stabilizing a particular—and particularly troublesome—relation among individuals, insurance companies, and healthcare providers. The hack confronts and perverts these relations.

The decision to engage in local storage practice is not always ideologically driven. Much data, including email, notes, and records, are simply local by default.

In summary, then, surveillant knowledge production entails the collection, storage, and dissemination of data, as well as the creation of data. Remote, jointly accessed data collections are essential for some kinds of knowledge creation, especially knowledge that requires analysis of population-wide data. But this entails significant organizational problems. Third-party service providers offer the expertise for this, but on their own terms. Deviation from those terms requires the development of novel organizational forms. Again, the infrastructural specifics of data access have implications for the construction of identity and for knowledge production. These will be discussed later.

Sense Making

Creating and accessing data are just preliminary steps toward the goal of QS—generating knowledge and making sense. We categorize these practices into four types: statistical description, statistical comparison, nonstatistical visualization, and conversation.

Statistical Description

Using statistical analyses to describe different aspects of one's life lies at the heart of the quantified self movement. For many participants, the goal is "a single interesting number about wellness" or some other ideal. Of course, a single number only whets the appetite for suites of numbers and cascading relations among them.

Examples of this kind of sense making are legion. The ZQ score produced by the Zeo device is determined first by determining the amount of REM sleep, deep sleep, and total sleep that a user gets during the night, then comparing that to the user's own baseline average sleep quality. Email archives were analyzed to elucidate evolving relationships: the gradual increases and decreases in contact with particular individuals from one month to the next, the emergence of new contacts into the top 10 category, and their disappearance as contact breaks off. They also made evident broader trends such as life's shifting priorities, from communicating primarily with friends to work-related contacts and then school-related contacts.

This kind of analysis creates knowledge that places the self in relation to the self, or in relation to some unstated or implicit ideal. More sophisticated analysis will place the self in relation to others, or will be explicit about the field against which sense is being made.

Statistical Comparisons to Self and Others

The "N=1" experiment relies on a scientific paradigm of independent and dependent variable, and the establishment of base cases against which comparisons can be drawn. For example, a prominent QSer noticed that eating pork fat caused him to sleep better and feel more energized and alert when awake. He attempted to duplicate this effect by designing an experiment, which involved consuming large amounts of butter then performing a set of arithmetic problems. Another example of the N=1 experiment is the self-administration of nonstandard treatment of Crohn's disease, mentioned earlier. Here, QSers carefully tracked symptoms before and after ingestion of two different kinds of parasitic worm.

Nonstatistical Visuals and Graphs

Many QSers are deeply interested in the relation between data, the sensory, and the affective. While numbers give some kind of ontological authority, they must be abstracted, arranged, and presented to elicit a visceral or cognitive response. Some QSers are professional graphic designers or visual artists and engage in this abstraction and presentation of numbers and data in quite sophisticated ways. Such abstraction and arrangement need not be statistical. For example, a QSer presented a map depicting the times and locations where he'd had sex during the previous year. Another was a visual artist who created and exhibited work derived from her self-tracking data.

Discussions at Meet-Ups

Finally, the QS conference itself and the semi-regular local meet-ups are essential in QS practices of sense making. It is at these face-to-face gatherings that participants attempt to "get down to … the meaning of personal data" by sharing personal experiences. All attendees are encouraged to speak from their own experiences. Although these meet-ups and conferences are becoming increasingly commercial as a result of attendance by those with a product or service to sell, QSers are encouraged to continue fostering the communicative structure that has been characteristic of these gatherings. This communicative structure facilitates "collaborative knowledge generation." In particular, the knowledge generated at QS meet-ups is meta-knowledge about the production of self-knowledge.

This section has outlined the practices of QSers, and the tools and resources called on in those practices. These span a great range, and while the use of off-the-shelf monitors and standard subscription services is very common, so is the use of hacked devices and found data for ad hoc knowledge generation. One general comment can be made, though. Participants often were troubled by the failures of statistical analysis. They either hadn't the chops to manipulate the data, or the data itself was too messy to subject to rigorous analysis. This was particularly the case for data generated from individual incidents. That data, and the incident that produced it, was unintelligible without benchmark data against which to compare it.

GOALS AND PURPOSES

This section describes the varieties of motivations, goals, and rewards that QSers experience in their practice. We do this to elucidate the ideological commitments of QSers and especially, as far as they are evident, the ideal identities toward which QSers strive and the social organization in which that identity is useful.

Reflective Self-Knowledge

Some QSers, when discussing the rewards of QS practice, mentioned the value of self-reflection for its own sake. Pausing to notice one's state changes one's sense of self. In itself, it reconstitutes identity. It "reassures you that you exist." This sense of bringing forth a new image of self and relating to the world though a mysterious interplay of data, perception, and pattern was described by some as the richest, most innate pleasure of QS practice.

Simultaneously, though, there runs through QS culture a more dominant ethos in the value of cutting through mystery, rather than engaging in it—of producing an "objective" self-knowledge, through verifiable measurement and formal analysis. Sensation and perception are to be distrusted unless accompanied by data. "Cognitive bias" is anathema. Numbers carry truth. They give an "empirical answer," so one can "act accordingly."

Of course, the belief that objective knowledge is better than subjective knowledge implies that the former is more useful. It allows one to act toward some goal. We classify the kinds of usefulness we observed into three broad categories: self-improvement, citizen science, and public visibility.

Self-Improvement

By far, the most prevalent purpose of QS practice in our observation is wellness and health—weight loss, more restful sleep, or a satisfying exercise regimen. Fitbit, Zeo, and other services were intended to help people "understand everything that goes into being happy, healthy, and productive; [to help you] understand where you score versus a healthy range and [to help you] choose some small behaviors … to improve." This emphasis on wellness and productivity speaks to the social position of many QSers. The QSers we met were, not universally but substantially, independent entrepreneurs ensconced in the political and cultural economy of Silicon Valley. They were contractors, consultants, hackers, and freelancers, attempting to become healthier, more energetic, and more self-motivated members of an economic order based on entrepreneurship.

While the ethos of the individualist entrepreneur was certainly prevalent, there was also a palpable crosscurrent of non-economic motivations for wellness. A few QSers strove toward pleasure and wellness not as criteria for productivity, but for their own sake. This was exemplified in projects that hacked sex toys to respond to biometric feedback rather than external control.

Citizen Science

Another impetus for QS practice was resistance to institutional processes of scientific and, especially, medical knowledge making. As an organizer put it,

"We're being judged by an inappropriate standard, so we're attempting to calibrate our own relations with those models." This scientific research was felt as an exhilarating intervention and engagement with the dynamics of real power. Most of this scientific practice, however, was individualist resistance to established orders of power. It was a renegotiation of one's place in relation to existing models. Engaging populations and subpopulations to create new models was much less in evidence. In part, this was due to the difficulties of creating, storing, accessing, and analyzing population-level data. This sort of population-level knowledge required a level of coordination that QS practitioners have yet to achieve. It's clear, though, that such kind of coordination is a goal and an ideal. CureTogether is an example of such a project.

Public Visibility

Some QSers engage in the practice not only for self-knowledge but also as a means of self-presentation. They engage in the practice from a specific identity position with the intent to speak, understand, and reveal the self from that position. This is similar in some ways to the personal science discussed in the previous section, except that the methods are not necessarily experimental, and the institutions engaged are more diffuse than the scientific or medical communities. For example, the life log of a child's terminal illness, mentioned earlier, was intended to give a holistic, impressionistic, affectively complex image of the child's life and to be "an icon of empowerment, community, and hope."

Of course, the pleasures of performance and self-expression suffused the entire conference. After all, these were people displaying and discussing the mechanisms and products of their self-knowledge. A developer of QS apps mentioned similar themes: "I did performance art … and there's [a] quality of self-performance and self-experimentation [in QS] that speaks to me."

As with much performance art, these performances often had a critical edge—they were aware of the audience and sought on some level to engage and trouble that relationship. This social critique was evident even in some apparently prosaic "self-improvement" applications. One female QSer engaged in QS for weight loss, not because of any perceived threats to her health or wellness but because of the new social position she felt herself occupy: "You gain weight and people just look through you. … So it's kind of a strange experience, and I really wanted to deal with this."

One QSer was quite explicit in his use of QS as performance and intervention, producing and exhibiting an "annual report on the sexual behavior of FreshenX, an HIV-negative, 37-year-old single gay man living in the Castro neighborhood of San Francisco, California." The poster noted that "95% of U.S. men have less than 5 partners per year [while] almost 50% of gay men in San Francisco have more than 5 partners a year." The primary visual element of the poster was a map of San Francisco on which FreshenX had identified the location and frequency of his sexual activities during the previous year. The poster also included summary graphs of total counts of these activities, representing the frequency, duration, and type of sex acts. While FreshenX's self-tracking was an individualized summary and representation of personally significant data and evoked the quantified self ideal of "self-knowledge," it also directly confronted the politics of statistics and normalization, as well as the cultural politics of privacy, publicness, and sexuality in a way that very few other QSers did. As FreshenX put it, "I based [the decision on what activities to track] off of … one, the kind of activities that I like to engage in, and number two, the most common types of activities that I know gay men do participate in. … Part of my agenda [was] to talk about something that is not talked about: … sex … that particular taboo. … It's an act of art … performance art. … Rather than altering me, it has finally expressed a part of me that I felt I wanted to express."

Why Not?

Finally, we must recognize that many reasons for QS practice are not just inarticulate, they cannot be articulated. The imperative "Know thyself" stands primal.

This section has discussed the range of purposes to which QS practice is put, and the usefulness of the knowledges that surveillance practice is capable of producing. That range is vast. Some produced selves are quite normative, striving toward well-established ideals. Others stand in stark contradiction to those ideals, adamantly claiming the position of the monster. Still others hold identity ideals in abeyance, always flirting with and refusing the truth of an objective self.

So, on one hand, QS practice seems to affirm that surveillance is not necessarily oppressive or normative, but may be used to produce queer knowledges. However, that this is possible does not mean that it is easy or probable. The next section explores the forces at work in institutionalizing and stabilizing QS practice, and the effects this stabilization is likely to have on the production of selves.

INSTITUTIONALIZATION: SEEKING INFRASTRUCTURAL STABILITY

Institutionalization seeks to forge and maintain relatively stable relationships to support practice. These relationships form a network of ideologies, laws, money, and machines. This heterogeneous networked infrastructure facilitates certain practices, while precluding others. Infrastructuring activity—negotiations over the creation of enduring relations among law, practice, machines, and money—was evident among some QS participant interactions. In interviews and at the conference, participants talked about several different models for these relations. One sort was informed by hacker culture, the other by a quest for business models that integrated with existing corporate and legal structures.

Hacking

The hacker ethos comprises several things, including a sense of individual agency and expertise, a sense of cooperative projects, and a commitment to "free" culture and open expression. Peer-based community organization is central to the hacker ethos, as are "open" practices. That is, in general, the idea that anyone's work should be available to others—not necessarily without cost, but without restrictions on adaptation or use.

QS hacking practice is particularly evident at the level of devices, which are either developed de nova or reverse-engineered to give the user access to the data she produces. This device-hacking practice is institutionalized in the OpenYou project—a platform for the development of code to access data from various devices, including the Fitbit and the Zeo EEG headband. Hacking devices require that they be reverse-engineered. This is almost always a violation of licensing agreements and, in the United States, of the Digital Millennium Copyright Act. It subjects the QSer to significant legal risk.

While there are many successful examples of open data repositories (e.g., OpenStreetMaps is a working open repository of geographic data), the hacking of repositories of QS data is a more difficult project. First, these projects contravene well-established interests and paradigms structuring the commercialization and commoditization of personal data. Second, QS data itself troubles notions of openness, publicness, and privacy, because it refers—often intimately—to an individual's actions and body. Skirting these concerns, some hacker effort was directed toward creating Personal Data Banks (PDBs), databases that could potentially conglomerate the data that each QSer was producing—whether from the Zeo, the Fitbit, or the cable TV box. In this case, problems of sharing or selling data do not arise. Indeed, the PDB was imagined as the platform from which novel practices of sharing might develop.

Integrated Proprietary Services

At the same time that QS facilitates this cooperative, peer-based, open-source infrastructure, another trend supports the development of proprietary systems that integrate data collection, management, and analysis in relatively closed, controlled, and explicitly profit-directed systems. At the QS conference, we identified three models for this integration of tools, data, and service.

The Web 2.0 Model

The first of these, and perhaps the most common, might be referred to as the Web 2.0, or mass media, model. A company operating with this type of business model recognizes three different markets: selling devices to QSers, selling data and services to QSers, and selling data and services to third parties. Though distinct, these markets are understood as interdependent. Finding a stable and profitable balance among these markets is not a simple problem, and it was the subject of significant discussion at the conference.

While device sales to QSers will generate revenue, that stream is not ongoing. People buy one, and once the market is saturated the revenue stream disappears. Subscription services potentially offer an ongoing revenue stream, but only if subscribers keep renewing. So companies try to incorporate both continuity and freshness, adding "social" features and incentives, like games and competitions, to keep their subscribers interested and involved. To keep new and interesting features coming, some companies position their service as a platform and rely on hackers and independent developers to generate novel means of engagement. Zeo, for example, facilitates third-party application (app) development by providing application programming interfaces (APIs) to access data records either directly from an individual's device or from Zeo's database (developers.myzeo.com). However, this tactic entails the risk that independently developed apps will eat into the profit stream generated by Zeo's own apps. Therefore, they restrict use of the APIs by terms of use that, among other things, forbid the development of any app that competes with any of Zeo's services (developers.myzeo.com/terms-and-conditions).

Another of the issues these companies face is the expense of distributing apps and devices. Developers look to increase distribution by affiliating with sympathetic organizations. National chains of fitness trainers, for example, may become retail outlets for some devices. This may work for products aimed at personal fitness or other goals that are already well integrated into the U.S. cultural economy. But Zeo, for example, cannot take advantage of this tactic, since there is no established industry supporting "sleep performance." There are no "sleep coaches" to act as retail conduits. And while there is a well-established medical field addressing sleep disorders, engaging that industry and positioning Zeo as a medical device entails enormous costs, since it invites the attention of regulators.

Work on the PDB is conceptually, though not organizationally, linked to this economic model, since the PDB is often imagined as the platform enabling the

QSer to enter the market for personal information as an agent empowered to "interact in a marketplace to trade slices of the data."

The Health Insurance Nexus

Another economic model also attempts to integrate QS practice with the U.S. industrial complex comprising healthcare and health insurance. This model targets employers as the primary clients. These employers contract with the QS company to provide their employees, as part of the employment benefits package, with self-quantification services, coordinating health screenings, fitness contests, and biometric monitoring. Benefits options may include coordination of coaching services for employees to address specific physical or emotional problems. This type of QS platform may bring to the individual employee's awareness the link between health, wellness, and lifestyle choices. It allows employers to monitor, promote, and reward behaviors such as abstaining from smoking or reducing cholesterol. This verifiable behavior change directly corresponds to a reduction in health insurance premiums, which are, in the United States, a substantial economic burden to the employer. More and more employers, insurers, and healthcare providers are adopting the "accountable care."

Institutional Research

A third model integrates the particular practices and tools of self-quantification into standard practices of large-scale medical research and population management. One cluster of projects attempts to design self-tracking apps to collect "observations of daily living (ODLs)" ("sensations, feelings, thoughts, attitudes, and behaviors that provide cues to a person about their health state") and integrate them with clinical management. These platforms direct data away from the user, and so they seem contrary to the concept of QS practice. Nevertheless, they are included in this analysis because they were present and visible at the QS conference, and also because this kind of project is integrated deeply into the U.S. healthcare nexus, enjoying funding from governmental agencies and very large nonprofit research foundations.

The infrastructural ideals discussed above are just that—ideals. In practice, the conceptualization and pursuit of those ideals is quite messy. Interests overlap, and relationships are vague, uncommitted, and exploratory.

DISCUSSION

Finally, we turn to a critical discussion of the ways in which trends toward certain institutional and cultural configurations of self-tracking integrate surveillance practice and the production of identities toward, within, or against particular systems of power. For each of the modes of institutionalization described above, we will discuss the kinds of identities and selves each tends to facilitate, and the resources called upon in the effort to stabilize that institutionalization in heterogeneous networked infrastructure. Remember that, as we understand them here, identities are always interactive. They are both subjective and objective, and both imposed and projected. They require both figure and ground.

The Commodity Self

The subscription model, exemplified by platforms such as Fitbit and Zeo, produces different tools of identity construction for actors occupying different positions in its stabilizing infrastructure. In general, though, we may refer to the self-produced identity as the *self as commodity*.

Those with access to the agglomerated data produced under this model are able to produce population data—norms, types, and patterns. These are the ground against which the figures of individuals become evident. They provide the vocabulary according to which individuals may be described and engaged. In general, these data are available to those who are willing and able to pay for it, or to those who have some sort of scientific legitimacy.

QSers using platforms in the subscription model are able to construct identities against the grounds of established cultural ideals (generally of health and wellness) or of prior personal, individualistic desires. In the case of the QSers informing this research, these are predominantly the ideals and desires of the individualist entrepreneur.

These platforms facilitate the construction of new norms, new desires, and new ideals to the extent that they are created by third parties, by the population data sent off-site, or by the participants through access to vocabularies, grammars, analytics, and data. This access varies considerably among platforms, from Fitbit's set of standard analytics to CureTogether's semi-controlled vocabulary of conditions, symptoms, and treatments, where any participant can add a new element to that vocabulary if it is not already present.

The context negotiated in this mode of institutionalization includes the users' cultural familiarity with the practices of social media and mediated publicness, a range of awareness of the value of data, and a well-established set of privacy principles instantiated in law and policy. First, the people who engage this model are comfortable with social media. They are used to assigning the traces of their lives to third parties and arranging and displaying those traces in a project of self-presentation. Second, that familiarity entails varying degrees of awareness of, and engagement with, the political economy of social media. This is especially the case with the negotiation of the value of personal data, and the tension between the value of that data to the individual, the community, and organizations such as corporations and state agencies. As with all capitalist media organizations, these platforms must play the tension between profit and legitimacy. That is, they must legitimate the privatization of the value of personal information by counterbalancing it with benefits that accrue either to the individual or to society. Legitimating it with respect to the individual is fairly straightforward (though not always easy)—if the self-knowledge that a QSer obtains from the service is worth the subscription price, then everything works out. Legitimating the sale of data (data that the platform acquired without compensating the source of the data) to third parties requires a bit more ideological work. This work involves the often-silent reiteration of capitalism as apotheosis of the common good. In the case of QS platforms, this can be seen in the justification of medical research by large profit-making pharmaceutical firms as an objective pursuit of the greatest good for the greatest number. It is also seen (as with all mass media) in the legitimation of advertising (and its attendant surveillance and knowledge of others) as a mechanism lubricating the invisible hand of the market. Supporting this work is an ingrained cultural eschewal of politics, a careful ignorance of the economics of manufactured identity, and a set of naïve privacy concerns. This is not to say that this cultural bent is omnipresent among QSers but it is present, and to the extent of that presence, the work of those instantiating this model is easier.

The Disciplined Self, the Corporate Self

The second model, situated in the U.S. healthcare/employer/health insurance nexus, may be said to facilitate the creation of the disciplined self and the corporate self. Individual employees are encouraged to monitor, understand, and act upon themselves with respect to the ideals and norms of standardized healthcare. Corporations are able to understand their employees as constituent parts of their corporate selves, and to manage those parts toward a more profitable whole.

Bringing about this mode of institutionalization calls on several resources. The most important is the economic self-interest of employees within a political economy that plaits profit-making healthcare, profit-making health insurance, health insurance as a perquisite of employment, and employment at the will of the employer. Also at play is the cultural phenomenon of deep branding and affective identification of individuals with corporate entities. Employees and employers valorize the team. And this notion of the team engages with the competitive ethos of capitalism and the habitus of social media. Together, these mediate the games, contests, and comparisons that support the figure of the individual, the ground of his or her similar others, and his or her ideal relation with respect to them.

The Atomic Self

The third model, which integrates QS practice with expert population management, produces what may be called *the atomic self.* This is the self as a unique constituent of the actuarial ground, but does not appear as a figure against that ground. It stands in relation to the model only as a part of that model. This identity is purely mathematical, statistical, and actuarial. It is useful to managers in the constitution of norms, types, patterns, and flows.

The maintenance of these selves requires that individuals sublimate their individuality to the construction of the abstract whole. Ideologically, it calls on a joy in numbers and a trusting pleasure in the God's-eye view. More than the previous models, it entails a trust in large organizations to produce objective, generalizable, beneficent truths.

This model requires access to big data, and that access is most often mediated through an ideology of big science, and particularly big science in late capitalism. That is, the risks of research are borne by public or quasi-public organizations like the Centers for Disease Control and Prevention (CDC) or tax-exempt nonprofits. The profit-bearing fruits are privatized. This trend is not absolute. Many in QS are involved in the political project of ensuring that big data is publicly collected and publicly available. This model also draws on the de-identification principle of privacy policy.

The Ineffable Self, the Queer Self

Finally, we consider the hacking model, by which we mean the institutionalization of artistry, artisanship, and community in self-surveillance practice. This is the model that facilitates the production of *the ineffable self* and *the queer self.* Through hacked devices, local data collection, and idiosyncratic analysis, individuals are able to see and present themselves as monsters against familiar ground, defying standardization and typification.

Quantified self meet-ups and conferences are themselves a resource in the institutionalization of this ethos, as practitioners are able to meet and talk in co-equal exchange. Self-quantification may seem at first glance to be keenly narcissistic, but the meet-ups are structured to facilitate a peer-based gift exchange of knowledge—not about the self, but about self-discovery. However, this relatively small-scale peer exchange is at odds with the prevailing "social-media moment [where] knowledge generation … is perceived [as something] that can only happen 'at scale' in this kind of blast-radius of a personal branding." Modern privacy regimes, too, are of little help in this institutionalization, since those regimes do so little to illuminate the nuanced and contingent exchanges involved in the recursive co-construction of individuals and communities.

CONCLUSION

This chapter has attempted to show how certain practices of surveillance and the production of self are structured and institutionalized in QS, and how that institutionalization is likely to constrain or enable the production of identities and critical engagement with that production. The analysis suffers in many ways, not least from an enforced brevity and oversimplification of complex relations and contradictions. It does suggest, though, and perhaps unsurprisingly, that the dominant form of institutionalization of QS practice occurs within the neoliberal project of increased commoditization of all aspects of social life, information, and knowledge. Within these institutions, selves are produced that are useful within that project. Still, queer forms of world making are alive at the margins, a margin that, so far, QS still inhabits.

NOTES

1. This research was supported by Social Sciences and Humanities Research Council Grant #487028 awarded to David J. Phillips.

BIBLIOGRAPHY

Agre, P. (1994). Surveillance and capture: Two models of privacy. *Information Society, 10*(2), 101–127.

Butler, J. (1998). Imitation and gender insubordination. In D. H. Richter (Ed.), *The critical tradition: Classic texts and contemporary trends* (2nd ed., pp. 1514–1525). New York, NY: Bedford/St. Martin's.

Foucault, M. (1977). *Discipline and punish: The birth of the prison* (A. Sheridan, Trans.). New York, NY: Pantheon.

Gandy, O. (1993). *The panoptic sort: A political economy of personal information*. Boulder, CO: Westview.

Giddens, A. (1984). *The constitution of society: Outline of the theory of structuration*. Berkeley: University of California Press.

Goffman, E. (1959). *The presentation of self in everyday life*. New York, NY: Doubleday.

Haggerty, K., & Ericson, R. (2006). The new politics of surveillance and visibility. In K. Haggerty & R. Ericson (Eds.), *The new politics of surveillance and visibility* (pp. 3–25). Toronto, Canada: University of Toronto.

Koskela, H. (2009). Hijacking surveillance? The new moral landscapes of amateur photographing. In K. F. Aas, H. O. Gundhus, & H. M. Lomell (Eds.), *Technologies of InSecurity: The surveillance of everyday life* (pp. 147–167). New York, NY: Routledge-Cavendish.

Lemke, J. (2008). Identity, development, and desire: Critical questions. In C. Calda-Coulthard & R. Iedema (Eds.), *Identity trouble* (pp. 17–42). New York, NY: Palgrave Macmillan.

McGrath, J. (2004). *Loving Big Brother: Performance, privacy, and surveillance space*. London, England: Routledge.

Norris, C., & Armstrong, G. (1999). *The maximum surveillance society: The rise of CCTV*. Oxford, England: Berg.

Star, S. L., & Bowker, G. (2002). How to infrastructure. In L. A. Lievrouw & S. Livingstone (Eds.), *The handbook of new media* (pp. 151–162). Thousand Oaks, CA: Sage.

CHAPTER TWELVE

The "Unobserved Observer"

Humphrey Spender's Hidden Camera and the Politics of Visibility in Interwar Britain

ANNIE RUDD[1]

> The basic force behind [the British documentary movement] was social, not aesthetic. It was a desire to make a drama from the ordinary to set against the prevailing drama of the extraordinary: a desire to bring the citizen's mind in from the ends of the earth to the story, his own story, of what was happening under his nose.
>
> —JOHN GRIERSON, "THE STORY OF THE DOCUMENTARY FILM," *FORTNIGHTLY REVIEW*, AUGUST 1939

On a dreary morning in January 1938, in a declining industrial city in northern England, Humphrey Spender loitered in a pub, sipping his beer and attempting inconspicuousness in his tatty mackintosh coat. Patrons, uniformly men and, with the exception of Spender, uniformly locals, gathered in clusters, engaged in conversation, around the barroom. Minutes passed. Eventually, having bided his time, and feeling that he blended into the background, he reached underneath his coat and grabbed hold of the Zeiss Contax that he was hiding there, allowing its lens to peek out between two buttons and positioning the apparatus on the counter of the bar in a well-practiced gesture. Tilting the 35mm camera just so, he framed his shot, sight unseen, in such a way that he knew he would capture the patrons sitting around a table 10 or 12 feet away. He snapped his picture.[2]

It was not a success. In carrying out the delicate negotiation that any surreptitious photographer must, between accurate framing and focus on the one hand and covertness on the other, Spender had erred on the side of visibility—he had

Fig. 12.1: Humphrey Spender, photograph of a pub in Bolton, 1938. © Bolton Council.

unwittingly revealed himself as an "observer," a member of the class of outsiders with which the town in question was, at this moment in history, crawling. The photograph that resulted bears the marks of this misstep: A patron in the back corner of the pub, seated with two associates, waves Spender off with exasperation on his face; others turn to stare (Figure 12.1). The unfamiliar young man has been exposed. Years later, Spender reflected on the circumstances of this picture, recalling, "This was a threat, this was 'get out', I probably felt nervous. I found that once I was noticed—once you were the object of everyone's attention—you'd finished. My main anxiety, purpose, was to become invisible and to make my equipment invisible" (1977).

This photograph is part of a collection of about 900 images that comprise Spender's Worktown series, which he produced over the course of several short, intermittent visits to Bolton, in the north of England, in 1937 and 1938. Spender took them while serving as the one-man photography division of Mass Observation[3] (MO), a grassroots sociological research group concerned with documenting everyday life in Britain. Influenced by socialist politics, experimental ethnographic methods, and a preoccupation with the unconscious, MO's social research—led by Tom Harrisson, an anthropologist; Charles Madge, a surrealist poet and sociologist; and Humphrey Jennings, a documentary filmmaker—was premised on the belief that ethnographic subjects could be represented with optimal authenticity only when they were unaware that they were being observed. The significance of Spender's project—initially conceived as a visual complement to MO's fieldwork—extends beyond visual ethnography, and even beyond photographic history: his photographs encapsulate a broader "way of seeing" that crystallized in the years between the World Wars, one premised on a belief that the camera could best expose socially and politically progressive truths only when it was itself hidden.

AGAINST THE PICTURESQUE: SPENDER BEFORE MASS OBSERVATION

Spender joined MO in the spring of 1937, at the age of 27.[4] "Guilt about my privileged status together with rather woolly motives to 'make the world a better place'" had moved him to take up documentary photography a couple of years earlier (Spender, 1987, p. 15). Hailing from a liberal-intellectual North London family, he was first introduced to the organization by Harrisson, who had become friends with Spender's eldest brother, Michael, while the two were on an anthropological expedition together. Humphrey Spender had trained at the Architectural Association in London and had had a brief career as an architect, but he had become increasingly frustrated with the stylistic orthodoxy that his job demanded; as an avowed modernist with an interest in Bauhaus architecture, he bristled at continually being asked to design staid, neoclassical buildings. He later claimed that after he included a dog urinating on a lamppost in one of his architectural drawings, he was let go (Spender, 1992). Deciding that architectural practice was not his path, Spender, who had long enjoyed photography as a hobby, opened a small photography studio on the Strand with his friend William Edmiston. Though Edmiston knew very little about photography, the studio ended up becoming quite successful, with lucrative commissions for commercial photography as well as assignments for the *Architectural Review* and *Harper's Bazaar* (1992). Spender lamented that much of his time was spent taking "incredibly boring pictures of batteries, of cold cream jars, of cosmetics"—unappealing subjects for Spender, who "thought that photographs were very, very dull without people in them" (R. Spender, 2011).

The following year, in 1934, Spender was recruited to work at the *Daily Mirror*, and he left the studio in Edmiston's hands. Handpicked for the job by the newspaper's editor, Guy Bartholomew, Spender worked under the alias of "Lensman" from 1934 to 1938.[5] Under Bartholomew's editorship, the *Mirror* was in the process of transforming from a conservative paper with a predominantly middle-class readership to a left-leaning tabloid aimed squarely at the working class.

It presented Spender as a roving chronicler who would, in his words, "inject … an element of Art" to accompany the "newsy and girlie-type photographs" that were more typical of the newspaper (1987, p. 11). Spender quickly lost his enthusiasm for this job. Despite the fact that he had been hired to take "artistic" documentary photographs, a designation that suggested that he would have a measure of creative freedom and that his photographs would have an element of truth-value, Spender became convinced that his editors appreciated neither aesthetic innovation nor unvarnished honesty. He was frequently pressured to stage his photographs in order to ensure suitably predictable and pleasant results, ones that would be consistent with the decidedly lowbrow orientation of the tabloid. In Spender's words, the desired aesthetic was one of "picturesqueness … caricature art … Welsh national costume, spinning wheels and so on" (1996). He was also consistently frustrated by the titles and captions that his editors presented alongside his photographs. In a representative example, one "Lensman study" depicts a road-sweeper on a dramatically lit road in Middlesex pausing his work "to greet an old pal and admire the glowing tints during a brief spell of sunshine." The headline accompanying the image reads, "Nice Mornin', Joe—No Fog Here."[6] Captioning photographs is always a fraught practice—in assigning a textual supplement to a photographic image, one invariably shapes the meaning of that photograph—and in this instance, the hackneyed nature of the sentiments that these captions expressed only added to the banality of the predetermined formula. Spender later elaborated on his frustrations with the *Daily Mirror*'s privileging of the cannily constructed, clichéd photograph:

> When I was working for the *Mirror*, I got to absolutely despise the set-up photography that was around with Fleet Street cameramen. … The "five-pound photograph"—you choose a character and you say "do this" and "do that" and "don't look at the camera" and "don't smile" and so on, that kind of thing. So that pushed me very far to the other attitude, that the people don't know they're being photographed, it's got to be a natural kind of thing. (1996)

The media environment of the 1930s had developed in such a way that there was both a widespread desire for, and a conceivable method of attaining, the kind of images that Spender wanted to purvey: unposed images of ordinary people who, far from being instructed on how to act in front of the camera, did not even know that they were being photographed. The camera that Spender used, a compact Zeiss Contax that used 35mm film, was one he had selected specifically for its discretion; Spender noted that it "was even quieter than a Leica; it had a shutter sound like a kiss" ("The Forgotten North," p. 86). This sort of camera was, at the time of these projects, a relative novelty, and Spender had been recruited to work for MO partly because he was one of the few professional photographers who could use one skillfully.

The Leica, the first widely popular 35mm camera, had come on the market in 1925.[7] For the news photographer, it had many advantages over the bulky, unwieldy plate cameras that most professional photographers used at the time. These large-format cameras required time-consuming setup, compromised the photographer's mobility, and ensured his or her visibility. The consequence for press photographs was that they lacked spontaneity: the photojournalism that predominated was necessarily "photography by consent," posed news images in which subjects lined up, said cheese, and had their likenesses taken. According to Tom Hopkinson, "One could no more 'steal' pictures [with a large-format press camera] than you could ride a motorcycle unnoticed into a cathedral" (1984, p. 6). With the emergence of the 35mm camera came many proclamations about the new possibilities that these apparatuses opened up for photographers, particularly news photographers. As one photojournalist of the era observed, "The Leica was the first miniature camera which the new photo reporter could use as the extension of his eye, instead of his eye being the slave of the instrument" (Gidal, 1999, p. 74). It became possible take pictures that were much more informal than had previously been possible—to capture everyday life in action, rather than posing it before the camera.

Spender's attitude toward photographing came to be predicated on his dissatisfaction with the *Daily Mirror*'s means of representing human life and customs, which he saw as a betrayal of the documentary photograph's obligation to represent reality in a truthful and unmediated manner. Initially at the *Mirror*, Spender was prohibited from using the 35mm camera, because the film that the camera required didn't allow for the careful retouching that the publication was used to practicing on the photographs it printed; as a tabloid, the *Mirror* was probably bolder than most newspapers in its doctoring of photographs. As Spender recalled later in life, "I'd had a great deal of trouble in getting the use of a 35mm camera involved in the *Daily Mirror*, because on a 35mm negative, they couldn't retouch—they couldn't slice large chunks of flesh off girlie-whirly thighs and so on" (1992). However, he persisted, and grudgingly, the *Mirror* increasingly accepted his undoctorable images. Spender remained staunchly opposed to acts of manipulation throughout his career as a photographer; Rachel Spender, his widow, recalls that he saw even the commonplace act of cropping photographs "as composing after the event, and extracting something that was actually there. He might actually have seen it as a lie" (R. Spender, 2011). Accordingly, he filed down his negative holders so that his negatives bore their natural edges and his prints were demonstrably uncropped. In subtly working to undermine the *Mirror*'s tabloid aesthetic, Spender saw himself as rejecting the tendency of the mass media to heavy-handedly "author" the lived experiences of real people. The ultimate antidote to the kind of misrepresentation he was pressured to practice in the *Daily Mirror* came through his work for MO, in the form of a scrupulously concealed camera. In order to offer what he saw as a more "authentic" and unauthored representation of everyday life in Bolton, Spender hid his camera, photographing his subjects unawares as they engaged in the activities that constituted their everyday lives.

"THE DRAMA OF THE DOORSTEP": BRITISH DOCUMENTARY AND THE EVERYDAY

Mass Observation's effort to ascertain and understand the will of ordinary British people was predicated on its founders' shared suspicion of the prevailing ways in which "the masses" were being represented by the political establishment and the mass media. This misrepresentation, Tom Harrisson writes, came in the form of:

> a very serious communications gap that divided the published opinion of political speech and press editorial from the true public opinion of the endlessly misrepresented "man-in-the-street". As for private opinion, it remained totally in private, obscure. The gap between leader and led, between publication and the mass of the public, between Westminster talk and Lancashire chatter, posed an invisible barrier, a danger in our democracy. (1974, p. 4)

There was great political urgency to the attempt to bridge these two worlds—and to the unprecedented public exposure of the personal lives of "ordinary people"—at this juncture in Britain's history. With the specter of Nazism weighing heavily on many Britons—and the British Union of Fascists, led by Oswald Mosley, boasting disconcertingly large numbers[8]—this moment saw the emergence of a counterbalance, a cluster of efforts to valorize the experiences of, and gain the support of, the working classes. MO was one element of this broader effort to assign ordinary Britons greater visibility. A similar set of priorities is discernible in organizations like the Left Book Club, a left-leaning book-of-the-month club spearheaded by the publisher Victor Gollancz that launched in 1936 and aimed at galvanizing British people, particularly the working classes, against fascism. This tendency is also clear in the populist tenor of many of the films to come out of the British documentary movement of the 1930s; a notable example, the MO cofounder Humphrey Jennings's 1939 film, *Spare Time*, which premiered at the New York World's Fair of that year, took as its subject matter the ways ordinary people—steelworkers, cotton mill laborers—spent their leisure time. Cultural forces like these imputed a new sense of urgency to the project of documenting, and implicitly attesting to the importance of, the everyman. John Grierson noted, in 1939, that he and others of the British documentary movement sought to draw the public's attention to "the drama of the doorstep": the profundity of ordinary life. This new attention to everyday life was believed to have far-reaching political implications: as Grierson recalls, "We were, I confess ... a little worried about the way the world was going. ...

We were interested in all instruments which would crystallize sentiments in a muddled world and create a will towards civic participation" (1966, p. 18).

The movement that emerged sought to expose and to valorize the experiences and sentiments of ordinary people—the collective—rather than focusing attention on a powerful and visible leader, and without recourse to the mythical "folk" of fascism.[9] In the first MO pamphlet, issued in 1937, the organization's founders stressed the historic significance of their moment: "The atavism of the new Germany and the revival of racial superstition have forced the issue home to many. We are all in danger of extinction from such outbursts of atavism" (Harrisson & Madge, 1937, p. 11). The rise of fascism in Germany and Italy galvanized many British institutions and groups on the Left to cast a critical eye on power imbalances within their own nation, and particularly on its deeply entrenched class system. Spender's photographs, for Mass Observation and elsewhere, offered a visual analogue of this development.[10]

"PROBLEMS OF ARTIFICIALITY" AND THE LIMITS OF OBSERVATION

With MO, Spender's role was to provide a visual corollary to the written records that the volunteer observers compiled in Bolton and Blackpool, and as with the textual records that the "observers" collected, Spender's photographs attempted surreptitiousness because this was seen as the only failsafe route to accurate representation. This anxiety around accurate representation—which the textual "observers" saw as the main problem with simply interviewing ethnographic subjects, and that Spender perceived in photographing people who were aware that they were being photographed—reflects an early awareness of what has come to be known colloquially, in the social sciences, as the "observer's paradox": the fact that in observing a foreign culture, the ethnographer inexorably alters it by the very fact of his or her presence. As Harrisson later wrote of his time "observing" in Bolton:

> We did not think that you could short-cut to the truth by asking strangers in the street or on the doorstep what they thought about every subject. What you say to a stranger is never going to represent the whole depth of your understanding or interest; and it may either consciously or unconsciously misrepresent it, sometimes very seriously … [therefore,] it was essential to do exactly the opposite of the modern interviewer. We must not produce "stranger situations." We must become assimilated into the society we were studying, and all the parts of it. Therefore, our observers joined each of the political parties, every conceivable club, pub, society, corner organization and gang that he/she could get into in the several levels of Worktown life. … Observers were trained to observe and record on the spot without being noticed, so that everything went on as if there was no stranger in

> the midst. He or she was not a stranger, merely a participant, invisibly controlled and disciplined from outside, reporting continuously to headquarters. (1943, pp. 9–10)

MO's approach, then, was one of participant observation: In the interest of attempting to offer an optimally "pure" depiction of the people of Bolton, one that was unaltered by the presence of foreign observers, the MO volunteers attempted to blend in seamlessly with the "natives" whose habits they studied. Often, this was difficult because of the extreme differences in accent and deportment between the working-class Northerners that comprised most of Bolton's population and the generally well-educated, well-off young men who were doing the observing. Spender recalled, "For me to go into a North Country pub and really speaking a completely different language, and to be a kind of 'Hail fellow, well met' person was very embarrassing" (1977, p. 3). Even so, in Bolton, the MO volunteers had one distinct advantage: Bolton residents' disbelief that anyone would visit the city merely out of a desire to learn about its people. Harrisson later recalled, "For one thing, no worker in their right senses ever supposed that anyone came to work in Worktown for any reason other than necessity. Likewise, it rarely occurred to anyone then that someone else might want to observe, let alone record, their common actions" (1943, p. 11).

The need to remain undetected shaped Spender's photographs in material ways. Certain places were simply off-limits, including, significantly, the interiors of people's homes, because here, "stranger situations" would invariably result. As Spender recalled, "Photographing of interiors implied setting up the whole scene. Because immediately you go into someone's house, they're very much on their pride, and they want the house to look good, and they'd probably delay your arrival until they'd considerably altered the whole arrangement of the house." This, in Spender's mind, amounted to a "problem of artificiality" (1996). Also unacceptable was the use of flash, since this inevitably stunned the subjects being photographed and exposed Spender as a photographer, which would likely lead to some uncomfortable confrontations. Spender, a retiring and rather sensitive individual, had no interest in interactions of this sort. Spender's photographs in Bolton, then, are overwhelmingly photographs of people in public places, shot with available light. Because of both the restrictions on where Spender could photograph undetected and the sorts of scenes he was encouraged to capture, Spender's photographs tended to be of communal events and venues that he and other MO members regarded as representative of ordinary Bolton life. In these images, prominent exposure is given to sports matches, political rallies, and scenes of street life, particularly markets, where Spender's subjects are often engrossed in signs, displays, and sales pitches (Figure 12.2). The emphasis, then, is necessarily on groups rather than individuals. For Spender, this focus on the collective was in part a consequence of his desire to be undetected as a photographer, to operate as a fly on the wall. He described his photographing methods, and the images that resulted from them, as "answers to the problem of people not looking at the camera" (1996). Interested

Fig. 12.2: Humphrey Spender, photograph of an open market in Bolton, 1937. © Bolton Council.

above all else in photographing his subjects unawares, Spender gravitated toward situations where those subjects would be less inclined to be paying attention to the unfamiliar man fumbling around in his jacket pockets. Rather than intimacy and individualism, then, Spender's photographs emphasize praxis and community, showing his subjects among their families, friends, colleagues, or simply fellow city dwellers. Capturing his subjects engaging in the activities that make up their quotidian existences, Spender's photographs suggest that selfhood is, in fact, constituted through the practice of everyday life.

While Spender was vehemently opposed to staging his photographs, he nonetheless struggled with the question of affective proximity to his subjects. While Harrisson, with his background in anthropology, stressed that Spender should operate at an ethnographic remove from his subjects—Spender described this as "a kind of innocent, as-though-from-Mars attitude" (1977)—Spender seems to have resisted the pressure to detach himself fully, perhaps because he knew that such detachment was ultimately impossible. He felt he could not fully heed Harrisson's call to "stand right outside [British culture] and look at it from a distance" (1982b), believing that Harrisson's impassioned bid for an estranged view of the English people was itself deceptive in its didacticism. Nor could he be confident that the photographs he offered were, as Harrisson had hoped that they would be, a neutral, unmediated, "pure recording" of their subjects. Harrisson's insistence was so strong that Spender's own attitude, he said,

> became rather obstinate. In a rather perverse way I think I was almost trying to disprove his points. So my own conclusion was that I would avoid loaded photographs, I would avoid caricature as far as I could. I would avoid picking out peculiar behavior. I would try and present general truths. (1982b)

Even so, Spender could not operate with the sort of detachment that he was told to practice. "Maybe this is one of the reasons why the photographs have been rather a success is that I do feel a kind of empathy towards—just looking at people," he later recalled. "I feel I don't want to do anything but sympathise with them" (1982b).

THE POLITICS OF VISIBILITY

In Spender's photographs, for MO and elsewhere, the photographer's sympathy is present at the level of form; in the illustrated press of the period, treatments of the rift between the powerful and the disempowered were frequently couched in a rhetoric of visibility. This is precisely what we see in Spender's photo essay, "The Men Baldwin Would Not See," which appeared in the *Left Review*, a journal associated with Victor Gollancz's Left Book Club, in 1936. Spender photographed the last leg of the Jarrow hunger marchers' journey to London to deliver their petition to Stanley Baldwin, then the prime minister. The marchers demanded manufacturing jobs in their region, which had recently reported an unemployment rate of 73% (Wilkinson, 1939, p. 256). But perhaps a more immediate aim was to gain acknowledgment—to be countenanced by a prime minister who had for many years turned a blind eye to the grinding poverty in England's industrial north. Baldwin refused to meet with the marchers, hence the title of the article. Spender's photographic chronicle of the march offered the marchers a degree of exposure—and recognition—that Baldwin had not granted them. It also couched in concrete, visual terms the power imbalance that typified the British political establishment's treatment of people living in Northern England's so-called distressed areas.

Picture Post, a singularly popular, photographically illustrated magazine that was launched in London in 1938, and which Spender began work for immediately after completing his Worktown photographs, offers a visual vocabulary that seems to reflect a growing understanding of the significance of the act of observing and being observed. A photo essay *Picture Post* published in 1938 foregrounds the acts of looking and of being seen, and the relationship of these conditions to power (Figure 12.3). Londoners stare expectantly at the door of the prime minister's residence, waiting for any kind of news, and we gaze at them who are in turn gazing at the house of their leader—who will not reciprocate their act of looking. Spender's photographs frequently feature this visual trope: the members of the crowd, standing and looking at some point that lies outside the frame.

Fig. 12.3: "The World Looks at No. 10," Picture Post, October 1, 1938, pp. 10-11. © Hulton Archive, Getty Images.

These citizens, rather than the prominent figures they are straining to see, are the subjects of interest. To represent the underclasses—to make them visible—was a strong political statement in itself at this time: as Stuart Hall has argued, the illustrated magazines of this period raised "the 'unnoticed subjects' to a sort of equality of status, photographically, with the heroic subjects (Prime Ministers) and the activities they elsewhere depict. This is the beginning of the democratization of the subject in photography" (1972, p. 83).

Clearly, though, merely taking photographs of the many, while a progressive step in the context of documentary photography in Britain, was not inherently tantamount to a democratic, participatory aesthetic. Just as important as the subjects of the photographs that Spender took were the visual modalities through which the photographs represented those subjects: the ways in which documentary photographs presented their subjects to the spectator, and the kind of relationship that this representation established between spectator and photographic subject. With the rise of *Picture Post* and other photographically illustrated magazines, readers were not only given access to a uniform repertoire of photographs—they were also, quite suddenly, brought into a newly immersive relationship to photography. While earlier magazines and newspapers had featured considerable numbers of photographs, nowhere was documentary and journalistic photography as copious and as widely accessible to the masses as on the pages of *Picture Post*, *Life*, and other magazines whose primary sources of interest were their abundant photo essays. Critical to the new modes of visual address that these magazines introduced was the reflexivity that they often demonstrated around the act of looking: within a couple of representative issues of *Picture Post*, the readership is called upon to look at the spectators at a wrestling match, to observe how Americans look at war, and even to guess what a smattering of lookers are looking at. In features like these, the power dynamics more traditionally associated with journalistic and documentary photography—in which spectators gaze reverently at the powerful or pityingly at the abject—are here confounded in favor of a documentary style that foregrounds proximity and contiguity rather than difference.

The same tendency is discernible earlier, in Spender's MO photographs. The modes of address that Spender employed in his Worktown photographs—the formal characteristics through which he represented his subjects—were as important as their content. To some degree, the photographing of bystanders engaged in the act of looking was simply a way of managing a lingering deficiency in the compact cameras of the 1930s. Because of the relatively long shutter speeds of even the best cameras at this point, Spender photographed people at moments of stillness rather than movement whenever he could, in order to achieve crisp and unblurred images. Frequently, he photographed onlookers with their gazes fixed on something beyond the frame: The photograph that results feels immersive; as if one is thrust into the middle of the scene rather than watching it at a remove (Figure 12.4). As the spectators, we see these images of people who do not meet the gaze of the photographer but are instead absorbed in the act of looking themselves. These photographs of people who, unaware of the photographer, do not meet his gaze, refuse to confirm existing power relationships seen in most documentary photographs by offering a clear distinction between the observer—an active subject—and the observed, who is passive. The spectator looking at Spender's photograph is not in a position of comfortable mastery anymore.

Rather than examining the photograph's subjects at a remove, we have the more empathic experience of feeling as though we, too, are within the frame. That seamlessness between the spectator and the people pictured was precisely Spender's goal, part of his project of making his images look natural, unposed, and unmediated, which often was, as he said, "all a matter of trickery, really, deceit. The great objective was usually to avoid suspicion, because people looking suspicious are people looking unnatural" (1982a, p. 19). Spender's photographs thus employ a particular, historically specific kind of realism: aiming for naturalness, they attempt to produce an anonymous yet empathetic record rather than a work that bears the mark of its maker. The frontal, forthright exchange that typifies many documentary photographs of human subjects, drawing attention to the photographic event's distance from "real life," is here elided in favor of a photography that attempts, with varying levels of success, to blend in

Fig. 12.4: Humphrey Spender, photograph of a Central League football game at Burnden Park, Bolton, in 1937. © Bolton Council.

seamlessly with the world it depicts. What Spender's hidden camera ultimately exposes is a constellation of heretofore hidden, yet immensely politically significant, acts of looking.

NOTES

1. This chapter owes a great debt to Rachel Spender, whose insight and generosity with her time enriched my analysis of Spender and his work. For their assistance as I conducted research on Spender's photography and on Mass Observation, I would like to thank the staff of the Mass Observation Archive, the British Library Sound Archive, and the Bolton Museum. Thanks are also due to the Bolton Council for permission to publish Spender's photographs in this volume.
2. The details of this occurrence come from Humphrey Spender's "Observation of Saddle Hotel [Saddle Inn]," written in January 1938. This document appears in the digital archive *Bolton Worktown: Photography and Archives from the Mass-Observation*. Mass Observation Archive, reproduced by Adam Matthew Digital. Retrieved from http://boltonworktown.co.uk/mass-observation-archives/saddle-hotel-3/
3. While the organization originally referred to itself as "Mass-Observation," I have here opted to employ the punctuation that the organization, and its archive, now use—"Mass Observation"—except where I would be manipulating source material in doing so.

4. For an excellent introduction to Spender's work before, during, and after Mass Observation, see Deborah Frizzell's exhibition catalogue, *Humphrey Spender's Humanist Landscapes* (New Haven, CT: Yale Center for British Art, 1997).
5. Spender would end up sharing the "Lensman" title with at least one other well-known photographer, Felix Man, but Spender was convinced that he was the original Lensman.
6. The *Daily Mirror* issue in question is that of December 4, 1934.
7. Oskar Barnack, of the German camera company Leitz, developed the Leica (a name derived from "Leitz Camera") around the idea of a still camera that made use of 35mm film, a film size that, at that time, was used primarily for cinema rather than still images. While Barnack began experimenting with this format as early as 1913, the First World War and Germany's subsequent economic strife delayed the release of the Leica, which ultimately came out in 1925. The Zeiss Contax, introduced in 1932, was another 35mm still camera that came to be a major competitor of the Leica. On the history of the Leica and the miniature cameras that preceded it, see Erich Stenger, *Die Geschichte der Kleinbildkamera bis zur Leica* (Frankfurt am Main, Germany: Umschau Verlag, 1949). In English, see Helmut Gernsheim, *A Concise History of Photography*, 3rd ed. (Mineola, NY: Dover, 1986).
8. Of the British Union of Fascists, Richard Thurlow writes: "There is some debate over how many members the BUF attained but if it is assumed that there were one and a half inactive supporters to every paid-up active member then the estimates that supporters in total amounted to between 40,000 and 50,000 in 1934, collapsed to about 5,000 in 1935 and gradually recovered to approach 20,000 in 1939, are probably accurate." *Fascism in Britain: A History, 1918–1945* (London, England: I. B. Tauris, 1998), 140.
9. Certainly, in the 1930s, photography also served as a potent means of establishing and entrenching a specifically Nazi ideal of "the people." German photographers like Erna Lendvai-Dircksen, who took photographs for the 1932 photo books *Unsere deutschen Kinder* (*Our German Children*) and *Das deutsche Volksgesicht* (*German Folk Faces*), among many others, offered an ideologically charged approach to representing the German populace; her photographs presented a racially homogenous rendering of the German people, one that was limited to subjects that looked "Aryan," strong, and healthy. Anne Maxwell writes of Lendvai-Dircksen that her photographs' "primary motivation … was to celebrate the purity of the bloodlines and the patriotic strength of the Germanic peoples living both within and outside the Rhineland, an idea that was very much in keeping with the concept of Volk, and indeed Nazi ideas about the racial unity of the Germanic peoples scattered throughout Europe." Maxwell, *Picture Imperfect: Photography and Eugenics, 1870–1940* (Eastbourne, England: Sussex Academic, 2008), 198.
10. The British Left and the British Fascists' clashing attitudes toward transparency became very clear to Spender when he attempted to photograph a rally led by Oswald Mosley of the British Union of Fascists. Spender recalls, "When I attempted to photograph the British Fascist Movement at Albert Hall, I was very forcibly removed although I was photographing objectively. No prints of that remain." The Forgotten North. (1982, April 17). *What Camera Weekly*, p. 85.

BIBLIOGRAPHY

The Forgotten North. (1982, April 17). *What Camera Weekly*, pp. 84–86.

Gidal, T. (1999). Modern photojournalism: The first years. In David Brittain (Ed.), *Creative camera: Thirty years of writing* (pp. 73–80). Manchester, England: Manchester University Press.

Grierson, J. (1939). The story of the documentary film. *Fortnightly Review, 152*(146), 121–130.
Grierson, J. (1966). *Grierson on documentary.* Berkeley & Los Angeles: University of California Press.
Hall, S. (1972). The social eye of *Picture Post.* In *Working Papers in Cultural Studies*, No. 2 (pp. 71–120). Birmingham, England: Centre for Contemporary Cultural Studies.
Harrisson, T. (1943). *The pub and the people.* London, England: Seven Dials.
Harrisson, T. (1974, April 20). *Looking at life: The eye and the camera.* Unpublished manuscript, Mass Observation Archive, Brighton, England.
Harrisson, T., & Madge, C. (1937). *Mass-observation.* London, England: Frederick Muller.
Hopkinson, T. (1984). *Picture Post 1938–1950.* London, England: Chatto & Windus.
Spender, H. (1938, January). Observation of Saddle Hotel [Saddle Inn]. *Bolton Worktown: Photography and archives from the Mass-Observation.* Mass Observation Archive, reproduced by Adam Matthew Digital. Retrieved from http://boltonworktown.co.uk/mass-observation-archives/saddle-hotel-3/
Spender, H. (1977, July 27). Interview with Derek Smith [Audio recording]. Brighton, England: Mass Observation Archive.
Spender, H. (1982a). Interview with Jeremy Mulford. In H. Spender, *Worktown People* (pp. 11–24). Bristol, England: Falling Wall.
Spender, H. (1982b, February 4). Interview on Kaleidoscope, BBC Radio 4 [Audio recording]. Brighton, England: Mass Observation Archive.
Spender, H. (1987). *Lensman: Photographs 1932–52.* London, England: Chatto & Windus.
Spender, H. (1992). Interview with Grace Robertson [Audio recording]. London, England: Oral History of British Photography Collection, British Library Sound Archive.
Spender, H. (1996, December 13). Interview with Ken Howarth [Audio recording]. Bolton, England: Bolton Museum and Archive Service.
Spender, R. (2011, July 12). Personal interview. Humphrey Spender Studio and Archive, Ulting, England.
Wilkinson, E. (1939). *The town that was murdered: The life-story of Jarrow.* London, England: Victor Gollancz.

CHAPTER THIRTEEN

Materiality

Challenges and Opportunities for Communication Theory

GINA NEFF, BRITTANY FIORE-SILFVAST, AND
CARRIE STURTS DOSSICK

Increasingly, communication researchers are issuing calls for attention to the role materiality plays in communication processes (e.g., Boczkowski, 2004; Boczkowski & Lievrouw, 2008; Leonardi & Barley, 2008; Leonardi, Nardi, & Kallinikos, 2013; Lievrouw, 2014). Resulting in part from the challenges of studying new communication and information technologies, this new focus on materiality offers opportunities for communication researchers to theorize beyond communication through, with, and, in some cases, without a medium to think about the material structures of mediation itself. In this chapter we propose a model for thinking through the communicative roles and functions of the materiality of everyday objects, by using one type of objects, documents, as an extended theoretical example of the importance of materiality for communication.

We argue that documents' material functions are distinct from (and occasionally orthogonal to) any textual or symbolic meanings those documents may convey. Without understanding the importance of material roles and functions for meaning, communication scholars cannot explain fully how people communicate with, through, and around everyday objects. While our field has a rich theoretical toolkit for understanding the meaning and meanings of things and representations, we struggle to make sense of what things can do in social settings. Material processes in communication have been undertheorized in contemporary communication scholarship, and when material processes have been addressed in our field, it has usually been through the lens of the social and cultural meanings and framings of those objects (Lievrouw, 2014). Our model focuses on the instrumental and functional roles objects play in social interactions, group settings, and institutional contexts. This chapter extends current communication theory on the material processes of communication by providing a detailed model for understanding documents' material roles, identifying the emergent tensions among them, and tracing dynamics of the social practices around, through, and with documents in these interactions. We include three key roles for objects in communication in this model: documentation, circulation, and conversation.

Documents—from the ephemeral to the contractual—serve as a useful example of everyday materiality. Our view sees documents as both mediated through a web of everyday objects to form "work-oriented infrastructure" (Nicolini et al., 2012; Star & Ruhleder, 1996) and as mediated through communication processes. Of course, documents convey textual and symbolic meanings and interpretations. Our goal here is to map a set of theories for scholars to begin including the communicative work that is accomplished through documents' material affordances, and hopefully by extension, through the material affordances of other kinds of artifacts. Documents are interesting because they are widely studied as texts, and yet relatively ignored materially as artifacts that operate in social settings. Documents must often serve multiple, conflicting roles, such as documenting decisions, establishing patterns of circulation among people and artifacts, and providing the material "sites" for ongoing conversations. While the use of documents as representing symbolic communication—what documents mean and "say"—is widely addressed in scholarly literature, documents' instrumental functions are also important for understanding the full complexity of artifacts within communication.

A media lens on documents focuses on their crucial roles in creating, stabilizing, and disseminating information. Documents form the basis of modern bureaucratic authority (Weber, 1947), the means of "control through communication" (Yates, 1989), and tools of "working knowledge" (Davenport & Prusak, 1998). As both tools of the process of organizing and products of that process, documents serve multiple roles within organizations and groups—as records or archives of decisions (what we term *documentation*), as communiqués connecting people and ideas across space and time (what we term *circulation*), and as tools of "epistemic cultures" (Knorr Cetina, 1999), or things to think with and through in what has been termed "sites of conversation" (Taylor & Van Every, 2000). Yet, the importance of materiality across these roles is often neglected, especially during the introduction of new information technologies and in organizational efficiency efforts when documents are framed as simply neutral artifacts that deliver neutral knowledge and information (Sellen & Harper, 2002).

Documents are a particular type of organizational artifact embedded in particular institutional contexts and social routines, and become "artifacts of modern knowledge practices" (Riles, 2006, p. 7). Our focus on documents emerges from an ethnography of information sharing in contemporary construction, where contract documents define the teams, building plans, and specifications communicate the workflow, sketching is a key visual communication technique, and new information technologies have disrupted long-established document practices (Dossick & Neff, 2011; Neff, Fiore-Silfvast, & Dossick, 2010). In our empirical work we define documents in a broad sense to incorporate paper documents, digital documents, and other material artifacts of organizing, such as logs, drawings, lists, meeting minutes, memos, sketches, and agendas. Documents can be intended as ephemeral tools for communication, such as quickly written notes or messages, or as durable records, as in the case of documents intended for legal purposes. In the process of studying a site as it struggled to replace paper documentation practices with new communication information technologies, we came to think through documents' material affordances, durabilities, and malleabilities. In this chapter we focus on theories of documents' functional roles, and, as such, address here primarily these material affordances of paper documents.

This is not to dismiss the textual and symbolic roles documents play in communication. Documents form the basis of shared understanding. Documents provide an important source of shared texts, establishing the surfaces for conversation and the coordination of organizational activity (Taylor & Robichaud, 2004; Taylor & Van Every, 2000). In other words, documents can give people a starting place for conversation, decision making, and action. Documents often integrate multiple conversations, perspectives, and dimensions (Pratt & Rafaeli, 2006, p. 285). For example, Kaghan and Lounsbury (2006, p. 275) describe the need for articulation work around a written contract both to provide a record of a legitimate "meeting of minds" while also helping to move the team forward. Similarly, meeting minutes can serve as a record to account for multiple interdependent agendas, as a legal record of decisions of the participants, and as a logistical tool for coordinating future action. Once created, documents such as contracts and meeting minutes can then be appropriated as a tool of authority to hold others accountable for tasks, both mediating and materializing distributed authority. How, then, do the material affordances of documents provide a way to think through these different functions? We saw many times through the course of our ethnography the need to reconfigure information among verbal, digital, and paper forms to serve different needs for different constituencies. There was a heightened awareness that written documentation was always also legal documentation. How, then, do the material roles documents play serve to communicate meaning in social settings? Does theorizing a role for materiality challenge existing communication theories or provide a useful extension at a point in time when scholars are grappling with how to think about materiality in a wide range of settings?

Our chapter proceeds as follows: First, we cover the existing theory on documents and material artifacts in organizations and teams to produce a typology of document roles and to propose a descriptive model of the material process of communication. Then, we present the theoretical implications of our model of document roles for bringing a lens of mediation to our understanding of the roles of material artifacts in organizations. People's social and material practices with, around, and through documents reflect and constitute the material structures of mediation. Thus, a lens of mediation reveals the importance of the social and material functions of documents, beyond just its textual meanings, in the process of communication.

A TYPOLOGY OF DOCUMENTS' ROLES

Reading the literature on communication and institutions, documents' material roles include three key functions: (1) documentation, (2) circulation, and (3) conversation. First, documents stabilize situations, groups, and organizations through the practices of recording and documenting. They are the material outcome of "communities of conversationalists" (Taylor & Van Every, 2000, p. 32), which provide a record of a meeting of minds (Kaghan & Lounsbury, 2006). Second, documents define circulation patterns and pathways within the organization—both the document distribution pathways and the ways people circulate around them. Documents carry information across contexts while "enforc[ing] humans to follow specific organizational pathways" (Cooren, 2004, p. 388). As such, a single document can embody multiple social courses of action (Harper, 1998). Third, documents activate the process of organizing by being the basis for multiple conversations among actors. Rather than functioning solely to document what is known, documents acting as sites of conversation are the material technologies that shape the process that Kuhn and Jackson (2008) call "accomplishing knowledge," in which people frame, reframe, and resolve problematic situations in order to realize a capacity to act (p. 461). Documents make problems and solutions visible and thinkable, functioning as "epistemic objects" (Knorr Cetina, 1999). Thus, documents can be both a way of communicating knowledge and a means of knowing (Whyte et al., 2008). In the rest of this section, we draw from the literature to characterize and define each of these roles in turn, and in Table 13.1 we summarize the communication literature around each of these three functions.

Documenting Organizational Decisions

Documents comprise organizational records. Documents inscribe, translate, and generate meaning, embodying organizational memory or local knowledge across time and space (Ewenstein & Whyte, 2009; Hutchins, 1995; Latour, 2005). They serve as "immutable mobiles" (Latour, 1987, pp. 226–230). As documentation, documents function to mediate organizational practices of producing authority

Table 13.1 Document Roles Defined in the Literature

Role	Documentation	Circulation	Conversation
Definition	Documenting decisions and history	Circulating among organizational actors	Conversing at a material site
Documents are ...	records of a "meeting of minds" (Kaghan & Lounsbury, 2006)	"institutionalized template[s] for social interaction" (Orlikowski & Yates 1994, p. 542)	"talking things" (Levy, 2005)
	material outcomes of "communities of conversationalists" (Taylor & Van Every, 2000, p. 32)	bureaucratic procedures, configurations of power (Becker & Clark, 2001)	"epistemic objects" (Knorr Cetina, 1999)
	organizational memories (Ewenstein & Whyte, 2009; Hutchins, 1995; Latour, 2005)	multiple social courses of action (Harper, 1997)	sites of organizational communication, informal interaction and "shared Talk" (Taylor & Van Every, 2000; Bechky, 2003)
	"response[s] to a query, pure function" (Riles, 1996, p. 27)	socially legitimated agents (Taylor & Van Every, 2000, p. 32)	"metaindexical," "reference and collaboration grounds" (Henderson, 1999, p. 54)
		"impersonal form[s] of social intelligence based on paper" (Mukerji, 2011, p. 243)	"holding ground[s] and negotiation space[s]" (Henderson, 1999, p. 54)
			conscription and inscription device[s] (Henderson, 1999)
			"social glue" (Henderson, 1999, p. 6)
Documents function to...	inscribe, translate, and generate meaning (Ewenstein & Whyte, 2009; Hutchins, 1995; Latour, 2005)	"enforce humans to follow specific organizational pathways" (Cooren, 2004, p. 388)	"accomplish ... knowledge" (Kuhn & Jackson, 2008, p. 461)

(*Continued*)

Role	Documentation	Circulation	Conversation
	stabilize organizational hierarchy, control information and communication flows, and produce distributed authority (Benoit-Barne & Cooren, 2009; Marvin, 1987; Yates, 1989)	guide and mediate the interactions of a group of people (Ashcraft et al., 2009; Corrent & Taylor, 1997)	enable people to explore what is unknown, contingent, and emergent (Cooren, 2004; Cooren & Fairhurst, 2009; Ewenstein & Whyte, 2009; Knorr Cetina, 1999; Star & Grisemer, 1989; Taylor & Van Every, 2000)
	maintain organizational authority and accountability (Cooren & Fairhurst, 2009; Cooren & Taylor, 1997; McPhee, 1985; Weber, 1947)	"anticipate and enable certain actions by others" (Riles, 2006)	embed or inscribe knowledge, represent ambiguity and incompleteness, move between "focused reasoning and free association" (Ewenstein & Whyte, 2009, p. 22)
	maintain or redistribute occupational divisions and control (Bechky, 2003; Yates, 1989)		capture an idea, enlist group participation, and represent the larger picture (Henderson, 1999, p. 53; Bechky, 2003a)
			support problem solving across organizational boundaries (Bechky, 2003a, 2003b)
			represent and constitute a world recursively (Putnam & Cooren, 2004, p. 324; Orlikowski, 2000)

and accountability and to constitute and maintain a source of organizational order (McPhee, 1985). Scholars have long studied documents' and other artifacts' roles in establishing and maintaining this order (e.g., Gagliardi, 1990; Pratt & Rafaeli, 1997; Kaghan & Lounsbury, 2006). As Weber (1947) reminds us, documents are one of the central communication structures necessary for bureaucratic authority. As a result of the role of documenting, documents define and stabilize organizational hierarchy, control information and communication flows, and produce distributed authority in organizational contexts (Benoit-Barné & Cooren, 2009; Marvin, 1987; Yates, 1989). Documents have affordances that enable them to dislocate interaction and stabilize specific schemas of action, extending into tools of organizational authority and accountability beyond the local interaction to mediate action elsewhere in space or later in time (Cooren & Fairhurst, 2009; Cooren & Taylor, 1997).

Defining Organizational Circulation

We define the circulation role of documents in two ways: (a) the movement of documents across organizational contexts and among stakeholders, as well as (b) the movement of stakeholders in relation to documents. Documents have both formal and informal circulation pathways that define knowledge boundaries. For example, who's in and who's out is defined in part through documents. People also gather around physical documents; libraries and plan rooms are places for both formal and informal gatherings associated with documents. In these ways, documents are genres of organizational communication that are "socially recognized types of communicative action," which can serve as an "institutionalized template for social interaction—an organizing structure" that recursively influences the community's ongoing organizational actions and the genres of organizational communication (Orlikowski & Yates, 1994, p. 542). Documents represent, reinforce, and challenge the distributed authority of a team or bureaucracy, guiding interactions even as they encapsulate the past (Ashcraft, Kuhn, & Cooren, 2009, p. 29). People often produce, circulate, and evaluate documents in anticipation of what that document will do or mean and these actions are often based on previous experiences with documents. How people think documents will be interpreted and received does not necessarily fit with actual practices. Suchman (2007) explains this as "the relationship between structures of action and the resources and constraints afforded by material and social circumstances" (p. 177). Architectural plans, as an example, "achieve their prescriptive efficacy through the contingent labors that they presuppose but leave unspecified" (Suchman, 2007, p. 200). In other words, how people communicate through or with documents is not magically inscribed by a document itself; rather, it is the mediating material structures and labor that make documents function in social interaction.

Thus, it is the social and communicative practices around documents that possess the power to structure patterns of team, group, and organizational communication. Building on Latour's (1994) theory of mediation, Cooren and Taylor (1997) suggest that "non-human actants," such as documents, can mediate the interactions of a group of people, transforming those interactions into a macro-level organizational actor, such as a firm. Vaughan (1997) shows in the case of the shuttle *Challenger* that the moment when objects no longer work is a key opportunity for observation—when the complex social networks and organizational structures in which objects are or cease to be embedded can be more readily seen. Collectively, the circulation of documents can begin to structure an organization, as theorists from the Montreal School of organizational communication have argued. Documents become the "socially legitimated agent or spokesperson that creates the structuring of the community of work into what we usually think of as 'the organization'" (Taylor & Van Every, 2000, p. 32).

Documents, as bureaucratic procedures, can establish and reinforce spatial configurations of power, such as the distancing between administrators and subjects, as well as produce an objective basis for intimate knowledge (Becker & Clark, 2001). Mukerji (2011) suggests subtle changes in the design and practices of paperwork in seventeenth-century France enabled documents to circulate among very different contexts of contracted technical expertise and official political power, allowing documents to function differently in different settings. That is, the communicative power of documents can only be understood in the contextually mediated networks in which they travel and the pathways people travel around them.

Establishing Sites for Conversation

Documents become tools for collaboration and knowledge production by acting as sites for conversation, enabling people to explore what is unknown, contingent, and emergent (Cooren, 2004; Cooren & Fairhurst, 2009; Ewenstein & Whyte, 2009; Knorr Cetina, 1999; Star & Griesemer, 1989; Taylor & Van Every, 2000). Conversation is conceptualized by Taylor and Van Every as the site of organizational communication, as the interaction and shared talk that represent and become the process of organizing. Documents are "talking things" (Levy, 2005); organizational tools and micro-material that people talk and think with, through, and around. Examining the use of visual representations among engineers, Henderson (1999) describes a visual culture whose way of seeing the world "is explicitly linked to actual material experience in rendering that world" (p. 9). Whether documents are capturing an idea, enlisting group participation, or representing the larger picture, in visual cultures documents are the primary means of communication, to the extent that "participants find it difficult to communicate about the design without them" (Henderson, 1999, p. 53; Bechky, 2003a, 2003b). It is often when problems arise or knowledge needs to be shared or generated that teams enroll documents as sites for conversations. Examining the use of artifacts among engineers, technicians, and assemblers in a manufacturing firm,

Bechky finds that knowledge is embedded in their respective occupational contexts of drawing work for the engineers and concrete work of building the machine for the assemblers, making it challenging to accomplish understanding between the two groups. The drawings and machines become useful in problem solving across occupational boundaries as they are enrolled as sites for informal interaction that helps develop common ground and shared understandings. Interaction through sketches or drawings enables their use as a "reference and collaboration ground to unite all these various forms of knowledge for negotiation" (Henderson, 1999, p. 54); the documents quickly become the "social glue between individuals and groups" (Henderson, p. 6).

As teams use documents to establish sites for conversations, they become a means for organizing, acting as epistemic objects for individuals to think with and as the locus of collective knowledge production and distributed cognition (Hutchins, 1995; Henderson, 1995, 1999; Knorr Cetina, 1999; Whyte et al., 2008). It is the conversations with, through, and around documents, in which organizing is made present, local, and emergent. To function as the starting point for further conversation, documents must be flexible and malleable and are by definition incomplete. Documents functioning this way not only embed or inscribe knowledge but also must represent ambiguity and incompleteness, which may be useful for supporting tasks that move between "focused reasoning and free association" (Ewenstein & Whyte, 2009, p. 22) and for problem solving across occupational boundaries (Bechky, 2003a). In the engineering context, documents are used as both conscription and inscription devices, simultaneously serving to capture information interactively and bridge knowledge boundaries as a boundary object (Henderson, 1999). Documents as sites for conversation are what Henderson (1999) calls "meta-indexical," meaning they have the ability to serve as "a holding ground and negotiation space for both explicit and yet-to-be-made-explicit knowledge" (p. 199). Not only do documents in this role both represent and constitute a world recursively (Putnam & Cooren, 2004, p. 324), they also form what Orlikowski (2000) might call "technology-in-practice," providing both the representation of what is possible and knowable and the material structures for the interactions around possibilities and knowledge (p. 410).

TENSIONS AMONG DOCUMENT ROUTINES AND ORGANIZATIONAL NEEDS

While one role may at times be more dominant than others, collectively, documents fulfill all three roles simultaneously. For example, tension arises when an organization becomes fixed in rigid documentation and formal circulation procedures. Documents fall into what Stohl and Cheney (2001) term "the formalization paradox," where "actors try to formalize a process that at its very heart needs to be informal and adaptive to changing situations" (p. 368). The material affordances of documents mean that their roles in providing sites for conversation and for circulating information can often be in tension with the formal, documenting functions of the paper trail. This tension between the need for institutionalized routines and formalized practices and the need for a range of informal, improvised, and spontaneous organizational actions is mediated and materialized in documents and the work people do with documents.

Challenges to the appropriation of authority embodied within documents arise when people circumvent, subvert, disregard, or adapt these documents for purposes other than those initially intended. However, while a document may shape, structure, or even direct organizational activity, its particular agency is not necessarily predetermined by its creators. We propose that rather than remaining fixed or immutable across interactions, documents often need to perform as a "medium of cultural persistence" (Cooren & Taylor, 1997, p. 247), while still maintaining a degree of plasticity and *interpretive flexibility* in both content and circulation that allows them to adapt to the needs of a local interaction or conversation. Dossick and Neff (2011) termed this tension between "clean tech" approaches to sharing information and the "messy talk" that is often required for knowledge creation. That is, to fulfill the multiple roles required for organizing, documents must move from formal to informal, from synchronous to asynchronous and from fixed to fluid and back again, depending on the task at hand. However, these aspects are in tension across the three document roles. For instance, documents need to serve as technologies of accountability (documentation and circulation) and as tools of local, emergent, distributed knowledge production (conversations), revealing a tension between the representation of work processes and the contingent nature of the work itself (Bardram, 1997; Bowers, Button, & Sharrock, 1995; Suchman, 1987, 2007; Turnbull, 1993). Bowker and Star (1999) describe this tension as the dual need for a global ordering system of classification (documentation and circulation) and the emergent local interaction issues (conversations) that continually thwart them.

DISCUSSION

The process of organizing depends on the capacity of documents to record actions, circumscribe the organization, and support collaboration. These three functions follow from documents' material capacities to act in social and communicative settings.

Understanding the roles that documents play in organizations shows how documents are active participants in the constitution of organizations. People do not merely push paper; paper, in the form of materialized organizational roles and routines, begins to push the people around it. This is, as Ashcraft and colleagues (2009) phrased it, how "various human and non-human agencies constitute organization through co-participation in communication" (p. 37). One need not subscribe fully to actor-network theory to begin to take seriously the ways people face material affordances and constraints from and with their documents and see that documents materially perform communicative functions within social settings that are not necessarily dependent on their textual or symbolic meanings. People gather around documents to talk. They pass documents around and in doing so circumscribe their groups, social movements, and organizations. And the material act of committing something to paper serves a powerful function for documenting and stabilizing conversations and their conversationalists.

Our work suggests that organizational failures and inefficiencies around documents have deep roots in the material and cultural practices and routines of document roles. Such examples do not represent breakdown of organizational routine but rather the opposite, an indication of the process of people organizing.

Roles and Fixity

Though malleable to some extent, genres of documents have a social, routinized fixity in their roles. Once documents are cast into a particular role, people need to exert effort to recalibrate or recast them into different ones. This tempers the notion of documents serving as boundary objects through their "interpretive flexibility." It is not merely how different people interpret information conveyed by documents differently that is the distinguishing characteristic for documents' social lives. Rather, the practices and routines around documents are key. How documents move through organizational and group circuits and what roles they play in those circuits could very well answer many of the thorniest problems in collaboration, problem solving, and information sharing.

Practically speaking, this means that innovation around documents may also happen in large part in material terms. For example, in teams we studied, people worked with, through, and around the routinized document structures to negotiate among the tensions that emerged as documents were called upon to serve multiple roles—logs were turned into agendas, whiteboards made into archives (Fiore-Silfvast, Neff, & Dossick, 2011). Our research shows that the organizational roles documents play for complex problem solving must simultaneously meet the needs of formal and flexible written communication. For example, maintenance personnel have relied on distributed professional knowledge networks of people who are uniquely qualified to provide the right kind of information because they have both personal experience with the buildings and an understanding of their context (Javernick-Will & Levitt, 2010). These knowledge networks developed around and relied upon paper documents such as drawings, operations manuals, and maintenance records. Not only were these paper documents effective medium for conversation, but they also functioned as social resources of organizational communication and circulation, and this may in some ways explain why paper persists as part of building maintenance records years after proponents declared paper records would be replaced with digital ones (Anderson, Dossick, & Neff, 2012). As Brown and Duguid (2000) assert, "Readers and writers have made [paper] a powerful resource for making, shaping, warranting, interpreting, and even protecting information," thus creating a social resource around paper (p. 244). By observing how people negotiate the tensions between document material roles, we gain a view of the material process of communication within social settings.

Research on materiality within the field of communication presents a challenge to thinking about communication as situated exclusively within human meaning. The material affordances and constraints of everyday objects serve powerful functions in the communication process, and communication theory needs to take up this challenge by expanding our notion of mediation to include things that are not necessarily thought of as media. This theoretical move may require new ways of conceptualizing agency within communicative actions, and it will almost certainly mean that communication scholars need to revisit and revise existing theories on sociomateriality, such as actor-network theory and cultural-historical activity theory, to better serve the theoretical needs within our discipline. Our model for documents represents only a start on this work and represents a call to action for other scholars to join us. Developing such theories of materiality for communication as a discipline, however, will expand our ability to address the powerful roles materiality plays in meaning making and organizing and help scholars make sense of the transformation of the material practices and processes as communication and media technologies change.

NOTES

1. This material is based upon work supported by the National Science Foundation under Grant Number SES-0823338.

BIBLIOGRAPHY

Anderson, A., Dossick, C. S., & Neff, G. (2012, July 15). Seeking new social norms: Facilities services organizational isolation in the University of Washington's digital transition. In *Proceedings of the Engineering Project Organizations Conference*, Rheden, the Netherlands.

Ashcraft, K. L., Kuhn, T. R., & Cooren, F. (2009). Constitutional amendments: "Materializing" organizational communication. *Academy of Management Annals, 31*, 1–64. doi:10.1080/1941 6520903047186

Bardram, J. (1997). *Plans as situated action: An activity theory approach to workflow systems.* Paper presented at the ECSCW 97, Lancaster, England.

Bechky, B. A. (2003a). Sharing meaning across occupational communities: The transformation of understanding on a production floor. *Organization Science, 14*(3), 312–330. doi:10.1287/orsc.14.3.312.15162

Bechky, B. A. (2003b). Object lessons: Workplace artifacts as representations of occupational jurisdiction. *American Journal of Sociology, 109*, 3.

Becker, P., & Clark, W. (2001). *Little tools of knowledge: Historical essays on academic and bureaucratic practices.* Ann Arbor: University of Michigan Press.

Benoit-Barné, C., & Cooren, F. (2009). The accomplishment of authority through presentification. *Management Communication Quarterly, 23*(1), 5–31. doi:10.1177/0893318909335414

Boczkowski, P. (2004). The mutual shaping of technology and society in videotex newspapers: Beyond the diffusion and social shaping perspectives. *The Information Society, 20*(4), 255–267. doi:10.1080/01972240490480947

Boczkowski P., & Lievrouw, L. (2008) Bridging STS and communication studies: Scholarship on media and information technologies. In E. J. Hackett, O. Amsterdamska,. M. Lynch, & J. Wajcman (Eds.), *The handbook of science and technology studies,* (3rd ed., pp. 949–978). Cambridge, MA: MIT Press.

Bowers, J., Button, G., & Sharrock, W. (1995). *Workflow from within and without: Technology and cooperative work on the print industry shopfloor.* Paper presented at the the Fourth European Conference on Computer-supported Cooperative, Stockholm, Sweden.

Bowker, G. C., & Star, S. L. (1999). *Sorting things out: Classification and its consequences.* Cambridge, MA: MIT Press.

Brown, J. S., & Duguid, P. (2000). *The social life of information.* Cambridge, MA: Harvard Business School Press.

Browning, L. D., Greene, R. W., Sitkin, S. B., Sutcliffe, K. M., & Obstfeld, D. (2009). Constitutive complexity: Military entrepreneurs and the synthetic character of communication flows. In L. L. Putnam & A. M. Nicotera (Eds.), *Building theories of organization: The constitutive role of communication* (pp. 86–116). New York, NY: Routledge.

Cicmil, S., & Marshall, D. (2005). Insights into collaboration at the project level: Complexity, social interaction and procurement mechanisms. *Building Research & Information, 33*, 523–535.

Cooren, F. (2004). Textual agency: How texts do things in organizational settings. *Organization, 11*(3), 373–393. doi:10.1177/1350508404041998

Cooren, F., & Fairhurst, G. T. (2009). Dislocation and stabilization: How to scale up from interactions to organization. In L. L. Putnam & A. M. Nicotera (Eds.), *Building theories of organization: The constitutive role of communication* (pp. 117–152). New York, NY: Routledge.

Cooren, F., & Taylor, J. R. (1997). Organization as an effect of mediation: Redefining the link between organization and communication. *Communication Theory, 7*(3), 219–260. doi: 10.1111/j.1468-2885.1997.tb00151.x

Cronen, V. E. (2001). Practical theory, practical art, and the pragmatic-systemic account of inquiry. *Communication Theory, 11*(1), 14–35. doi:10.1111/j.1468-2885.2001.tb00231.x

Davenport, T. H., & Prusak, L. (1998). *Working knowledge*. Cambridge, MA: Harvard Business School Press.

Dossick, C. S., & Neff, G. (2011). Messy talk and clean technology: Communication, problem solving and collaboration using building information modeling. *Engineering Project Organization Journal, 1*(2), 83–93. doi:10.1080/21573727.2011.569929

Ewenstein, B., & Whyte, J. (2009). Knowledge practices in design: The role of visual representations as "epistemic objects." *Organization Studies, 30*(1), 7–30. doi:10.1177/0170840608083014

Fairhurst, G. T., & Putnam, L. (2004). Organizations as discursive constructions. *Communication Theory, 14*(1), 5–26. doi:10.1111/j.1468-2885.2004.tb00301.x

Fiore-Silfvast, B., Neff, G., & Dossick, C. S. (2011). From conversations to structures: The material social life of documents in organizational communication. International Communication Association Virtual Conference, May 23–June 10.

Gagliardi, P. (1990). *Symbols and artifacts: Views of the corporate landscape*. Berlin, Germany: W. de Gruyter.

Glaser, B. G., & Strauss, A. L. (1967). *The discovery of grounded theory: Strategies for qualitative research*. Hawthorne, NY: Aldine de Gruytner.

Goodman, R. A., & Goodman, L. P. (1976). Some management issues in temporary systems: A study of professional development and manpower—the theater case. *Administrative Science Quarterly, 21*(3), 494–501.

Groleau, C. (2006). One phenomenon, two lenses: Understanding collective action from the perspectives of co-orientation and activity theories. In F. Cooren, J. R. Taylor, & E. J. Van Every (Eds.), *Communication as organizing: Empirical and theoretical explorations in the dynamic of text and conversation* (pp. 157–177). Mahwah, NJ: Lawrence Erlbaum.

Groleau, C., Demers, C., Lalancette, M., & Barros, M. (2011). From hand drawings to computer visuals: Confronting situated and institutionalized practices in an architecture firm. *Organization Science, 23*. doi:10.1287/orsc.1110.0667

Harper, R. H. R. (1998). *Inside the IMF: An ethnography of documents, technology, and organisational action*. San Diego, CA: Academic Press.

Henderson, K. (1995). The political career of a prototype: The importance of the visual in design engineering consensus and conflict. *Social Problems, 42*, 274–299.

Henderson, K. (1999). *On line and on paper: Visual representations, visual culture, and computer graphics in design engineering*. Cambridge, MA: MIT Press.

Hutchins, E. (1995). *Cognition in the wild*. Cambridge, MA: MIT Press.

Javernick-Will, A. N., & Levitt, R. E. (2010). Mobilizing institutional knowledge for international projects. *Journal of Construction Engineering and Management, 136*(4), 430–441.

Kaghan W. N., & Lounsbury, M. (2006). Artifacts, articulation work, and institutional residue. In A. Rafaeli & M.G. Pratt (Eds.), *Artifacts and organizations: Beyond mere symbolism*. Mahwah, NJ: Lawrence Erlbaum.

Knorr Cetina, K. (1999). *Epistemic cultures: How the sciences make knowledge*. Cambridge, MA: Harvard University Press.

Kuhn, T., & Jackson, M. H. (2008). Accomplishing knowledge: A framework for investigating knowing in organizations. *Management Communication Quarterly, 21*(4), 454–485. doi:10.1177/0893318907313710

Latour, B. (1987). *Science in action: How to follow scientists and engineers through society*. Cambridge, MA: Harvard University Press.

Latour, B. (1994). On technical mediation: Philosophy, sociology, genealogy. *Common Knowledge, 3*(2), 29–64.

Latour, B. (2005). *Reassembling the social: An introduction to actor-network theory.* Oxford, England: Oxford University Press.

Leonardi, P. M., & Barley, S. R. (2010). What's under construction here? Social action, materiality, and power in constructivist studies of technology and organizing. *The Academy of Management Annals, 4*(1), 1–51. doi:10.1080/19416521003654160

Leonardi, P. M., Nardi, B. A., & Kallinikos, J. (2012). *Materiality and organizing: Social interaction in a technological world.* Oxford, England: Oxford University Press.

Lievrouw, L. (2014). Materiality and media in communication and technology studies: An unfinished project. In T. Gilespie, P. Boczkowski, & K. Foot (Eds.), *Media technologies* (pp. 21-51). Cambridge, MA: MIT Press.

Lindlof, T. R., & Taylor, B. C. (2010). *Qualitative communication research methods* (3rd ed.). Thousand Oaks, CA: Sage.

Marvin, C. (1987). *When old technologies were new.* Oxford, England: Oxford University Press.

McPhee, R. (1985). Formal structure and organizational communication. In R. McPhee & P. K. Tompkins (Eds.), *Organizational communication: Traditional themes and new directions, Vol. 13.* Sage Annual Reviews of Communication Research. Beverly Hills, CA: Sage.

Miles, M. B., & Huberman, A. M. (1994). *Qualitative data analysis: An expanded sourcebook* (2nd ed.). Thousand Oaks, CA: Sage.

Mukerji, C. (2011). Jurisdiction, inscription and state formation: Administrative modernism and knowledge regimes. *Theory and Society, 40*(3), 223–245. doi:10.1007/s11186-011-9141-9

Neff, G., Fiore-Silfvast, B., & Dossick, C. S. (2010). A case study of the failure of digital media to cross knowledge boundaries in virtual construction. *Information, Communication & Society, 13*(4), 556–573. doi:10.1080/13691181003645970

Nicolini, D. (2010). Practice as the site of knowing: Insights from the field of telemedicine. *Organization Science, 22*(3), 602–620. doi:10.1287/orsc.1100.0556

Nicolini, D., Swan, J., & Mengis, J. (May 01, 2012). Understanding the role of objects in cross-disciplinary collaboration. *Organization Science, 23*(3), 612–629. doi:10.1287/orsc.1110.0664

Orlikowski, W. J. (2007). Sociomaterial practices: Exploring technology at work. *Organization Studies, 28*(9), 1435–1448. doi:10.1177/0170840607081138

Orlikowski, W. J., & Yates, J. A. (1994). Genre repertoire: The structuring of communicative practices in organizations. *Administrative Science Quarterly, 39*(4), 541.

Osterlund, C. (2008). Documents in place: Demarcating places for collaboration in healthcare settings. *Computer Supported Cooperative Work, 17*, 195–225. doi:10.1007/s10606-007-9064-1

Pratt, M. G., & Rafaeli, A. (1997). Organizational dress as a symbol of multilayered social identities. *The Academy of Management Journal, 40*(4), 862–898.

Pratt, M. G., & Rafaeli, A. (2006). Artifacts and organizations: understanding our "object-ive" reality. In A. Rafaeli & M.G. Pratt (Eds.), *Artifacts and organizations: Beyond mere symbolism* (pp. 279–288). Mahwah, NJ: Lawrence Erlbaum.

Putnam, L., & Cooren, F. (2004). Alternative perspectives on the role of text and agency in constituting organizations. *Organization, 11*(3), 323–333. doi:10.1177/1350508404041995

Putnam, L. L., & Nicotera, A. M. (2010). Communicative constitution of organization is a question: Critical issues for addressing it. *Management Communication Quarterly, 24*(1), 158–165. doi:10.1177/0893318909351581

Riles, A. (2006). *Documents: Artifacts of modern knowledge.* Ann Arbor: University of Michigan Press.

Schmidt, K., & Wagner, I. (2004). Ordering systems: Coordinative practices and artifacts in architectural design and planning. *Computer Supported Cooperative Work: The Journal of Collaborative Computing, 13*(5–6), 349–408. doi:10.1007/s10606-004-5059-3

Sellen, A. J., & Harper, R. H. R. (2002). *The myth of the paperless office.* Cambridge, MA: MIT Press.

Sillince, J. A. A. (2007). Organizational context and the discursive construction of organizing. *Management Communication Quarterly, 20*(4), 363–394. doi:10.1177/0893318906298477

Star, S. L., & Griesemer, J. (1989). Institutional ecology, "translations" and boundary objects: Amateurs and professionals in Berkeley's Museum of Vertebrate Zoology, 1907–39. *Social Studies of Science, 19*(3), 387–420. doi:10.1177/030631289019003001

Star, S. L., & Ruhleder, K. (1996). Steps toward an ecology of infrastructure: Design and access for large information spaces. *Information Systems Research, 7*(1), 111–134.

Stohl, C., & Cheney, G. (2001). Participatory processes/paradoxical practices communication and the dilemmas of organizational democracy. *Management Communication Quarterly, 14*(3), 349–407.

Stradtman, L. R. (2012). *Online reputation management for dummies.* Hoboken, NJ: John Wiley & Sons.

Strauss, A. L., & Corbin, J. (1990). *Basics of qualitative research: Grounded theory procedures and techniques.* Newbury Park, CA: Sage.

Suchman, L. (1987). *Plans and situated actions: The problem of human-machine communication.* New York, NY: Cambridge University Press.

Suchman, L. (2007). *Human-machine reconfigurations: Plans and situated actions.* Cambridge, England; New York, NY: Cambridge University Press.

Taylor, J. R., & Robichaud, D. (2004). Finding the organization in the communication: Discourse as action and sensemaking. *Organization, 11*(3), 395–413. doi:10.1177/1350508404041999

Taylor, J. R., & Van Every, E. J. (2000). *The emergent organization: Communication as its site and surface.* Mahwah, NJ: Lawrence Erlbaum.

Turnbull, D. (1993). The ad hoc collective work of building gothic cathedrals with templates, string, and geometry. *Science, Technology, and Human Values, 18*(3), 315–340. doi:10.1177/016224399301800304

Vaughan, D. (1997). *The* Challenger *launch decision.* Chicago, IL: University of Chicago Press.

Weber, M. (1947). *The theory of social and economic organization* (A. M. Henderson & T. Parsons, Trans.). London, England: Collier Macmillan.

Weick, K. E. (1995). *Sensemaking in organizations.* Thousand Oaks, CA: Sage.

Whyte, J., Ewenstein, B., Hales, M., & Tidd, J. (January 01, 2008). Visualizing knowledge in project-based work. *Long Range Planning, 41*(1), 74–92. doi: 10.1016/j.lrp.2007.10.006

Yates, J. (1989). *Control through communication: The rise of system in American management.* Baltimore, MD: Johns Hopkins University Press.

Yates, J., & Orlikowski, W. J. (1992). Genres of organizational communication: A structurational approach to studying communication and media. *Academy of Management Review, 17*(2), 299–326. doi: 10.2307/258774

Biographical Sketches

Ekaterina Balabanova is a lecturer in the Department of Communication and Media at the University of Liverpool. Her work explores the intersection of international politics and international communication, particularly the relationship between news media and politics; the media's role in humanitarian crises and war; and the communication of conflict. She has published extensively on the influence of the media on foreign policymaking, and how military interventions are portrayed and shaped by media coverage. Her most recent work addresses the interplay between media and human rights, and the impact of nongovernmental organizations on public debates, policy agendas, and public understanding of human rights issues. Another long-term interest is media coverage of migration in the enlarged Europe; she is also collaborating on projects to develop and construct cross-country comparative analyses of press coverage.

Alex Balch is a lecturer in the Department of Politics at the University of Liverpool. His research investigates international mobility and security, particularly the politics of hospitality in Europe, and rights-based approaches to problems of forced labor and human trafficking. Dr. Balch has published extensively on the development of immigration policies in the UK, Spain and the EU, and worked with a number of public and third-sector organizations such as the Joseph Rowntree Foundation (JRF), the UK Human Trafficking Centre (UKHTC), Gangmasters' Licensing Authority (GLA), and the International Centre for Migration Policy Development (ICMPD) in Vienna. Current projects include research funded by the EU on corporate social responsibility and human trafficking, and international collaborative projects studying various aspects of immigration. In 2009–2010 Dr. Balch received an ESRC postdoctoral fellowship, which included a visit as guest scholar at the Center for Comparative Immigration Studies (CCIS) at the University of California, San Diego.

Carrie Sturts Dossick is an associate professor in the Department of Construction Management in the College of Built Environments, and director of the Pacific Northwest Center for Construction Research and Education, at the University of Washington. Dr. Dossick's research interests include data practices, collaboration, technologies, and building information modeling (BIM). Her current research projects focus on technology and collaboration strategies for green building design and construction; global virtual teams; applications of technology for building operations; and Integrated Project Delivery. She has received funding from the National Science Foundation, the U.S. Army, the U.S. Department of Education, Hewlett-Packard, Skanska Building USA, the University of Washington Royalty Research Fund, and the College of Built Environments' BE Lab. In 2005, she received the ASCE Best Peer Reviewed Paper award from the American Society of Civil Engineers, for her article on pricing engineering services.

Nora Draper is a PH.D. candidate at the University of Pennsylvania's Annenberg School for Communication. Her research investigates political, economic, and historical factors that shape the Internet industry's approaches to norms of privacy, surveillance, identity construction, and reputation. Her work has been published in the *Journal of Children & Media*, *Critical Studies & Media Communication*, the *International Journal of Communication*, and *Surveillance & Society*.

Brittany Fiore-Silfvast is a doctoral candidate in the Department of Communication at the University of Washington. Her research focuses on the relationship of technology and emerging cultural and organizational forms; her projects include examinations of how media and communication practices are shaped in moments of technological change and through processes of informationalization in arenas such as health care, global development, building design and construction, and warfare. She received a National Science

Foundation Doctoral Dissertation Research Improvement grant for her study of the social and organizational implications of digital health in the United States and India. As part of an Intel-funded research project, she studied the social and institutional arrangements around emerging consumer-oriented digital health and wellness tools and the production of new forms of patient- and consumer-generated data. Her previous work on a National Science Foundation–funded study examined collaboration and new technologies in green building design and construction.

Udo Göttlich is a professor of Media and Communication Studies at Zeppelin University in Friedrichshafen, Germany. He studied comparative literature, sociology, and political science and received his doctorate in sociology from RWTH University in Aachen, Germany, followed by his habilitation at the University of Duisburg-Essen in Germany. He has held guest and visiting professorships at the Alpen-Adria University, Klagenfurt, Austria; the University of Hildesheim, Germany; and the Bundeswehr University, Munich, Germany. His main research interests and publishing focus on the sociology of culture, media and communication studies, and cultural studies.

Brian Harding is completing a master's of information at the University of Toronto. His research focuses on sociotechnical practices such as self-tracking and the formation of literacies through these practices.

François Heinderyckx is a professor in the Department of Information and Communication Sciences at the Université libre de Bruxelles (Belgium), where he teaches media sociology and political communication, and a Chang-Jiang Scholar Professor at Communication University of China (2013–2016). He is the former director of the Department of Information and Communication Sciences at ULB, and is a member of the High Council for Media Literacy, government of the Wallonia-Brussels Federation, and the Brussels Platform for Journalism. Heinderyckx's research interests include journalism and news media, political communication, audience studies, and media literacy. He is an editor of the *Routledge Studies in European Communication Research and Education* and serves on the editorial boards of numerous journals. In 2005, Heinderyckx was one of the founding members of the European Communication Research and Education Association (ECREA) and was president of ECREA from its creation until 2012. He is the 2013–2014 president of the International Communication Association (ICA).

Martin Rolf Herbers is a research assistant to the chair for Media and Communication Management at Zeppelin University in Friedrichshafen, Germany. He studied communication science, German philology, and psychology at the University of Münster, Germany. His dissertation research examines the production of political entertainment media in German television. His further research interests include (political) entertainment research, the political public sphere, and visual communication.

David Karpf is an assistant professor in the School of Media and Public Affairs at George Washington University. He teaches and conducts research on the Internet and organized political advocacy campaigns. He is the author of *The MoveOn Effect: The Unexpected Transformation of American Political Advocacy* and his research has been published in the *Journal of Information Technology & Politics*, *Policy & Internet*, and *Information, Communication, and Society*.

Daniel Kreiss is an assistant professor in the School of Journalism and Mass Communication at the University of North Carolina at Chapel Hill and an affiliated fellow of the Information Society Project at Yale Law School. His research explores the impact of technological change on the public sphere and political practice. He is the author of *Taking Our Country Back: The Crafting of Networked Politics from Howard Dean to Barack Obama*. His work has appeared in *New Media & Society*, *Critical Studies in Media Communication*, the *International Journal of Communication*, and other academic journals.

Mark Latonero is a research director and deputy managing director at the Annenberg Center on Communication Leadership and Policy, and a research assistant professor at the University of Southern California Annenberg School for Communication and Journalism. His research focuses on emerging communication technology and social change with a specific interest in technology and human rights. Recent research examines the role of digital and networked technologies in human trafficking and exploitation. Latonero's work has appeared in *Information, Communication & Society*, *Information Systems for Crisis Response and Management*, and *Communication Research*, among other publications.

Danielle Leighton is a technical business analyst with the technology consulting firm T4G, and in 2012 earned a master's of information degree from the University of Toronto. Her professional and academic research and consulting have focused on a range of applied communication problems, including intra-organizational communication and information services, the communication of academic standards and requirements, academic information services, and the impact of online, computer-based aural rehabilitation on hearing aid success rates.

Leah A. Lievrouw is a professor in the Department of Information Studies at the University of California, Los Angeles. Her research and writing focus on the relationship between media and information technologies and social change. Her most recent book, *Alternative and Activist New Media*, explores the ways that artists and activists use new media technologies to challenge mainstream culture, politics, and society. With Sonia Livingstone of the London School of Economics, she is coeditor of the four-volume *Sage Benchmarks in Communication: New Media* and *The Handbook of New Media*. Works in progress include *Foundations of Communication Theory: Communication and Technology* and *Media and Meaning: Communication Technology and Society*.

Gina Neff is an associate professor of communication at the University of Washington. She studies the contemporary economics of media production and the political economy of communication with a focus on work and technology in both high-tech and media industries. Her book *Venture Labor: Work and the Burden of Risk in Innovative Industries*, examines the risk and uncertainties borne by New York City's new media pioneers during the first Internet boom. She also coedited *Surviving the New Economy*. With Carrie Sturts Dossick, she runs the Project on Communication Technology and Organizational Practices, which focuses on communication technology in the innovation of complex building design and construction. Her work has been funded by the National Science Foundation, and she is currently at work on a three-year project funded by Intel studying the impact of social media and consumer health technologies on the organization of primary care.

Rasmus Kleis Nielsen is an associate professor of political communication at Roskilde University and a research fellow at the Reuters Institute for the Study of Journalism at the University of Oxford. His work focuses on political communication, the use of digital technologies by political campaigns, and changes in news media around the world. *Ground Wars: Personalized Communication in Political Campaigns* is his most recent book. His work has appeared in various academic journals including the *International Journal of Press/Politics*, *New Media & Society* and *the Journal of Information Technology & Politics*.

Sean Phelan is a senior lecturer at the Wellington campus of the School of Communication, Journalism and Marketing, Massey University, Aotearoa New Zealand. His publications include *Discourse Theory and Critical Media Politics*, coedited with Lincoln Dahlberg, and *Scooped: The Politics and Power of Journalism in Aotearoa New Zealand*, coedited with Martin Hirst and Verica Rupar. He is currently writing a book about neoliberalism, media, and the political.

David J. Phillips is an associate professor of information at the University of Toronto. His work brings together queer theory, technology studies, media studies, surveillance studies, and political economy to study issues of surveillance, identity, and identification. His research articles and other works exploring the relations among information, economics, ideology, policy, culture, identity, and technology have been published in *Social Text*, *Information, Communication & Society*, and numerous other venues. He is currently exploring theater as a vehicle for research, pedagogy, and fun.

Joan Ramon Rodríguez-Amat is an assistant professor at the University of Vienna. His research interests combine cultural and media studies and issues of media governance and the public sphere. He is the book reviews editor of the *International Journal of Media and Cultural Politics.* He has held teaching appointments at the University of Vic (Barcelona, Spain), the University Alpen-Adria, Klagenfurt (Austria), and in the United Kingdom and France. He has also worked as a researcher at the University of Jena (2007) and the Hans-Bredow Institut in Hamburg (2008) in Germany.

Annie Rudd is a Ph.D. candidate in communications at Columbia University, and a Mellon/ACLS Dissertation Completion Fellow for 2013–2014. Her research focuses on the history of visual culture, and her dissertation traces the history of the hidden camera in documentary, journalistic, and amateur photography. She has twice received the ICA Communication History Division's Top Student Paper Award, in 2012 and 2013. At Columbia, she has taught in the university's undergraduate core curriculum, and worked on digital humanities projects and archival processing at its Rare Book and Manuscript Library.

Katharine Sarikakis is a professor of Communication Science and Media Governance at the University of Vienna. She has held tenured and visiting positions at the University of Leeds, UK; Karlstad University, Sweden; McGill University, Canada; and is an honorary research fellow at Hainan University, China. She is the founding coeditor of the *International Journal of Media and Cultural Politics*, and has written extensively on media and cultural policy and international communications.

Adrienne Shaw is an assistant professor in Temple University's Department of Media Studies and Production. She received her Ph.D. from the Annenberg School for Communication at the University of Pennsylvania. Prior to joining the Temple faculty she held postdoctoral posts at the Mudra Institute for Communication Ahmedabad, the University of Pittsburgh, and Colorado State University. Her research and teaching focus on popular culture, the politics of representation, technology, cultural production, and qualitative audience research, with a particular emphasis on video games, gaming culture, and gender and sexuality studies. In addition to authoring several book chapters, her research has been published in *Ada*, *New Media & Society*, *Critical Studies in Media and Communication*, *Games and Culture*, among other journals. Her forthcoming book is tentatively titled, *Playing at the Edge: Gender, Race, and Sexuality in Video Games.*

Aram Sinnreich is an assistant professor at Rutgers University's School of Communication and Information, in the Department of Journalism and Media Studies. He is the author of two books, *Mashed Up: Music, Technology and the Rise of Configurable Culture* (2010) and *The Piracy Crusade: How the Music Industry's War on Sharing Destroys Markets and Erodes Civil Liberties* (2013).

Ruxandra Trandafoiu is a reader in communication at Edge Hill University, UK, where she teaches political communication, identities, psychology of persuasion, and research methods. Her research interests include diasporic media, migration and nationalism, European Union politics, and Eastern European societies. She is a former journalist and art critic. Her books *Diaspora Online. Identity Politics and Romanian Migrants*, and *The Globalization of Musics in Transit: Music Migration and Tourism*, coedited with Simone Krüger, were both published in 2013.

Anita Varma is a doctoral candidate in the Department of Communication at Stanford University. Her research area is cultural studies of media, particularly the power dynamics that operate through corporately controlled media and how global media flows in the new digital landscape may contribute to cultural homogenization. Her undergraduate research on the politics of difference was funded by the Ford Foundation and published in *Young Scholars in Writing: Undergraduate Research in Writing and Rhetoric.*

Katharina Wolf is a lecturer at Curtin University in Perth, Western Australia, and course coordinator of the public relations program there. She is also a Ph.D. student at Murdoch University, where she is completing her thesis on activist communication. Her research interests include activist and political communication, the integrated use of digital technologies, work-integrated and blended learning, as well as professional development and graduate employability in public relations. She is the immediate past state president of the Public Relations Institute of Australia (Western Australia) and a director on the Institute's national board. Ms. Wolf has also received a number of local and national teaching awards.

Index

SUBJECT HEADINGS

NAME HEADINGS

international
communication
association

Annual Conference Theme Book Series

As of 2013, ICA and Peter Lang Publishing started co-publishing papers from ICA's annual conference theme sessions in the form of edited collections. Written in an engaging style, these volumes are meant to appeal to a wider audience and to reach scholars in other disciplines outside of Communication Studies. As such, the collections are not conference proceedings per se but a unique set of selected essays that capture the insights and agendas of the discipline's top scholars.

For additional information about this series, please contact Mary Savigar at Mary.Savigar@plang.com.

To order other books in this series, please contact our Customer Service Department:

(800) 770-LANG (within the U.S.)
(212) 647-7706 (outside the U.S.)
(212) 647-7707 FAX

Or browse online by series at www.peterlang.com

www.ingramcontent.com/pod-product-compliance
Ingram Content Group UK Ltd.
Pitfield, Milton Keynes, MK11 3LW, UK
UKHW021851100926
8556IPUK00020B/1172

9 781433 125355